D1120394

Karl Bushby was born and brought up in Hull, East Yorkshire, in 1969. His father was a professional soldier for twenty-four years, twelve of them in the Special Forces, so was often away for long periods. After his schooldays, Karl joined 3 Para. By the age of twenty-one, he was married with a young son, but by twenty-six had divorced. He left the army in 1998. Six months later, he began the Goliath Expedition and left Punta Arenas, Chile, pulling a small two-wheeled trailer.

RECEIVED
AUG 1 7 2006

GIANT STEPS

**An American Odyssey from
Punta Arenas to the
Edge of Alaska**

Karl Bushby

TIME WARNER
BOOKS

property of
L.E. SHORE
MEMORIAL LIBRARY
THORNBURY, ONTARIO, N0H 2P0

TIME WARNER BOOKS

First published in Great Britain in April 2006 by Time Warner Books

Copyright © Karl Bushby 2006

Maps © John Gilkes 2006

The moral right of the author has been asserted.

All rights reserved. No part of this publication may be reproduced, stored in a retrieval system, or transmitted, in any form or by any means, without the prior permission in writing of the publisher, nor be otherwise circulated in any form of binding or cover other than that in which it is published and without a similar condition including this condition being imposed on the subsequent purchaser.

A CIP catalogue record for this book is available
from the British Library.

ISBN 0 316 72958 2

Typeset in Sabon by M Rules

Printed and bound in Great Britain by
Clays Ltd, St Ives plc

Time Warner Books
An imprint of
Time Warner Book Group UK
Brettenham House
Lancaster Place
London WC2E 7EN

www.twbg.co.uk

For Adam, the son I left behind

Until there is commitment, there is hesitancy, the chance to draw back, always ineffectiveness.

Concerning all acts of initiative (and creation), there is one elementary truth the ignorance of which kills countless ideas and splendid plans: That the moment one definitely commits oneself then the providence moves too. All sorts of things occur to help one that would never otherwise have occurred. A whole stream of events issues forth from the decision, raising in one's favour all manner of unforeseen incidents, meetings and material assistance which no man could have dreamed would have come his way.

Whatever you can do, or dream you can, begin it.

Boldness has genius, power and magic in it.

Begin it now.

Goethe

Contents

Foreword

There are virtually no undiscovered places left to find, no unclimbed mountains left to scale, no new rivers left to cross. It seems there may be no challenges left to face.

Yet every now and again we find someone who has noticed a new challenge hitherto unthought of, and we think: it may be crazy but he must have a lot of bottle to undertake it.

Such exploits may last hours, days, even weeks. To fly non-stop around the world on a single tank of fuel; to sail alone on the same lonely journey; all demand a 'Wow' of admiring surprise.

But Yorkshireman Karl Bushby has no time for blink-and-you-miss-it chores. This thirty-five-year-old former Red Beret decided eight years ago to undertake the longest march ever tried, in effect to march around the world. He has been marching for nearly eight years, pulling his entire life in a hand-cart behind him. Sixteen thousand miles have passed under his feet, twenty thousand more to go, and another six years out of his life.

In order to avoid crossing the oceans by boat or airplane; in order to keep the route to marching only, he picked the longest single unbroken trek he could find. He started from Punta Arenas, southernmost point of Chile. At the time of writing he has reached Alaska and waits for the ice to form a bridge to take him across to Siberia.

From there the route will take him west, west, always west towards his home; through the eleven time zones of Russia, across Poland, Germany and France, until some time around 2011 he sees the white towers of Dover's cliffs

He will not see Australia, Africa or the southern half of Asia, but the circumference of the world is about 24,000 miles, and he will eventually accomplish one and a half times that. The route will finally have involved three continents (four if you count the Americas as two, north and south), twenty-five countries, a frozen sea, six deserts and seven great mountain ranges.

Already he has overcome the freezing gales of Patagonia, the fetid jungle swamps of Colombia and Panama, the 50°C of the Mojave Desert and the –40°C of Canada's winter. There have been terrorists to face, other bandits, filthy jails, disease and death in Central America; but also kindness, curiosity, hospitality, friendship and shared food from those along the road.

It is an odyssey worthy of Ulysses himself, a saga fit for the old Nordic gods. From the nightly diary of Karl Bushby this first-half story has been culled, to tell us safe here at home that the spirit of young British men and women to do amazing and slightly crazy things is not yet crushed, but still alive and well.

Frederick Forsyth
18/5/05

Acknowledgements

It is almost customary at this point to state that there are so many people to whom I owe a debt of gratitude that to name but a few would be to upset a great many. To this I will add it would be impossible to mention everyone simply because of the massive number of good people that have stopped my world from becoming unglued over the past six or seven years. I have been constantly spurred on, and always amazed, by the support and good wishes of ordinary folk around the world. Since I took that first of many steps hundreds of people have contributed towards the expedition, for no other reason than they believe my dream is a worthy one. I will endeavour to make the dream a reality. There have been some dark periods and without your support, just knowing that you were rooting for me, the going would have been very hard indeed.

While I sailed on, across a sometimes choppy sea, taking in many experiences and beautiful vistas, there were those down in the 'engine room' of the expedition slaving away in their various efforts to maintain me in the field. The backroom boys and girls without whom nothing would happen. My parents, who swung in behind my madcap scheme and have beavered diligently away, out of the spotlight, securing sponsorship and funding. In return I have given them headaches, heartaches and worry, yet they carry on managing the 'business', simply because that's what parents do! Andy Cooper, who came on board back in the 'early days' and created my marvellous website at his own expense, before donating funds and becoming a director of our then newly formed company, Goliath Earth Trek UK Ltd. I am also indebted to Jonny Beardsall, initially for spending a couple of days walking with me in the burning Mojave Desert prior to completing the exercise by writing a cracking article in the Saturday *Telegraph*

Magazine. Then latterly for taking on the awesome and unenviable task of editing my diaries down from over 500,000 words to a more manageable 100,000. Our thanks to Sally Holloway, literary agent, who took control of our wayward attempts to attract anyone in the publishing world to the diaries, then steered us down the road to success. I would especially like to thank Frederick Forsyth, who has supported the Goliath Expedition for a number of years now and has kindly offered to write a foreword for this book.

The expedition is obviously greatly indebted to those companies that supply both equipment and funding. Members of staff with whom we deal could be said to be members of our team now and could have not been more helpful. It's a very grateful thanks not only from me but the expedition as a whole to the following companies: Softcom Technologies (Mail2Web); Superfeet; The North Face; Zamberlan.

Finally, my heart goes out to the people of the Americas, from the southern tip of Chile to the Bering Strait. Many nations, many races but overall all human. For every one person that did their best to disrupt my day there were thousands of complete strangers that went out of their way to lighten my load. I was just some guy on the road, mostly dusty and dirty, always tired and hungry, a foreigner who couldn't speak the language in a number of cases. Yet they would cross the road to shake my hand. They would take me into their homes, sharing their sometimes scant food and possessions. There are those who took me in for days and even weeks, looking after me as though I was a prodigal son. Those who took me in and cured my ills. Also those many good souls who put up with my black depressive moods, countering them with humour and above all tolerance. I cannot start to name you here, I dare not, I could not mention one without mentioning all. Some will get a place in the book, but please understand strict editing has had to remove a lot of others whose acts of kindness remain detailed in the original diaries. From everyone who gave me a smile or wave, to those who made their homes mine, I would like to say you will never know how much it meant to me, I can never repay you. My adventure through the Americas should restore in all of us our faith in human nature.

Thank you.

Introduction

Nine years in 3 Para and I was going nowhere. I was twenty-six, I had been married, divorced and had a son, Adam, who was five. I was a corporal and, because of my partial dyslexia, would stay one. I was frustrated and unfulfilled. I had always believed that others in the battalion didn't think I could cut it. What I needed was a huge test, one that would prove – more to myself than to them – that they were wrong about me once and for all. It had to be something extraordinary, a challenge way beyond the levels of normal human endurance. I'd read and re-read books by explorers like Charlie Burton and Ranulph Fiennes and these men really inspired me. I decided that I, too, was going to go on a *very* long walk.

The seed for this journey was sown long ago. Although I grew up on a housing estate on the outskirts of Hull, I always loved the great outdoors. As a child I was never happier than when trudging over the fields on imaginary expeditions with my younger brother, Adrian, in tow. We would build dens, trap creepy-crawlies and look for birds' nests. Once I brought home a baby jackdaw that had fallen from a nest. I kept it in our garage until it could fly and then I let it go. By then it was very tame and it even started following me when I walked to school and would wait around for me in a tree overlooking the playground. But the trouble was the teachers didn't like it – they called the RSPCA and they took it away. I was about ten and was heartbroken. It had meant something to me. I was always more content around animals and birds than in any classroom. I will try to explain.

I have one abiding memory from Sutton Park primary school – I was made to stand on a chair in front of the whole class because I couldn't spell, which was hurtful and frustrating. In fact, I was dyslexic but no one realised until I was much older. Because of this, I didn't do very well at my comprehensive but, like my father and grandfather before me, I knew I was destined for the Army anyway and joined as soon as I could. I joined aged sixteen.

My father was a professional soldier for twenty-four years, twelve of which were spent in the Special Forces and, naturally, I always looked up to him. I craved his approval but I found it hard because, as a teenager, I was physically immature compared to my peers. Between the ages of sixteen and eighteen, I grew five inches, and because I was doing so much growing, I couldn't keep up and carry the weight over long distances during the training. For two and a half years I struggled as a recruit, eventually passing P Company – the test phase for a place in the Parachute Regiment – at my fifth attempt. This was unprecedented, but they held on to me, seeing potential in my determination and soldiering skills. In the end, others suspected that I was given a discretionary 'pass' by my commanding officer. Though I was able to meet the standards on my final attempt, my previous failures lived with me.

But you don't drag yourself through those two and a half long years and emerge unscathed. I was labelled and, for a while, it stuck. It always bothered me that other soldiers had made it known that they didn't feel I had earned my place in the battalion. In truth, I was more aware of it than others and once I'd shown that I was a capable soldier, most had likely forgotten about it. I hadn't. Coupled with how I'd felt at school, I had something to establish. I still have.

During a Northern Ireland tour in 1996, I began to think hard about mounting a solo expedition. Working in the Battalion Int. Cell (Intelligence Section), I was able to order maps as a matter of course. Without any eyebrows being raised, I amassed a collection covering most of the world and spent months poring over them as I looked at possible routes for a long-distance walk. Then, slowly, I came round to the idea of linking numbers of routes together. This could be it. In my room in barracks, I remember drawing a line on a wall map from the southernmost tip of the Americas to the west coast of Alaska. It was then I had a letter from my father. In it, he related how two Special Forces guys had been toying with the idea of crossing from America to Russia via the Bering Strait, when it freezes for a few weeks of the year. If I could walk across these fifty-eight miles of

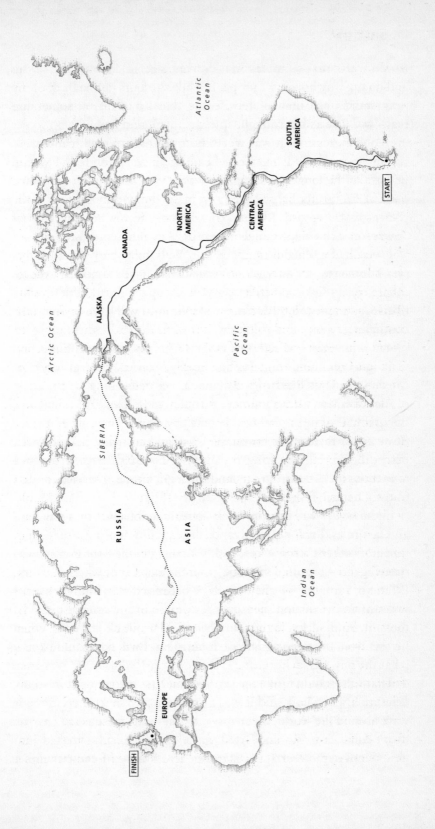

frozen water that separates Alaska from Siberia, I would be in Asia and on my way home to Europe. It made the hairs on the back of my neck stand up. I immediately sensed that I had hit on something really big. It was big enough, stupid enough and bad enough to get everyone's attention. It was worth putting years of my life into.

This was where I had been heading since childhood. I would undertake the longest walk in the world *ever*, leaving an unbroken path of footprints behind me, and in so doing almost double the present world record. I would travel from the southernmost tip of South America back to England, entirely by foot, entirely alone.

I soon had a schedule mapped out. Walking twenty miles (thirty-two kilometres) a day, with necessary rest days, I aimed to average 3000 miles (4800 kilometres) per year so, by the time I have finished this 36,000-mile (58,000-kilometre) journey, I will have crossed four continents, twenty-five countries, a frozen sea, six deserts and seven mountain ranges. I would start in Punta Arenas, southern Chile, and walk in a continuous line through South America, Central America, Mexico, the United States and Canada, before heading for the coast of Alaska where, after a journey of 16,000 miles (26,000 kilometres), the first half of my story would come to an end. Then, when the ice flows are at their most 'hospitable', I would cross the Bering Strait, before beginning the long trek home. I would, with a massive amount of luck, return to England through, I hope, a service conduit of the Channel Tunnel in around 2011.

In the field, I will have no back-up team and I abide by a few hard and fast rules. I will never advance the expedition using *any* form of transport other than my feet, and, if I must detour – for example, to renew a visa – I resume the walk from the exact spot where I left off. If I'm not camping – I usually will be because I have little money – I will stay in the dirtiest, cheapest rest-house in the roughest part of town or, if I'm lucky, in the spare bed of a hospitable stranger. When I crawl from my sleeping bag each morning, I will never quite know what the day has in store.

That others didn't take me seriously at first merely reinforced my determination. Many said it was not possible to make a continuous walk around the world; the maps said otherwise – just as long as you didn't mind crossing uncharted wastelands, guerrilla-infested jungles, windswept deserts and a frozen sea. I didn't. I can remember sitting in a bivouac staring across a Norwegian ice field in 1997 and thinking that, one day, and soon, I might find myself alone in such an environment – for that, surely, would be the greatest test. I knew that whatever came my way I would have to take on the chin. This was all or nothing. There would be no turning around – once I left I was on a one-way ticket. I've never forgotten this.

I gave the endeavour a name – the Goliath Expedition – and began discussing it with the Regiment. After all, this was what being a paratrooper was all about: endurance, self-sufficiency and the ability to go it alone on foot. They seemed to like the idea, so I got cracking. I began plotting more detailed routes across countries, then continents. Then, when I had nearly completed my initial twelve years' service, I was given some fantastic news – the Army had agreed to keep me on as a serving soldier for the first three years of the expedition. Now my dream *could* become a reality. I would have a solid foundation on which to build the expedition, the credibility I required and some money in the bank to get me rolling. Everything looked very promising. The *Soldier* magazine ran a piece about the expedition and, because I was planning something extraordinary, I even had an invitation from 10 Downing Street to attend the Queen and the Duke of Edinburgh's Fiftieth Anniversary dinner at the Guildhall.

Extending my engagement in the Army meant a bonus of £6000, on the strength of which I bought some extremely expensive equipment: satellite phone, laptop computer and a solar-panel charger. But then my hopes were dashed. On the morning I was due to sign on for another three years, the Army had changed its mind. I was faced with the choice of the Army or the expedition. Bitter as the disappointment was, in a sense I couldn't blame them – there was very little to inspire confidence and the prospect of losing a lone serving soldier in some out-of-the-way corner of the Americas would have given them a few headaches. By lunchtime, I had passed through the main gate at Aldershot and was on the train home to Hull, unemployed, in debt and about to move in with my mother, Angela.

Still I wouldn't let it go. Despite this blatant setback, my preparations began to take on a momentum of their own. I wrote so many letters to companies large and small in an effort to find sponsors but, in the event, found just two at an equipment exhibition in Harrogate. Zamberlan – the Italian footwear-maker – agreed to provide boots,

Panama

Medellin

Trujillo

SOUTH
AMERICA

Pacific

Ocean

Arica

Antofagasta

South

Atlantic

Santiago

Esquel

N

Piedra Buena

W   E

Punta
Arenas

S

0   250   500   750   1000 miles

0   400   800   1200   1600 km

START
November 1998

—— Route

Wales

Fairbanks

Whitehorse

Fort Nelson

Dawson City

Calgary

Pacific

Ocean

**NORTH
AMERICA**

Salt Lake
City

Las Vegas

Nogales

North

Atlantic

Culican

Manzanillo

Tecun
Ulman

N

W   E

S

| 0 | 500 | 1000 | 1500 | 2000 miles |

| 0 | 800 | 1600 | 2400 | 3200 km |

and Superfeet, special insoles. I wondered how many pairs I would go through in the next twelve years. But as far as sponsors went, that was it. Though I was making some money doing part-time surveillance work for a private detective, there was little in the kitty. Bailiffs were after my satellite phone and laptop because I was falling behind with the payments. I realised that to wait in the hope that someone would come on board was to wait forever and it was only a matter of time before all the equipment I'd bought would be repossessed. I trusted that, as the expedition progressed, others might sign up at a later stage.

Fortunately, support from both my parents – they had been divorced for several years – never wavered. While my mother started a collection for me among her workmates at the Nestlé factory in Hull, my father, Keith, now living in Hereford, became the expedition's 'base camp', promising to monitor my progress, keeping me re-supplied and to log the diaries and photographs that became the material for this book.

Although equipment had to be simple, lightweight, dependable and basic, I would not be able to carry it all in a rucksack, so I began designing a trailer. Though it would later earn the title the 'Beast', I eventually settled on a bog-standard golf trolley cart – the cheapest option – which I had customised. Pulled by a single shaft and set on two bicycle wheels, all my essentials – tent, sleeping bag, stove, maps and food – would be stuffed into large bags strapped to the frame.

My preparations were complete. I was 'good to go'. That said, I had no life or medical insurance – I couldn't afford either – and, once I was in South America, didn't have a single contact, a letter of introduction, or a friend of a friend to call if things went belly up. All I did manage was a carefully worded card printed in Spanish explaining my intentions, which ought to impress even the most reluctant of officials. It wasn't much.

So why did I still crack on, you may be wondering? Why did I go it alone without a safety net? Why, when no major sponsors appeared, was I still willing to start walking in the first place? I admit that I was in too deep. I asked myself questions but I was committed – I was going, come what may. I admit that I found the prospect pretty frightening.

As a warm-up, I walked from Hull to Dover to expose any weaknesses in myself or in the kit. Apart from a couple of punctures to the tyres on the Beast, there were no obvious problems. I felt that a regime of intensive physical training was pointless, as in truth with so much in front of me I didn't need to be 100 per cent physically fit at the outset of my journey. It was my mental approach that needed honing.

One dark afternoon in October 1998, I was met at Swindon station by my father and driven to RAF Brize Norton in Oxfordshire. With just £500 in my pocket and clutching a one-way ticket to Chile via the Falkland Islands, paid for by my father, I said goodbye to him and my brother in the terminal. I was well over the weight allowance but father chatted up the duty sergeant on my behalf and there was no problem. There wasn't much time to spare and I guess I'm not one for emotional partings. I just smiled and shook their hands. I had a plane to catch.

Chapter One

SETTING OUT: PUNTA ARENAS AND ARGENTINA

Sunday, 1 November 1998   **Punta Arenas**

A nightmare. I miss the last bus and the ten-mile taxi ride from the airport to Punta Arenas is $4000 Chilean (£4). After changing some money, I put the trailer together, which takes me three hours. I must find somewhere to sleep but get just twenty metres before catastrophe. The trailer wheels tighten, crushing the ball bearings and ripping the thread from the spindle. After stripping everything down, I sense I'm in a whole heap of trouble. Everything I try is turning to rat shit. I'm gripped by panic and fear – I am immobile. To top it all, today is Sunday and – get this – the 'Day of the Dead', a Chilean holiday on which they decorate graves and have large parades around the cemetery, so there is plenty to see but nowhere to shop. I must wait another day for trailer spares.

So here I am sitting in the street. There is a clear blue sky and warm sun, but it's blowing a gale, and an icy one too. My hands are numb with cold and it's hard to write. I daren't move the trailer far in case I damage it further. I meet a lad from Canada who has been working here for three years. He invites me to his place for something to eat, which I gratefully accept. I find somewhere to pitch my tent on a patch of grass between the two main roads leading out of town, where others in tents are selling flowers to those visiting their dead relatives. They will be here all night so I shouldn't stick out too much.

It's only day one . . . God help me!

San Carlos
de Bariloche

Esquel

ARGENTINA

Pacific

Ocean

South

Atlantic

CHILE

A
n
d
e
s

Perito Moreno

PATAGONIA

N

W   E

S

Piedra Buena

0   100   200   300 miles

0   100   200   300   400   500 km

Punta
Arenas

*TIERRA
DEL FUEGO*

**START
November 1998**

—— Route

Cape Horn

Monday, 2 November 1998   **Leaving Punta Arenas**

I find a bike shop first thing for spares. I re-thread the spindles, fit new ball bearings and new nuts and get under way by 10:36. Walking north along the road, everyone in vehicles waves or toots their horns and appears very friendly. The roads are more like rough tracks. They don't relate to my map so, at times, I'm not sure if I'm heading the right way. I learn not to listen to locals – they know where they live but can't tell you where that is on a map. Most directions I've had are a bag of bollocks.

By mid-afternoon, I feel weak as, but for two hot dogs, oranges and a few cups of coffee, I haven't eaten in two days. I find a nice place off the road to pitch the tent. Pushing through the trees, I find I'm actually on the edge of a sheer cliff top, looking down on the Straits of Magellan. Tierra del Fuego is in the distance: an awesome sight. I light a fire and get some pasta on.

Sunday, 8 November 1998   **Leaving Chile**

All week, the land has been flat, dry and dusty, and the days sunny and bright. But I've had a first taste of the wind, which increases as the day wears on. Gale-force gusts have stopped me dead in my tracks and being blown sideways for seven hours every day means you soon lose your sense of humour. I've left my sunblock at home, so use toothpaste instead (it seems to work) and wrap myself in a shamag.

Nights are cold. Normally it's tent up and straight inside to get out of the wind. On Friday, though, I pitched next to a filling station. To my delight, some bloke who stopped to refuel spoke English. He looked at my map and told me there is only one road to Argentina and I'm on it. Just as I was about to start cooking, he came over and offered to take me to the refinery where he works, for a coffee in the canteen. While the man on the pumps watched my kit, my new friend urged me to get stuck into a plate of ham. I did so with gusto, appreciatively.

Tomorrow, after seven days on the road, I intend to cross into Argentina.

Monday, 9 November 1998   **Crossing the border**

It's 13:30, my passport is stamped. The Chileans are very friendly, wishing me luck and, as I pull away, are banging on the windows giving me the thumbs up and waving. Just a hundred metres on, the Argentines are somewhat more sober. Two soldiers look over my documents and read the card in Spanish that explains what I'm up to before disappearing into a room at the rear of the checkpoint. Ten minutes later, they're back, smiling, shaking my hand and wishing me luck. They don't even want to check my gear. I pass a sign that reads: THE MALVINAS ARE ARGENTINIAN.

The landscape changes from hills to table-top flat with the odd dead volcano on the far horizon. As I write this, the wind is picking up but it's warm. The kit is still OK and the trailer, henceforth to be known as the Beast, is also fine. Both of my little toes are blistered but they don't hurt. Hopefully, they'll dry out. My wind-up radio is a morale boost at the end of a day but, annoyingly, I can't pick up BBC World Service here so I feel a bit cut off.

THE BEAST

The Beast is Karl's first trailer. In 1998, he asked a light-engineering firm in Hull to see if they could convert an aluminium-framed golf trolley into a trailer in which he could carry his essentials. With a central shaft and yoke, which Karl attached to the frame of his rucksack, it cost £100 to build and would be abandoned in Sullana, northern Peru, in May 2000 when he would buy a donkey.

Wednesday, 11 November 1998   **Rio Gallegos**

I have only come three miles this morning and I am still fifteen from the next town, Rio Gallegos, when I hear a distinctive 'pling', the sound of the spindle snapping as a wheel literally falls off. 'Please God, no . . .' I say to myself. I now see how much damage I caused trying to move my trailer in Punta Arenas with no wheel bearings. For nine days, I've been on borrowed time. I think what to do. The spindle has snapped just inside the wheel bracket. If I can force what is left of it through the bracket, then maybe I can join the two ends with a wheel nut? Will it hold the weight of the trailer and handle the rough track? It's worth a shot.

It is still only 09:38 as I gingerly set off down the track. The next five hours are pretty tense. I feel every bump on the road and I am conscious of every squeak the wheels make. I can see the town in the distance but it never seems to get any nearer. Now I know how it feels to bring a crippled aircraft home on one engine. I slow to a crawl as the track becomes cratered and strewn with large rocks. This is a sick joke – I'm convinced the Beast won't make it.

Then, just two miles from town, the potholes turn to sealed road and, after eighteen hellish miles, I check in to the cheapest hotel I can find.

Sunday, 15 November 1998   **Rio Gallegos**

So far, my diet has been poor, with only pasta keeping me going. I have been consuming just 600–800 calories per day, which is crap, so from now on, I'm aiming to take in 2000 per day. This consists of 200 grams of peanuts, four cups of pasta and a handful of dried fruit. People tell me it will get cheaper further north. I hope so. I have little money. It is expensive here and food for the next leg costs me US$60.

I rest up for three days, spending my last night on a campsite just across the road from a nightclub. It doesn't kick off until midnight and my tent is thirty metres away from this all-out, rocking party. I've not a cat in hell's chance of any sleep so, at 03:30, get dressed and join the party. It's a good night and I don't return to the tent until 07:00. I doze for an hour before packing up and pushing on.

Monday, 16 November 1998   **Entering Patagonia**

The west wind is the strongest I've experienced so far. For hours I am forced to walk – or rather stumble – at an angle of forty-five degrees to my left, which is playing havoc with my ankle joints. I notice llamas cope by lying flat out on their sides – either that or they're stone dead, killed by flying debris. In the afternoon, the wind increases and flips the Beast over and off the road. Enough is enough and I wait for it to ease off.

An hour later, I try again. I haven't got far before a large coach pulls up beside me and scares me half to death – I hadn't even heard it in the roaring wind. I expect some verbal about walking on the road, but instead, a passenger hands me a two-litre bottle of spring water. Proves how wrong I can be. That person will never know how grateful I am. I battle for a few more hours then find a scrape in the ground just off the road. I am knackered but must get the tent up. Out of the bag, it becomes a rampant wild animal and fights me like a tiger. What normally takes two minutes takes an hour. Pegs will not stay in the stony ground and the fabric lashes about in the air with poles flying in all directions. I am close to snapping. Welcome to Patagonia!

PATAGONIA

The southern part of the continent of South America as far as the Magellan Strait is known as Patagonia. Since 1891, the land has been split between Argentina and Chile. The Argentine section – through which Karl walks – extending 1000 miles (1600 kilometres) north to the Colorado River, is a tract of more than 300,000 square miles (480,000 square kilometres), nearly one third of the whole of the republic. It is home to millions of sheep. It is also prone to a boisterously strong wind, which raises a haze of dust in summer. In winter this dust turns to mud.

Friday, 27 November 1998   **Piedra Buena**

I make many new friends in Piedra Buena, as the town is known, and stay almost a whole week. At first I pitch the tent at a camping ground out of town – I don't have the energy to look elsewhere. I check out the local nightclub, getting there early – midnight – and soon two guitarists are bursting into song and people are dancing on the tables. It is shit-hot. This goes on till 02:00 when they attempt to start the disco. I meet an Argentine soldier who speaks a little English. I crash at his place at 07:30 and I'm able to base myself there for the rest of the week. I am given a space at the back of a storeroom, which suits me fine. He shares with two friends – really good lads. I get hammered with them again at the same disco later in the week.

I also meet a local girl in a restaurant who speaks good English. She invites me for lunch at her mother's place. Fantastic food – how kind they are. I am invited to the girls' secondary school. With a map of the world, I give my first lecture on the 'Goliath Expedition' to a class of teenagers, with the headmaster as my interpreter. I'm nervous, but as I get into my stride I enjoy myself more and can tell that the kids are genuinely interested. I get a photograph of myself, surrounded by kids, holding up the map. As I leave I'm mobbed by girls; I sign hundreds of autographs on school bags, footballs, T-shirts and countless bits of paper. I feel like a soccer star.

Thursday, 3 December 1998   Leaving Piedra Buena

The wind never lets up this week. I'm barely making fifteen miles a day, and once as few as eight. It seems to increase in the early afternoon. It's as if someone throws a switch that operates the lungs of the Andes and back comes an almost hot wind. It whips up clouds of dust and debris like grass and tumbleweed which pass you like bullets. If I'm heading due west, it sometimes stops me dead in my tracks. Progress is a slow plod. Heavy rain also turns the track to mud which sticks to the tyres so I feel like I'm hauling a truck. My shoulders ache like hell.

Last night at 22:00, a car pulled up and this bloke got out and came over for a chat. He asked how I was. I was lying in the tent at the time making a brew before trying to get my head down. He sat down and asked 'was I alone?', which always make me nervous. He spoke no English so I'm only guessing here. He gestured as to whether there was room for another in my sleeping bag. No, I must have got it wrong . . . surely this wasn't what he was asking? I hoped he'd piss off. He then asked for some toilet roll and disappeared for, I assumed, a crap, only to return and sit down in front of me with his trousers round his ankles. Well, I was gobsmacked. Before I knew, he turned round and stuck his bare arse into my tent and pointed at my crotch! He soon got the picture and fled in his car.

Friday, 4 December 1998   Gobernador Gregores

Yesterday, still thirty miles from town, a second spindle snapped . . . and so did the wheel fitting. I've a spare spindle but the bracket is more serious. The broken spindle is stuck fast so I use my jet cooker to heat it up to try and loosen it. I merely burn my hands, melt a hole in my fleece and bend the cooker in the process. I decide to pitch the tent and, in doing so, manage to break two more poles. All the time, I'm blasted by sand and dust; my eyes are red raw and tears are streaming down my cheeks. I'm extremely pissed off.

I phone home using the sat-phone to boost morale. It works. Using my Leatherman tool, I estimate – or rather, guess – where I think the spindle ends within the axle and begin sawing through. I guess right. The broken spindle is free and I've only lost an inch of axle.

I wake early and resume repairs, trying to fit a new spindle. In effect, what I'm struggling to do is fit two tubes of almost equal diameter inside other. I try in vain, even resorting to brute force, hammering it with a rock. I only manage to push a few millimetres of spindle inside the axle but it seems to hold. Bashing it has, of course, damaged the screw threads so I must file new ones. As for the bracket, I decide simply to bind it tightly with para-cord. It looks a pathetic solution but it's noon so I should crack on. I set off. I give my lashed-up wheel not more than a hundred metres but fourteen miles later, I trundle into Gobernador Gregores almost drunk with happiness.

Wednesday, 9 December 1998   Gobernador Gregores

When I arrive, I meet an old boy – Carlos – who stops his bike to talk to me. He speaks some English and at first I do wonder if I've run into the village mad man – he is quite a character. He soon introduces me to Mrs Helen Gibbs, an elderly woman who, besides teaching English at an adult's night school, is something of an administrative genius. She is a great help in finding me forwarding addresses for my mail. When I later ask her if she knows any mechanics, she says there is just one and we've already met ... Carlos. He makes a cracking job of fixing the trailer and machines a new modification, which I've called the Carlos Fandango. He won't accept any payment and even invites me for lunch. He is seventy-five – what a terrific guy.

I've been resting here for four days. All the time I've been in town, the weather has been calm and sunny, but within a few hours of getting moving again, it's a howling gale. It is yet another full frontal assault into the devil's breath ... and more bad tracks.

Thursday, 10 December 1998   Beyond Gobernador Gregores

Last night, the wind flattened my tent and I hardly slept. It was blowing a hurricane and I just lay there waiting for things to start coming apart. Many things played on my mind – food, memories of family, friends at home. It was a long night.

Once on the road, the stiff headwind reduces me to a crawl and makes even simple 'admin' tasks much harder. Going to the toilet becomes a messy affair. Obviously, it's unwise to aim into the wind but when you face the other way, your body creates a vortex and the urine is just whipped into the air and all over you. The wind makes my eyes water and my nose runs constantly. I end up blowing snot all over my face – trying to blow my nose through one nostril doesn't work because the wind simply wraps it around my entire face. Attempting to wipe it off spreads it everywhere, so I just let it dry and scrape it off at the end of the day.

Then, just after midday, the wind changes direction and is behind me. I really start to motor and the track is also downhill for miles – it's heaven and it feels like I've never made so much rapid progress.

Friday, 11 December 1998   Beyond Gobernador Gregores

When I come to pitch my tent at 16:00, there is no shelter from the gale and I can't get any pegs into the ground. The wind is very cold, numbing my hands and face so I back-track two miles to a road junction I passed close to a derelict house, where I'll spend the night. It's a real snapper retracing my steps but I need to get out of this wind. At least I'll get some sleep.

Late last night, I found two chicks, about the size of chicken chicks, cheeping outside my tent. I looked through the door at them and they scurried away. This morning, I find them looking worse for wear at the side of the track so I carry them in the top of my rucksack all day. As I write, they're sitting in one of my pans.

Monday, 14 December 1998   **Las Horquetas**

I can now see the snow-capped Andes rising in the west through the heat haze. There are three small places marked on my map that I will pass through before I reach the bigger town of Perito Moreno. I need to buy rations at one of these places, as what I have won't last much longer.

Even though it has been signposted for 150 miles, Tamel Aike turns out to be just a single forlorn house. No one is at home but I refill my water bottles from a pipe overflow round the back. Las Horquetas is not much better. It is a poky, run-down hotel with two men sitting at the bar, one who speaks a little English. I eat a huge mountain of spaghetti then buy bread and a tin of ancient-looking peaches to keep me going. The walls are hung with animal skins: foxes, some very large wild cats, llamas and an extremely large puma – I wouldn't like to meet that after dark.

Tuesday, 15 December 1998   **Towards Bajo de Las Caracoles**

Today I see something strange on the road in the far distance. In the heat haze, it is hard to say what it is. Tall, thin and black, it is moving quite fast in my direction. I feel the hairs on the back of my neck stand up. I've seen nothing else all day. Now it is just me – and this silently moving black shape. It still has no features – it's just a dark shape hovering above the ground. My eyes widen and my heart is pounding. Then, at four hundred metres, the shape is suddenly recognisable – it is just some bloke on a bike.

Harold from Munich is peddling from Tierra del Fuego to Bolivia. It is taking him three months. It is good to spend an hour or so with an able English speaker. We've both shared the same experiences, met the same people and had the same difficulties with the wind. Harold has followed my twin tracks for days and was puzzled by the two bike wheels running in parallel. The word is, there is a small shop two days' walk from here at Bajo de Las Caracoles – a massive relief as I'm low on rations.

Thursday, 17 December 1998   Bajo de Las Caracoles

Last night I had visitors: mice. Once I had my tent up I was infested with them and these boys are as bold as brass. They sit in groups of five or six in the entrance of my tent and watch me. Anything I put down, they are into; my boots, mess tins and rucksack, anything I leave for a moment. They eat peanuts from my hand and keep me amused for ages. That is, until I want to sleep. These little shits keep me awake all night. It sounds as if they are chewing holes in everything and they are still at it first thing this morning.

Just before I make Bajo de Las Caracoles, I pause at the head of a huge valley. I have the most incredible view of the Andes stretching away in front of me, pale blue and topped with snow. The valley is ten miles wide. I can see for miles and stand here for a while taking it all in. It is a rare moment when I know why I am here.

In the town, I meet some Italian tourists at the local store. They seem dead impressed with what I am doing and take pictures and videos of me. One old guy gives me 100 pesos – he will never know just how much that meant to me. I can now buy enough food for six days, enough to get to Perito Moreno.

Tuesday, 22 December 1998   Perito Moreno

Total distance to date: 681 miles (1097 km)
Each day I think the winds are the worst I'll ever have to face but twenty-four hours later I'm always proved wrong. Those today – my last day's walking before Christmas – are straight from the depths of hell. Reaching the top of a re-entrant, I can see a radio mast in the distance – it must be the edge of Perito Moreno, but it's hard to tell: the wind is screaming around, kicking up huge dust clouds.

When a destination is in sight, it is usually the time a wheel decides to fall off and, guess what . . . yes, one does. I can't believe that it has happened again. This time, I've no spare spindle and still eight miles to push so, yet again, I'm crawling around on my hands and knees, amid swirls of dust, trying to undo nuts and bolts. I pick a large nut and manage to join both ends of the broken spindle together. The rough track, of course, isn't helping and I feel every lump and stone beneath the wheels as I creep slowly forwards again.

The wind has, of course, spotted my difficulties and after circling for a few minutes, comes in for the kill. I must stop and dig out my goggles as I can't open my eyes with all the dust and grit being thrown in my face. When the track swings east, the gusts hit me sideways on and I stumble all over the place. Reaching the head of another valley, a huge gust turns the Beast right over, dragging me with it. I struggle to climb out of my Bergen straps, cursing as I do so.

Amazingly, the broken spindle holds. I right the Beast, but only take two steps before there is a lurch behind me. I turn around, expecting to have lost the right-hand wheel only to find it is the left wheel that has come off. If I were religious or faintly superstitious, I should take this as a sign of some sort. This is the third time that this has happened when I've been in sight of my goal. There's nothing else for it – I get to work and make a running repair on the second spindle and continue. Two hours later, I creep into town. It has taken five hours to cover ten miles.

Friday, 1 January 1999   Perito Moreno

Considering the number of tourists that pass through it, Perito Moreno is a very run-down town to spend Christmas in. It has a campsite but this is expensive so I build a discreet hide in some nearby bushes and play cat and mouse with the owner, who can't work out where I have been sleeping.

The travellers I meet here – from Brits and Israelis to Germans and Dutch – are a good source of information. It may be a bit strong, but I almost feel as if we're all part of some tribe. We've all come from different parts of the world, but we look and sound quite alike in many ways, having lived through some similar experiences. There is a British lad – he's ex-45 Commando – who has been running tours for three years. He and his Aussie girlfriend have driven a group of eleven down from Ecuador. I meet another Brit from Wembley who has been travelling for a year in Central and South America, and who isn't looking forward to heading home in March. He says I'm 'quite a celebrity' with the groups touring this part of the world as I'm in all the local papers. They all tell of some Englishman who can be seen walking and walking, pulling the strangest thing behind him. He says he is 'glad to have met me'. It is so strange to hear that from someone.

I meet Jesus. She is a passenger in a car of young people who spend all their free time 'hamster-wheeling', the term I use to describe the way the locals cruise up and down the main street. Jesus speaks good English but is only around for a day because she has to leave to see her family. No matter, I meet several other local girls and see the New Year in at the disco, which doesn't stop until 08:00. These girls like a dance and I have several good nights there. I've quite a fan base and when I turn up, always get a rowdy reception and a Coke thrust into my hand. I also utter my first complete sentence in Spanish. It's great to get a reply rather than blank looks. I will miss the new friends I've made in Perito Moreno.

Saturday, 9 January 1999   Rio Mayo

Conditions under foot are appalling all week and – no surprises here – I lose another wheel. I was expecting it to happen. I only have the one spare spindle, but this holds until the road turns to tarmac on the outskirts of my present location, Rio Mayo. Just before I reach the town, another van chock-full of tourists pulls over. Although the driver and guide know all about me, the passengers don't. One American woman asks me where I am going. I tell her I am walking home.

'Ha ha, no really,' she asks. 'Where are you going?'

'I'm walking back to England,' I reply.

'Oh, my God!' I hear someone shriek, and another gives the command, 'De-bus'. The doors fly open and Americans, Italians and some Argentines spill out and I am mobbed with questions and asked to pose for endless photographs.

Wednesday, 20 January 1999   Rio Mayo

I have the best three days in Rio Mayo. Camping in a park, I immediately fall in with a group of soldiers who are just like soldiers the world over. We end up in the local discothèque where, surprise,

surprise, they put away a shed-full of beer. They get very loud and stupid, so much so I wish that I was alone again although it does mean they keep buying me burgers. The conversation extends to the Falkland Islands, but they are too young to recall it and their interest is more out of curiosity than anything else. As the night wears on, one collapses so I lay him on a bench with his head propped on my jacket. Big mistake: he vomits all over it.

Gabriel, the local English teacher, invites me to put up at his place – the lure of home-cooking and a proper bed is irresistible. He's very interesting and we click straight away; he has been a traveller in the real sense of the word and has lived with people from different cultures. I admire his outlook on life. He has a girlfriend, Natalie, and we hang out at her place. Problem is, she's a flirt. She needs no excuse to hang around my neck. I don't know whether it's because I'm the only blond guy around or what but it makes things tense at times.

I am trying to get a lift to the border this morning to renew my visa but the lift I am promised never materialises. I decide to get going and hit the road at midday. I don't get far before my latest mates ambush me in a car with some ice creams.

Thursday, 28 January 1999   Costa Gorda

With no wind all week, it is brutally hot. One night, the thermometer reads 50.01 °C. I just lie in a pool of sweat but even this is preferable to being plagued by the buzzing outside: the flies here are horrendous. I'm also getting a little worried by the numbers of black widow spiders I keep encountering. I have to watch where I sit and where I put things, particularly after dark.

In Costa Gorda I camp in the garden of an abandoned house near the centre of town. I find the police station to see if there is any chance of movement between here and the border fifty-five miles (ninety kilometres) away. Trouble is, it's a small place where no one goes, or so I'm told. I should reach Esquel in six days – which is close to the border – so this will then give me three days to fix my visa before it expires.

While I'm sitting tight, I try to make a bow and arrow. Not that I have much success. I manage to fire a stick thirty feet or so but there's no real power, certainly not enough to put one in a sheep. I know it's not right – the sheep out here belong to someone – but I have been getting very hungry at times. All through my journey I have seen them dotted about, far from human habitation and wonder if I might bag one if ever I'm desperate. So far, the morality of such an act is not an issue because I can't get near the buggers.

Monday, 1 February 1999   Beyond Costa Gorda

Lying in my sleeping bag, I feel a little cold this morning. I can hear what sounds like rain falling on the tent but it is strangely dark outside. Through sleepy eyes, I peer at my watch – it's 06:30 so why is it still dark? I lie there for another moment then notice the tent roof is a touch saggy. Sitting bolt upright, I sense the space in my mobile home has decreased, as if I am being squashed. I push against the tent side only to trigger an avalanche of snow . . . yes, snow. Quickly unzipping the entrance, I emerge into a winter wonderland although I can't see beyond a hundred metres as the clouds are low and the snow is still falling.

The thermometer is at freezing. Just a few days ago, I was coping with 45° C – I had been short of water and dreaming of cold drinks and ice – but now I'm in the foothills of the Andes. I don't feel as if I've climbed at all and I'm still in the valley bottoms but this shows me just how unpredictable Patagonia can be. Shivering, I pull my Gore-Tex coat from the Beast. It's as if I've emerged from a dream and was back in England.

This morning I am interrupted by more travellers who are following me in the local papers along my route. I always stop and pose with them for photos, even in the snow. The sun comes out again at 16:00. In one burst of steam, all trace of the snow vanishes and the land turns to dust again. This evening, camping in a culvert under the road, it is still warm.

Wednesday, 3 February 1999   Towards Esquel

15:00: a yoke on the Beast snaps clean off. Completely immobile, I pull off the road. Once again, I must solve an ugly problem while being hammered by wind and dust. I trawl the roadside and hunt around an old earthworks – perhaps used when the road was built – where I find a piece of old black plastic piping. It might be just the ticket. Cutting it to length, I squash one end of the tube and bend it to match the angle of the broken pieces then lash it to the frame.

The plastic pipe is hard and very rigid. Using the blade on my Leatherman tool, I begin to bore and whittle a hole through which to thread a small length of bungee that I'll use to fix it to my rucksack. I am pressing on hard when the knife slips . . . straight into my left wrist. I flinch and withdraw the blade. As I do so, a bright red jet of blood shoots across the ground for about a metre. Wide-eyed, I jam a thumb over the cut. Shit . . . Shit . . . Shit. I sit in stunned silence for a moment. Slowly I release my thumb to look again. The blood spurts so back goes the thumb.

I've done one of two things: I've either severed or just nicked an artery. If it's the former, I'm in for an interesting time. If I've just nicked it, my prospects are substantially improved. I feel a touch queasy, which is to be expected – how often do you see your own blood jetting from your wrist? I lie back and look skywards. Relax, just relax, I mutter. I decide to give it a few minutes of pressure and have another look. If I can't arrest the flow, I'll need assistance.

It's all right, I tell myself. I'm only sitting out a sandstorm amid the debris of my wrecked trailer and I have just slit wrist my wrist. All I need now is to step on a forgotten landmine. I sit up and the queasi-ness fades. I slowly lift the pressure on the wound. It is a clean cut one centimetre long. I move my wrist a touch. The wound re-opens and, although more bright red blood bubbles, it doesn't spurt. It is clotting – I replace my thumb. This is good, I tell myself – I can cope with this.

It is a deep cut and it will need a stitch or two. Trying to shelter from the wind, I dig out my medi-pack in which I find a threaded 22mm needle, alcohol and gauze pads. I wash the wound so that I can see what I am doing. It bleeds quite badly. I am aware of the risk of infection; as fast as I clean it up, dust blown up by the wind sticks to it again. After much swabbing and fumbling, I manage to get a stitch into the centre of the wound but tying it off in these conditions is a fiddly job if you're only using one hand and your teeth. I get a second stitch in but, drawing my third and final one together, I pull too hard and the skin tears. I need a fourth. Bright blood still wells

between my handiwork, but after a minute, it is clotting nicely . . .
the job's a good 'un. Dressing it with the gauze and a crêpe bandage,
I have the situation under control.

I'm back in business. With the bungeed pipe in place and attached
to my rucksack, I walk for another forty-five minutes before I camp
under some trees where the valley narrows. Despite life's minor problems I am happy again. I've won the day.

Saturday, 6 February – Monday, 22 February 1999   **Esquel**

Two days after my injury – and with a grand total of 1170 miles
(1882 kilometres) behind me – I walk into Esquel. It's a big place and
I don't like big places. There's too much traffic and nobody gives a
shit, it's just rush rush rush, with a 'get out of my way' attitude. The
point is, I've all but run out of money so must stay in town until my
mum sends me some. I'm told it may take fifteen days for a letter
from England to arrive.

First stop is the hospital. My cut looks to be healing well and I'm
impressed that two of my stitches have held. No one speaks English
here, but the nurses are a good laugh; they redress my wrist and ask
me to return the next day.

Finding somewhere to stay is the next priority and, as always, I'm
in luck. A truck slows down alongside me. William's a tall, hand-
some Argentine – an architect working on a nearby construction site
on the edge of town – and he speaks some broken English. He says
he has room for me to pitch my tent so I make my way there. Besides
needing Mum's money, I must fix the Beast and also get to the frontier to sort my visa.

In town I run into Walter, whom I met a few days earlier on the
road. In his late fifties, he's from Belgium and is cycling down from
Lima, Peru. He sold his business to fund his travels, most of them in
Asia, and has an overwhelming desire to spend the rest of his days
travelling. He's a good sort; a stocky chap with dark hair and a grey
beard and the eyes of a wolf. Sitting outside a restaurant, we take the
piss out of tourists in their Jesus sandals with socks pulled up to their
knees, khaki shorts, camera jackets and bush hats. Rarely do they
step off the tour buses. It's arrogant of us, I suppose, but we enjoy it.
Walter is something of a gourmet and stands me an expensive dinner

inside. It costs him US$64 but he says he is 'sponsoring' me . . . what a bloke.

I get a lift there and back to the closest border crossing. It's a tiny post with a barrier but despite its remoteness, the guards are still smartly turned out with pressed shirts and trousers. All goes swimmingly well. When I get back, William has found someone to repair the Beast and generously pays the rest of the US$15 bill as I've only four dollars to my name.

Mum's letter eventually arrives as well as one from a member of my new fan club, Victoria Gonzales, a fine young lady I met in Piedra Buena, whose envelope has been to Hull and back again. I've cash at last so the pressure is off, at least for now. My last night in town with William ends at 06:00 in the Argentino pub and I leave town three hours later. I've been like a child waiting for Christmas, actually getting excited about walking again, which is a good omen.

Thursday, 25 February 1999   Beyond Esquel

From my tent last night, the forest fires burning on the slopes of a valley in the distance are dramatic. They started two days ago and, glowing red with clouds of smoke, resemble a volcanic eruption as they look to be spreading to a second mountain. The night turns into a hellish one. The wind picks up and, although I secured the tent sides with rocks – I can't get pegs into the rocky surfaces – it is soon being forced flat by almost hurricane-scale gusts. It is at its worst at 01:00. The tent loses its fight; the poles snap, the fly sheet is loose and the whole right-hand side of the tent lifts, rolling me in my doss bag on to all my kit within.

I thrash around in the dark trying to get boots on. Kit is flying everywhere and once outside, I'm hit by a blast of stinging dust. I just throw myself on the tent fabric to prevent it from vanishing before pinning it down with more rocks. In desperation, I crawl into my bag in the open air and beg this night to end. Before it does, it rains. Wet and shivery, with my eyes swollen and burning from the dust inside them, I chuck some more rocks on the plane crash that was my tent and crawl underneath to wait for the dawn.

Saturday, 27 February 1999   **El Bolson**

I feel I am leaving the deserts of Patagonia behind now and everything is becoming greener. As I drop into a bottomless valley lined
with pine trees, I walk into El Bolson just as a national festival is getting under way. Ninety per cent of those attending appear to be
hippies and New Age types so, looking as I do, I guess I fit in. I meet
New Earth people and Star children and infiltrate them, introducing
myself as Carlos the wood gnome. One is a Brit – Katherine – who is
a well-to-do sales and marketing person travelling with Victor, her
Aussie boyfriend. I like them – we get on well.

In the night, a sixth sense tells me something is up. I'm in my tent
next to the Beast when I disturb some creep helping himself to my
gear. I challenge the figure and he bolts with my ice axe and shamag.
Leaping from my bag, I give chase barefoot. My blood is up and I'm
gaining on him when he drops the axe. He can keep it – I just need
that shamag to keep the sun off me. I'm closing only to lose him
when he bursts on to a gravel road littered with sharp stones. Bugger.

Monday, 1 March 1999   **Beyond El Bolson**

Another altercation today. I stop outside an old house on the roadside to ask for water and can't find anyone about. It is then I notice
the apple trees growing on the other side of the road along the verge.
These are first class and taste very nice when I try one. I bag a few
but just as I'm loading them into the Beast, an old gaucho comes
down the hill ranting at me in Spanish. He is short and stocky,
dressed in a poncho, with a scarf around his waist and a large hat. A
rough old beggar, he is blind in one eye and hopping mad. Had the
trees been on his side of the fence, I would have offered to pay but
they are just growing in no man's land.

As I try to depart he reaches into the small of his back and pulls
out a commando-style dagger and waves it at my belly. I grow a
touch apprehensive as he continues to threaten me and demand
money. I have a good look at him; no doubt he's tough but I assess
he's past his best knife-fighting days. Taking a step back, I reach
down the side of my rucksack and whip out my machete. He gets the
message. Life in the valley is becoming quite an adventure.

Sunday, 7 March 1999   **San Carlos de Bariloche**

Nestling in the mountains, Bariloche is known as Little Switzerland – you can guess what it looks like – and I rest up here for three days. Friends I make always seem to pass me on to another contact and William – the architect I stayed with in Esquel – has urged Rodrego, also an architect, to look out for me. Not only do I stay at his house – and sleep on a proper mattress, albeit on the floor – but he also buys me a new set of tyres for the Beast. What can I say, what a bloke!

The roads are getting busier and I encounter irate drivers who sound their horn as they swerve round me. I pass a police checkpoint on the edge of town, where I'm ordered off the road and instructed to walk on a dirt track at the side. This is strewn with broken rocks and sprinkled with broken glass. I argue, then rant in a mixture of Spanish and English but the copper looks blank with a 'I couldn't give a rat's arse' expression. The track shakes my wheel nuts loose and I have to struggle on for over a mile before I'm sure the police can't see me anymore and I can get back on the decent surface.

Thursday, 11 March 1999   **Chile–Argentina Border**

Yesterday, I joined a queue at the Argentine border. This takes for ever but I have no problems and eventually inch my way through amid a stream of cars and wagons. Once across, an elderly couple heading the way I've just come hand me a heap of fresh food that they can't take over with them. I gratefully accept corn on the cob, ham slices, a wedge of cheese, vegetables, fruit and even bread – will make a sandwich or three. Sod making sandwiches, I think before long. I just find the nearest shady tree and stuff my face there and then.

This morning, I puff and pant my way uphill towards the Chilean border. If the stiff climb isn't bad enough, I am in a foul mood because I have to keep stopping to tie the wheels to the axle with para-cord. I've a sharp pain in my stomach, which is, I guess, just due to the stress I'm under. I must calm down. I am developing an intense hatred of the Beast and wish it would break beyond repair so that I can bin it. I am sick and tired of it but in my heart of hearts, I know I can't do this walk without it.

Then things don't seem so bad after all. I thought I had another twenty miles to push when a workman I stop to speak to tells me the frontier is less than two miles from here. The unmade surface turns to tarmac. A sign – Welcome to Chile – looms into view.

Chapter Two

CHILE

Chile, and more crucially, a smooth road. Unlike Argentina – where roads zigzag up and down the hills – here they just run straight up and down. It's all I can do to stop the Beast from burying me on descents. It is causing wear and tear on my knees and ankles, which are very sore. My toes are also being crushed into the fronts of my boots when I try to hold back the weight of the trailer.

It's also far more tropical than I have been expecting – it rains most nights. I begin to notice soil rather than sand; there are flowers, with a multitude of silvery-green hummingbirds darting between them; there is the high-pitched croak of frogs coming from murky pools along the roadside; and, of course, the decaying smell of the jungle. Roads passing through deep valleys are flanked with trees and brambles, all dripping with ripe fruit – I know what I will be living on. I also come across the bodies of tarantulas that have been run-over. I wasn't expecting any of this until Ecuador.

Resting at a roadside café, I meet some carpenters from Mendoza, who invite me to join them in their fry-up. My plate is piled high with steak, potatoes and bread, washed down with a glass of wine. No sooner have they left than another family walks in and sits at a table next to mine. They are all smiles and waves as if I'm the boy next door. I can make out that they're talking about me and say, 'Hello, how are you?' Before I blink, they invite me to eat with them ... I've died and gone to heaven. A tray of steak, sausages, pork with fried onions, tomatoes and potatoes arrives and my meter

BOLIVIA

PARAGUAY

BRAZIL

Pacific
Ocean

ATACAMA

La Serena

ARGENTINA

URUGUAY

Santiago

CHILE

South
Atlantic

Arica

Tocopilla

Antofagasta

Temuco

Los Lagos

San Carlos
de Bariloche

N
W — E
S

| 0 | 100 | 200 | 300 | 400 | 500 miles |

| 0 | 200 | 400 | 600 | 800 km |

is soon showing full. They've seen me on TV in Esquel. It's amazing what a bit of publicity brings . . .

Monday, 22 March 1999   Los Lagos

My left knee is playing up. I notice it most when I'm going downhill. It is becoming a real worry so I am stopping for a couple of days on the edge of Los Lagos, as I'm sure it will get better if I rest. But I can't hang around for too long as I'm nearly out of grub. I am given six peaches at a farm where I call for water. At first, I think that they are potatoes, which I would prefer. All I seem to eat right now is fruit. I only have one Chilean dollar left and two left over from Argentina, which I'll change in a bank.

The bank in Los Lagos is busy and I queue for ages. From the looks I'm getting, you would think I've escaped from somewhere – it's clear the locals don't see many gringos in these parts. Boredom is temporarily relieved when there is a power cut – these are not uncommon in this part of the world. Alarms go off and security men run around in a tizzy while they try to sort it out. Once the fun is over, I find they can't change my few dollars for some reason, but the supermarket does and I spend US$3 on pasta, sugar, two eggs and some bread. Now I'm dead broke.

Saturday, 27 March 1999   Beyond Los Lagos

Right now, my diet is 80 per cent fruit. As it is autumn, it's easy to exist on it but soon it will be winter so what do I do then? I keep thinking about eating meat and whenever I pass a herd of cows, I go into hunter mode. Sachets of army-issue coffee found on the verge are an absolute gift from God because I ran out a few days ago. I also pick up two bread rolls that are barely a day old. It makes my day.

Last night, I sat by the fire, considering future plans. I wonder what I will do when I get to Ecuador. I will have to give up the Beast and forward it and the heavier kit on when the way gets too steep. Then I'll consider using a pack animal, probably a donkey. This should save my knees from a hammering in the mountains. I hear it will be even cheaper to live once I get to Peru so I might be able to afford to buy some creature to haul the kit.

Tuesday, 30 March 1999   **Beyond Los Lagos**

Happy Birthday to me! I'm thirty. I wake and open my card and present from Emma, my last girlfriend back home. She has sent me coffee – spot on! It's just what I need as I am running out again. It is a little something but it has a major impact. I am happy again, and consider taking the day off but eventually decide against. I tab seven kilometres and come across a small town. At a filling station on the outskirts, I curse that it has no café . . . bollocks! What I really need is some young blonde to appear and say 'Hey, fancy some breakfast at mine?' And what do y'know, one does.

Her name is Barbara and her mother owns the gas station. She invites me to her grandmother's place just next door where I am treated to toast, jam and scrambled eggs and lots of coffee. Apparently, Barbara's late grandfather always invited travellers in for something to eat so this tradition continues in his memory. God bless him.

Having refilled my water bottles, I return to the Beast only to find Barbara is waiting – her mother insists I stay for lunch seeing as it's my birthday. I have a shower and change my clothes before I meet grand-mother, a very nice elderly lady. Soon the food is ready and I sit down with the three generations. Each place is laid with several pieces of cut-lery, side plates and two wine glasses. We have a starter, a main course and a pudding – roast apple in custard – and then the table is cleared and a single candle lit. A cake appears and I blow out the candle as they all sing happy birthday. What a bizarre time I'm having. Not only that, but Barbara is studying architecture in Santiago – she's home on holiday – so I have my first contact in the capital.

It's now 16:30 so I have to get going again. An hour later, I pull into a large open field, which has a small copse in the centre. It's on the edge of a small town and no sooner have I got the tent up than I'm sur-rounded by kids playing football and riding their bikes. I am also being watched by some grown-ups which is bad news. As a precau-tion, I remove anything of value from the trailer and put it in the tent. This is a good move, because just after midnight, I see a figure walk past the tent some fifty metres away. It is an obvious 'recce' but he doesn't spot me slipping out through the flap of the tent.

Crouched in the shadows, I see him meet another. The pair speak in hushed voices before the second man begins to creep very carefully towards my tent and trailer. I stand, hidden behind a large tree trunk and smile as he sneaks right past me. He is so close I can smell him . . . a teenager. He kneels next to the Beast and as he does so I lean over his shoulder and quietly ask him what he is going to do now. He leaves his skin behind as he leaps skywards – he and his mate leg it. This is good fun but I can't get back to sleep. I'm on edge.

Thursday, 1 April 1999   Towards Temuco

The alarm on my watch wakes me. 04:00. It is an icy cold night lit by a full moon and an absolutely awesome display of stars. I crawl from my tent and melt into the early morning like a hungry vampire. My Softie jacket is an excellent garment for nocturnal raids as it is dark green and has a drawstring around the waist, making it easy to stuff 'things' down the front. Like maize.

But no sooner do I enter some nearby fields than a flock of birds – I think they're called 'Triostrios' – give me away. They circle overhead making a God-awful noise that is surely enough to wake anyone asleep at the farm. Damn. I cross fences and ditches, sticking to the tree-lines and manage to find my way into the maize field, which is very small. It is literally next to the farmhouse so I begin painstakingly cutting the maize heads from the stalks. It takes time but I manage to cut a dozen and my jacket is bulging.

On my return route, I jump a steep-sided, water-filled ditch and grab a fence-post on the landing side to steady me. Unfortunately, it's loose. Bit by bit, it slowly leans towards me, lowering me gently into the ditch until I am up to my tits. I gasp as the ice-cold water floods through my layers of clothing. I climb out and squelch my way back to camp . . . at least I've found something to eat.

No chance of any sleep after my dawn dip. As the sun comes up, I get a fire going and boil two corn-cobs for an hour until they are soft enough to eat. I don't leave until noon as I've clothes to dry.

Sunday, 4 April 1999   Towards Temuco

Total distance to date: 1543 miles (2485 km)
I'm not far from Temuco – the next main town – but I don't want to be there too soon as my mail is not due for a few days yet. With this

in mind, I camp in a pine forest two hundred metres uphill from a cluster of wooden farm shacks with the usual selection of chickens, pigs and dogs running about outside. I ask at the farm for water and they oblige, and also give me some bread. The next day, I'm still resting here when the one of the younger men from the farm – Patsicio – brings me more bread and stops for a chat. I show him my newspaper cuttings. This is it – I'm famous. He asks me for lunch and says I can sleep on the farm.

Guarding the farm are two old dogs with bad attitudes. I don't like them and the feeling's mutual. I am given a wooden shed, the doorway of which is too narrow to fit the Beast through. The next thing I know, the farmers crowbar the door frame. I protest that it isn't necessary but they'll have none of it. It is a stinking hovel: I am kept awake by the rodents trying to get at my food and, on one occasion, at me!

In the morning I have breakfast in bed, brought by an old guy, who lives next door to Patsicio. At lunch-time, it is the turn of the people next door to feed me and I am served a plate of liver and lemon. I am also introduced to a fruit called a membrillo – it's nice, if a little bitter. After lunch, a potato farmer drops by, this time with a pile of family photo albums. Aaah! I view pictures of his tractor, a field, a pile of potatoes, more tractors, him and his tractor . . . need I go on? Now that I've been shown so many photos of his tractor, we are almost blood brothers . . . when he leaves, he gives me his address, more photos of himself, his family and, you've guessed, his flippin' tractors.

I'm eaten alive by fleas in the night. I itch like crazy. Again, I have breakfast in bed, this time it's bananas, bread and coffee. Christ! This is the life. Mid-morning, Patsicio's wife cooks up a plate of chicken and mashed potato. I feel so guilty. All this from people who have so little themselves. I guess they'll never know just how much it means to me. I don't finally leave for Temuco – just six kilometres away – until 14:00 because I've had to wait two hours for the bread they were making for me.

Thursday, 15 April 1999   Beyond Temuco

Outside my tent this morning everything is covered with a layer of frost until the sun breaks the horizon and it all turns to steam.

Compared with how I felt a short time ago, I'm not only physically better, I'm mentally much happier. I've been eating more fresh vegetables, which could have something to do with how well I feel.

I notice changes in the land again. The soil is dry and sandy, a lot like it was on the other side of the mountains I've just crossed. This is the 'dry country' before Santiago, something I remember others have told me about. Besides the odd dead skunk – which you smell well before you get to it – I only seem to see birds. Birds of prey are very common. Flocks of large brown hawks sit on every fence-post for several hundred metres, just watching me pass. The roads are littered with dead ones hit by cars, so many that you wonder how the species survives at all.

A couple in a minibus stop to invite me for a coffee. I can't really work out what they are trying to suggest, but it turns out that they are teachers and that the coffee stop is at a school just a kilometre away. They are waiting outside when I arrive. It is extremely small and very run-down. A large group of kids, ranging from toddlers to teenagers, welcome me and lead me into the school – two classrooms, a dusty yard and a kitchen, where an old woman is standing over a large cauldron of rice. I am given VIP treatment. The teacher explains that I'm an 'Anglo-Saxon', and how we 'are all tall and have blond hair'.

The children's eyes are on stalks. I tell my familiar story and where I've come from and where I'm going . . . more whoops of incredulity. The elderly teacher speaks some English so relays their many questions. I end up emptying the Beast and showing them all my kit. They love it. I have coffee and biscuits then a dinner lady gives me bread to take with me. The children give me apples and those friendship bracelets.

Friday, 16 April 1999   Pablo's

A truck stops me. The driver climbs out and introduces himself in English as Pablo, Chilean and in his mid-fifties. He owns the land I'm passing through and asks me to stay at his place a kilometre away. What a result.

His house is a hundred years old and in a beautiful setting. Tropical plants grow in the large garden, and inside the walls are hung with strange heirlooms, which makes it interesting to wander around. Pablo leaves me resting on the porch in the early evening. I sit alone as the sun is setting, casting a deep orange light through the trees that encircle the house and garden. Golden leaves are falling like snow upon the lawn and I notice autumn has suddenly arrived. I think about my son, Adam, and the fact I don't know where he is right now. It is playing on my mind so I ring Mother. The first thing she says is 'I've just been speaking to him.' A weight from my shoulders is lifted.

This weekend is Pablo's fifty-sixth birthday party and I am invited to stay for it.

His two sons – in their mid-twenties – and daughter – she's nineteen – come down from Santiago, bringing with them the obligatory pack of dogs (four of them). Other relatives and friends appear and it is becomes quite a party. At one stage, I can hear Pablo's pro-Pinochet friends discussing the former dictator. I understand more than they think I do and I know what is coming. I'm asked – in English – for my opinion and I give it as I see it. It's not what they wanted to hear but I don't think I've put my foot in it.

Crossing into Chile, I admit that I was glad to see the back of the deserts of Patagonia, but I'm starting to look forward to the next challenge . . . the Atacama. Deserts are a hellish challenge – I'm already looking forward to this one.

Wednesday, 21 April 1999   **Beyond Pablo's**

Around noon, a black VW Beetle pulls off the road and into a lay-by ahead of me. I can see that the man tinkering with his engine is a gringo. When I draw level with him, he asks, 'You are walking?'

His name is Uwe Quist; he's Hungarian but lives in Germany, and looks like the rugged guy in the Marlboro advertisement. He has been driving between Alaska and Ushuaia for two years, and is now on his way back up north as far as Arica, the last place in northern Chile before Peru. There, he plans to leave his car with the girl he has been travelling with and then return to Europe. He's dreading going home.

Uncorking a bottle of wine, we hop over a fence and sit under a tree where we swap adventures. Uwe's favourite place is Colombia;

he liked the people and never had any trouble but didn't feel the same about Peru, which sounds very dodgy. He has a good attitude to life and to people; Uwe is one of the 'Wild Bunch', characters that can't settle, who just have to keep travelling. There is always real fire in their eyes. When they describe their adventures, the passion and enthusiasm shine through. No doubt, I'll meet many more.

Friday, 23 April 1999   Chillan

Chillan is a textbook town 'occupation': someone who can speak some English spots me in a café, and offers me a place to stay. This time it is Jimmy; he lives in the suburbs with his parents, two brothers and a sister in a house adjoining a car repair garage where he works. Susan, his sister, is thirty-one and studying veterinary medicine. I stay the weekend and, at times, I find myself alone with her. Bluntly, she asks me what I intend to do about a girlfriend? There is a long silence.

This question has been weighing heavily on my mind for some time. It's not the fact that I haven't had sex for five months . . . anyone can abstain for that long, or longer. It isn't purely physical, it runs deeper. It has to do with time and space; I'm here today – gone tomorrow. One-night stands are always a possibility, but this is not what it's about. I just don't see there's room in my life for anything more. Perhaps this is the price I pay for living my dream.

It's a constant dull ache being alone. Were love to find a way, it would bring conflict into my life; to find someone and then to be forced apart would be like being skinned alive, but to give up my dream for someone is unthinkable. What's it to be then, a rock or a hard place? Not that Susan is playing.

Tuesday, 27 April 1999   Parral

Very wet morning. Everything is cloaked in thick fog, but it all disappears when the sun comes up. It gets hot today and I have a good view of the Andes as I walk a dead straight road. At times I manage to slip into a trance-like state. This is great when I can manage it: I just fold my arms across my waist, drop my head and the autopilot switches on. I disappear inside myself. I'm able to keep the same pace going and the hours just fly by.

I stop at a café next to a gas station, just short of a place called Parral, where I spend time catching up on my notes. I down a glass of Coke and the girl behind the counter brings me a free sandwich. It is, apparently, just one of the perks of having a striking resemblance to Kurt Cobain . . . whoever he is. God bless him all the same.

Saturday, 1 May 1999   **Beyond Parral**

I asked at a nice-looking house if I might sleep on some nearby ground last night. The owner, Ted, is Canadian – his wife is Chilean – and they seem relatively well off. As I set up camp, three young girls emerged and asked if I'd like some soup. The eldest returned carrying a large pan. The others reappeared with trays of sandwiches and cakes, and bags of tea, coffee and fruit-flavoured powdered drinks.

When I leave this morning, the housemaid tells me those inside are still sleeping so I ask her to pass on my thanks. But I've only been walking for twenty minutes when a truck pulls over in front of me – it's Ted. He's sorry he wasn't up before I'd left and was intending to ask me to stay for a while. I had come at a bad time yesterday when they were preparing a family birthday party for their fifteen-year-old daughter, which is an important celebration out here. He asks me if I'd like to come back with him, and hits me with the magic words . . . 'You can have a shower, wash your kit and eat lots of food.' How could I resist?

Ted left Canada ten years ago and settled here with Viviona, working as a safety specialist in a copper mine. He's tall, slim and a very pleasant guy. Viviona gives me some of her husband's trousers, a top and some socks: she also starts putting together some packs of cereals for my journey. They both insist I keep telephoning them to let them know how I'm doing and even say they'll give me some change for payphones . . . this is too much. They've persuaded me to stay until after the weekend.

Tuesday, 4 May 1999   **Beyond Parral**

I only left them yesterday but apparently Irma (Viviona's mother) misses me. It's 16:00 and about time to knock off when she and Viviona turn up in their car with a load of food. We sit on the roadside where I am given hot dogs and more birthday cake while they take endless photographs. Just to add to the occasion, Pablo also spots us on the roadside as he drives past on his way down from Santiago, so we have a strange reunion on the verge.

Wednesday, 5 May 1999   Towards Rancagua

Tea-time again and who should turn up but . . . Viviona. This time the whole family piles out of the car. Viviona produces a huge casserole in a pan and a pile of fruit, bread, yoghurt, crisps and chocolate, which we all get stuck into. Viviona's father, Omar, also returns my Leatherman tool that had gone 'missing' when I was staying with them. He had taken the likely suspect – a lad from the adjacent farm – for a drive and convinced him that the missing tool ought to be returned.

They leave me with more food than I can carry. Before they say goodbye – yet more photographs – Omar and Irma get quite emotional and I can see Omar starting to fill up. They are calling me their adopted son.

Thursday, 6 May 1999   Towards Rancagua

This is not over yet. It's fifty-eight kilometres to the next decent town, Rancagua, and 158 to Santiago, which is the halfway point of what I'm calling 'Stage One'. I'm close to the mountains now, so enjoy splendid views, and the road itself undulates like a rollercoaster. The further north I go, the more habitation I pass and it is harder to find secure-looking places to sleep.

Just when I think I've found one, along comes Viviona and her mother – or rather, my mother, as Irma is known. They want to show me the photos from the previous two reunions and insist on feeding me to bursting point. We sit by the roadside while I'm force-fed a box of fried chicken in breadcrumbs and a large bowl of rice which I can't finish. I'm stuffed. They also give me a bag containing soap, shampoo, a new toothbrush, a new small towel, more food, two bottles of wine and one of Ted's old jumpers. My God! They even try to make me take a pair of Ted's old trousers . . . please, enough already. They promise to help me at any stage while I'm still in Chile. How can I ever repay such wonderful people?

Friday, 7 May 1999   **Towards Rancagua**

Mid-morning. I'm sitting in a car hoovering a bowl of lentil soup because the 'family' has just shown up . . . again. Irma has made me boiled eggs. I am soon in pain and reaching critical mass . . . I can eat no more! They try to give me the trousers again . . . 'no more trousers,' I insist. Viviona gives me a roll of masking tape and two tubes of superglue, just the things to patch my decaying tyres. Roderego, Irma's brother, slips me more money before we finally part. What a guy.

It's tea-time when I chance upon a Shell station. Rather than a scruffy café, this place has a smart-looking restaurant. I pause and look around – it's quite busy. There is hot food on display with trays of fruit and racks of wine and spirits. Tables are set with shiny cutlery and wine glasses. Soft classical music is playing and a drop-dead gorgeous waitress is beaming at me with a dazzling smile. Then I notice everyone has stopped eating and talking and is looking at me. I contemplate just walking out again but that would make me look even more stupid. Instead, I ask a smartly dressed chap at the counter for a Coke and walk to an empty table as if I own the place.

'You have come from Punta Arenas?' asks my man with the Coke.

'You are going to Alaska,' he continues. 'And it'll take you five years, yes?'

We shake hands. He knows all about me.

'Ah, we hear from the people that come here, they all talk about you.'

A waitress appears with a plate of beef, chicken and rice. It is followed by a pudding and some chocolates . . . on another plate.

'On the house,' he insists. I hear him telling other customers all about me as I thank his staff and leave.

Wednesday, 12 May 1999   **Santiago**

Total distance to date: 1910 miles (3076 km)

I reach the outskirts at 10:00, but it is early afternoon before Pan American Route 5 reaches the city. I couldn't find a street plan anywhere so have sketched a map from a phonebook. When the hard shoulder runs out I become part of a fast-moving cloud of eighteen-wheelers, the trucks whipping past my left earlobe. I feel the heat from their engines – this is putting years on me. Add to this the fact that the roadside is carpeted with the carcasses of dead dogs and the smell blends nicely with the carbon monoxide. Dogs around here must breed like flies just to keep the numbers up because so many die on the roads.

Santiago is a huge city, one great concrete jungle from horizon to horizon, above which hangs a blanket of smog. The air quality is made worse by the fact that Santiago is a city in a basin, surrounded by mountains and there is virtually no ventilation: every day certain numbers are read out on TV and radio and cars with these registration numbers are not allowed into the city, in an attempt to cut pollution.

I tab like a madman to Avenue El Bosque Norte where I will find the British embassy which closes at 17:00. I'm there by 16:00. I speak to staff behind bullet-proof glass and ask for some water while I wait for my letters and parcels. I'm not made to feel welcome.

SANTIAGO

A bustling, noisy capital, it is the fifth largest city in South America, and stands in a wide plain, 600 metres above the sea. Graced with tree-lined streets, parks and distinctive neighbourhoods, it covers 100 square kilometres and is crossed from east to west by the Mapocho River, which passes through an artificial stone channel, spanned by several bridges. The magnificent chain of the Andes, with its snow-capped peaks, is – rain and smog permitting – always in full view, for much of the year.

Thursday, 13 May – Monday, 31 May 1999   **Santiago**

I move in with Pablo – the bloke I stayed with a month ago in his hundred-year-old house in the country. His place in town is a contrast but it's perfect. An hour's walk from the centre, it's a cramped chalet in the grounds of someone else's home and one of Pablo's sons, Christian, is also staying here. He's a frustrated teenager and I don't think he likes having me around.

THE PAN AMERICAN HIGHWAY

This is a network of roads connecting North America with South America. Since 1923, there have been plans to create this route – a continuous road running 16,000 miles (26,000 kilometres) from Alaska to the bottom of Chile. Now all but fifty-four miles (eighty-seven kilometres) are complete, so aside from a detour by boat to avoid the notorious Darien Gap on the Colombian–Panama border, it is possible to drive the whole way.

I've never found a city where it is so easy to meet girls. I often go to bars and, by 04:00, I've always got a pocket full of phone numbers, but it is the same old story . . . young women live with their parents. There is Katherine – waitress at the 'Louisiana', and Claudia – an Italian working at her embassy, as well as Marcella – she speaks good English, and Elizabeth – she speaks none at all. I even meet someone called Tamel, who turns out to be a bloke (at least he has his own place). But these beautiful girls are a helluva job. They're very complex and nearly all still living with mother, even at the age of thirty.

Then I meet Treiz, who is my age and very attractive. She is single and says she has a place of her own. We both know what we are getting ourselves into but it doesn't make it any easier because I will be leaving. Treiz begs me to stay longer. She says I am okay at her brother's place and that she will pay for me. But I have to play hardball now. If I give in, it will only happen again somewhere else. I feel as if I'm being pulled in all directions but I just have to deal with it. I have to go when I say I will go.

Saturday, 5 June 1999   **Beyond Santiago**

The desert again: large hills, rocks, sand, scrub and cactus. Sheep have given way to goats and, compared to the south, there is very little traffic heading for the capital. Yesterday, when a bus pulled over in front of me, I sensed it was Treiz (as I'd called her on Friday). She'd left Santiago at 08:00 asking the driver to keep a lookout for the blond gringo. 'Yes, we know him,' the driver replied.

We walked together for fifteen kilometres until we reached the edge of El Melon where we camped in a dry stream-bed. This morning, we're up at 06:00 because this crazy girl must catch a bus back to Santiago and go to work. 'Nina de Luna' or 'Child of the Moon' is what I call her.

Monday, 14 June 1999   Los Vilos

On my first night here a taxi-driver, Sergio, puts me up. Then Treiz drops in again. She is unimpressed when I admit I slept with a girl I'd met at a disco on Friday night – telling her just seemed the right thing to do. We spend the night in a hotel but neither of us is sure we'll ever see each other again. Before we part in the morning, we play like children on the side of the road. The bus comes and she is gone. Perhaps she'll take a holiday in January and join me when I get to Peru? Who knows?

I discover I'm missing US$100. The little green-eyed beauty from the disco on Friday night is looking 'favourite'. I live and learn but I'm relaxed about it. Luckily, I've enough money left to get me to La Serena but a hundred dollars . . . I could weep.

Thursday, 17 June 1999   Towards La Serena

I meet a topographer, who's working for a road builder and has seen me in the papers. Impressed with my plans, he informs me that, basically, the road ahead undulates as it does now for the next 2000 kilometres. Isn't this just what I want to hear. I guess I'll spend the rest of my time in South America doing hill 'reps' while pulling a tank with its brakes on.

In the afternoon, I stop for a map check, when a truck pulls in on the other side of the road. Two men are waving at me from the cab – I wave back and turn back to my map. Then they come over and hand me an envelope with 'Mrs Karl Bushby – Present' written on it.

How bizarre. I look at the two who are grinning at me. They also hand me a letter. It reads:

Dear Sir,
Bavaria Restaurants chain invites you to enjoy one hot meal in each of the northern cities you expect to stop in. We have

food services in seven northern towns, so some of our lorry drivers will stop you on the road and give you the invitation tickets, please accept them.
Yours sincerely,
Christian Kast.

Inside the envelope are seven tickets for restaurants in La Serena, Vallenar, Copiapo, Antofagasta, Tocopilla, Iquipue and Arica, all towns I intend to pass through. Christian Kast, it seems, is the restaurants' owner and has read about me in a colour piece in the Santiago paper, *The Mercury*. I'm beginning to understand the power of publicity.

Saturday, 19 June 1999   Towards La Serena

I'm about to begin writing up my notes in a grotty restaurant next to a Copec filling station, but I think I'll grab a coffee first. I am just thinking what to do about my tyre – it has blown again as I entered the forecourt – when, as if from a movie script, one of the lads from the garage comes over and hands me a brand new 24in. x 1.95in. tyre. I look around. Nothing. An old gas station and a tatty restaurant, all in the middle of a desert, and some bloke hands me a new tyre. Right now, it is the one thing I need in life. I could turn religious. He explains that a man had dropped it in here with instructions to hand it to the gringo heading north.

A girl of about eight – a daughter of the owner – beckons me to follow her. Behind the restaurant, the rest of the family are trying to pin a struggling sheep to the top of a makeshift table. They want me to give them a hand. A large bucket sits under the head of the now wide-eyed sheep as a man produces a large knife – I know what's coming. The family, meanwhile, is discussing the TV, as their father sticks the beast with the blade and saws through its throat. The animal gasps, wheezes and shudders as its steaming blood gushes into the bucket. It fights like hell in its last moments and makes very disturbing sounds. This seems to take about three minutes. At last, the blood has stopped pumping and it hangs limp.

I try to imagine a similar scene happening at home. Most British kids wouldn't sleep for a month if they saw this. Out here, not a murmur, no deviation from what was happening on TV last night.

Wednesday, 23 June 1999   La Serena

La Serena is a tourist town with a beautiful beach. No buildings are over four storeys high and all must conform to traditional styles. I get a great welcome here: as I head for the post office to find the mail, a stream of well-wishers stops me and offers me food, water, money and a bed for the night. One woman – Claudia, who speaks perfect English – offers me a room for free at her hotel.

Four letters are waiting for me, including a rather odd one from a Dr Michael Bier. He had apparently seen me passing his home way back, then read about me in the newspaper. Attached to his note is a cheque for US$100 and a postcard to his friend in Austria, which I am asked to deliver by hand in a decade or so. Dad has sent me a new shamag – it's pale pink – so I look like a cross between Lawrence of Arabia and Quentin Crisp. All the same, I have been badly in need of one.

Claudia's hotel is actually a homely bungalow with a few spare rooms to let. She has a boyfriend, David, who is North American, and they have two children, a boy, five, and a girl, two. They also have rats. I sit and listen to them all night, running around the roof space.

Thursday, 25 June – Saturday, 10 July 1999   La Serena

Treiz, ever resourceful, tracks me down. She stays for a few days and I'm sad to see her go when she catches the night bus to Santiago. The bus station reminds me of a battlefield, packed with confused people wandering around as if lost, and so many tearful people bidding each other farewell. I'm alone again.

There is no one else in the bungalow during the day so I find myself doing housework. I soon have the place gleaming. This is a side effect of having been in the British Army – I'm forever on the lookout for something or someone to 'get a grip' of. Claudia, meanwhile, likes to talk and unburdens all her personal problems – everything from money to the kids – and admits things are going badly with David. It makes me feel uncomfortable that she is telling me. What would David make of this?

I meet Kay from New Mexico, who is travelling with a friend, Megan. Both are teaching English to keep themselves going. Kay and I click – she's gorgeous – a bundle of fun and I enjoy her company. At a barbecue the next evening, I'm in the kitchen munching on a cracker when she walks past, pauses on tiptoes and bites off half of it with a semi-kiss. All done in one stylish movement and it leaves me quivering. I wasn't expecting it. I awake next morning staring across the pillows into her large brown eyes. She has to leave, of course, which is the way the story always goes.

Things come to a head between Claudia and David. They've decided to split. She has my sympathy but I don't have any answers. I've become the innocent catalyst for their breakup; David's calling me her 'toy-boy' and tells her I must pay for my room if I'm staying any longer. But funnily enough, he isn't really blaming me and we shake hands. Making up, we get steadily inebriated one afternoon on pisco and Coke. 'Piscola' is 35 per cent proof so we don't need to drink much.

'You have a great image and you carry a million men's dreams,' David says. 'But buddy, you have got to get a tooth!' (I lost a front one in the Army and rarely bother wearing the false one).

'I know TV people, I know how they think. If someone does an interview with you, they could decide to drop it because of that tooth. It may seem trivial but you've gotta believe me. It's the first thing I thought when I saw you ... it's a great story pal, but please, get a tooth.' Hmm, I will keep it in mind.

Friday, 16 July – Wednesday, 28 July 1999   Vallenar

Vallenar's a small town and isn't busy on a Friday night. I book into a grotty but dirt cheap hotel – it's 3000 pesos (approx £3) per night – which, believe me, is as cheap as it gets. Inside, it's a mess and stinks of urine. The cold-water shower is outside and the temperature falls rapidly as it gets later. Fortunately, the light isn't working so I can't see how blue I'm turning. I re-emerge, convulsing, hyperventilating and feeling like I've got frostbite, only to find three cats curled up on my clothes. This is the end – more bloody fleas.

I need to eat. I get very chummy with Marcela, the attractive girl on the till in the restaurant I eat in and, because of her, I stay in town longer than I had intended. I must balance my desire to get to know her with the urge to crack on. Still, I've become convinced that I mustn't push myself quite so hard, that I must make the most of any opportunity that comes my way . . .

Marcela's restaurant becomes my 'home'. I spend a lot of time here and I get VIP treatment. Trouble is, I begin to hate it when they give me free food and fuss over me the whole time. I'm too proud for my own good. I can't take this brand of charity when I don't really need it. No doubt when I'm broke and in a shit state in some far-flung place, it won't be there for me but right now, I'm fine. For the first time in this expedition, I feel guilty.

I slip further into a decline, aggravated by the fact I spend hours waiting, hanging around in the street, often in the freezing cold, waiting for Marcela to knock off from work. It doesn't help that she can't speak much English. My growing sense of isolation is intense and I begin a downward spiral to a point where I actually start to feel as if I'm having a panic attack. Never before have I felt half so bad. Everyone around me wants to know what's wrong but this only makes it worse. I'm stir-crazy. Definitely time to say goodbye.

Sunday, 1 August 1999   Copiapo

Total distance to date: 2400 miles (3865 km)
Another hot sunny day, another flat tyre. I'm in a really foul mood as I wobble, squeak and clank down the road. Just before I reach town, there's a beast of a hill. I stop to re-apply new para-cord – the first bit has worn through – then start to drag the carcass up the slope. As I do so, a camera crew shows up . . . for the love of God, why now? Here I am, puffing and panting, the Beast in a shit state, making a right noise and one wheel a mass of chewed up rubber and string. Ahhh.

Monday, 16 August 1999   Chanaral

Yesterday, I reached Chanaral, beyond which is 400 kilometres of nothingness . . . just desert in one of the remotest stretches of the Atacama. I'd showered at an Esso station then moved down to the beach to sleep. Just as I thought I'd found the perfect place, I stumbled across someone sleeping under a blanket. He's an Indian with no legs and a wheelchair – he's bumming his way around the country. We talk and he's glad to have me as a neighbour. I know this because he scrounges half my evening meal. He looks a bit rough and he walks around using his hands. Kind of reminds me of R2D2.

This morning, the sun is hot in a big, bright blue sky. Two weeks ago, to lighten my load and make room for more food and water in the desert, I boxed up my less essential kit and sent it on to Antofagasta. I hope it gets there before me. I've spent any remaining cash on more pasta and cross my fingers I've enough on board. I trace a valley east for most of the day, but the last six kilometres is all uphill, a long slow climb that near finishes me.

As I make camp just before sunset, the valley below to the north fills with clouds of fog. Looking out across these dense clouds is just like peering through the window of an aircraft. Distant peaks are bathed in a red glow: it's very impressive.

ATACAMA DESERT

A sparsely populated, virtually rainless elevated desert that extends from Chile's coast to the foothills of the Andes. Although it is less than 100 miles (160 kilometres) wide, it extends 600 miles (960 kilometres) south from the Peruvian border and includes the main cities of Arica, Iquipue and Antofagasta. Made up of salt basins, sand and lava flows, it is often described as lunar in appearance and is a desolate piece of country. It is a very cold place with daytime temperatures ranging between 0° C and 25° C. In the highest places, snow falls, and excavated bodies of buried Indians – perfectly preserved by the cold – are thought to be 9000 years old.

Tuesday, 17 August 1999   **Towards Agua Verde**

Today's route is downhill at first before I turn into a seven-kilometre killer of a climb to a height of 895 metres. I'm in a shit state at the top. The Beast seems so heavy, making life damn hard. I sit down and take a break at the twenty-kilometre mark, not far from the next summit, 'Satan's Hill'. I am reminded of just how quiet it can get in the desert when there is no traffic. It's absolutely silent – all I can hear is the blood banging through my ears. There are no signs of life, just the two large black vultures that seem to be following me. Perhaps they're hoping I'll drop something, or maybe drop dead myself. I feel as if I might.

I'm stopped by a family looking for their mentally ill son; he's in his forties and has gone missing. They're searching the length and breadth of Chile and gave me a photocopy of his picture (and two oranges). If I do come across him out here, I guess the only way he'll be identified is by his dental records – that's if those vultures haven't removed his teeth.

After 'Satan's Hill', I have another ten kilometres to push before I achieve my thirty-kilometre target. I am shattered when I get there. My clothes are run through with white veins of dried salt, so much so that my trousers have gone stiff. Looking out across the valley to the east, I can see that it will be the same tomorrow, and the next day. I sit for an age on my arse and I can barely motivate myself to pitch the tent.

Monday, 23 August 1999   Beyond Agua Verde

Bitterly cold and very windy this morning. My home is covered in a layer of ice and freezing droplets of water rain down on me from the trees I'm under as I pack up my kit. My hands and face are numb and I can't wait to retreat into the restaurant to beg some hot water for a brew.

I am straight into a slow climb. Up ahead of me, the clouds of fog meet the warmer air and explode into huge spirals, moving so quickly that they look like giant flames, before they evaporate into nothing. On the hills to my left, huge dust devils are whipped into mini-tornadoes, sending columns of dust hundreds of metres into the sky. The cold wind coming from behind me begins to give way to a much stronger warm wind from the north. It's here to stay and is horribly familiar. Suddenly I'm pulling hard uphill and being battered by winds that are turning gale force. I meet false horizon after false horizon. My legs are burning up with the lactic acid my effort is pro-ducing but I push on even harder. As I close on the top of the final crest, the wind is so strong it almost stops me in my tracks. After three hours and twelve kilometres, I'm there, absolutely destroyed. I've climbed 1998 metres and I'm looking out across the Atacama's plateau with snowy mountains to the east and the road still turning north.

The wind doesn't relent. Bits of rubbish wing past me like bullets. A litre plastic bottle comes from God knows where, bouncing along the road towards me as if powered by a rocket. It hits the embankment on the roadside, and clips past my ear. Blimey, I don't want to get in the way of one of those. Sand stings my face and hands so I mask up. I struggle on then take a breather. I want to get a photo so dig into the top pouch of my rucksack for my camera. As I do so, I remove a cassette, my faithful U2 tape, and tuck it under one of the bungees on the Beast.

With the wind still roaring away, I haven't noticed the huge truck that's pulling over in front of me. Suddenly, from out of the gale, I feel a presence beside me. I look up to see a girl standing there with a beaming smile. She is wearing a loose-fitting cotton dress over a Lycra body with heavy boots and carries a huge rucksack.

'What the . . .?' I mouth.

'You're the Englishman walking round the world, right?' she begins.

I confirm. She then whoops with joy, gives me a hug then turns to wave to the truck driver who pulls away . . . leaving her, with me . . . in the middle of nowhere. I find this a touch disconcerting.

Poula is a twenty-year-old cookery student from Vina del Mar. She's on the return leg of her month-long solo hitch-hike around Peru and Bolivia and has been reading all about me. Although she speaks no English, we get by and I warm to her strong, bubbly character. She's banging on when, abruptly, she points to the trailer where, still tucked under the bungee, the entire length of my tape has unravelled and is streaming in the wind. There is no saving it – my beloved U2 tape is ruined.

I decide I might as well try and camp here. The problem is . . . where? The wind still howls and the ground is flat in every direction so I can't begin to think of erecting the tent in this. A hundred metres further on is a scrape where a bulldozer had pushed some stones during the building of the road. My plan is to build a stone barricade in the hollow to try and get out of the wind and, hopefully, then get the tent up. Poula thinks it's a great idea (you can't knock enthusiasm), and we work our arses off building it.

It's pretty harsh out here, everything is a mass of dust and sand, a real mess, but Poula isn't complaining. While I cook some pasta, she begins to make some scoff from a cactus she calls 'San Pedro', several larges pieces of which she produces from her bags. She sits for ages, cutting up the cactus; she peels off a thin outer layer of skin to reveal a layer of dark green flesh which she drops into a pan. This, I discover, must be boiled for hours. I tell her to stuff it after fifteen minutes – she's not using any more of my precious fuel.

Poula explains that, were she to boil it a little longer, crystals will form in the base of the pan. These, it turns out, are hallucinogenic and the Indians use them to visit the spirit world. I sit with my head in my hands, as she searches through the goo with a spoon to see if any crystals have appeared.

'Hey, let's just have pasta,' I offer. She agrees. Besides, the goo stinks.

Poula shows me various things that she has collected during her travels; lots of rocks, various edible plants and beans, and lots of souvenirs from Peru and Bolivia.

'Look at this,' she urges, and shows me a chunk of volcanic rock.

'Very nice, where's it from . . . Peru?'

'No, just by your tent,' and she sticks it in her bag.

She makes me laugh, that's for sure.

Later, I watch her as she sits outside the tent, huddled in my Softie jacket, staring at the stars and a full moon. She notices how still and silent it is, awestruck by the intense isolation. She's right.

Tuesday, 24 August 1999　　　　　　　　　　Towards Antofagasta

The wind returns in the night with a vengeance. Poula wakes me, clinging to me like a demented fruit bat, terrified that the tent is about to disintegrate. I reassure her that it has been through much worse. The morning start is slow. In the wind and swirling dust, my 'admin' is chaotic; I had buried all the kit under rocks to stop it blowing away, all the cooking pans are filthy – covered in burnt cactus – and there's not enough water to clean them.

I sling everything into the Beast and haul it back on to the road. This, believe it or not, is where we part in the place we met . . . the middle of nowhere. Poula is more than happy for me to leave her here, assuring me that she will get a lift 'no problem'. There she is, her dark hair thrashing in the wind, the dust caked across her face, wishing me well. She belongs on the road. Before I move, she removes one of her necklaces and ties it to my ankle.

There is a lot of traffic heading south. After fifteen minutes, I pause and scan into the distance behind me with my monocular. She's not there.

DUST DEVILS

These are a type of whirlwind. Caused by extreme surface heating, these funnel-shaped columns of air occur in dry places, such as deserts. Smaller than tornadoes, they rise from the ground and are not associated with cloud. Moving spirally round an axis, their diameter is three to ninety metres and their height 150 to 300 metres. More often, they appear in the afternoons, when there is a lot of surface heating. Their speed can be up to 95kph (60mph). They last only a few minutes, but all loose objects around the dust devil, such as dirt and dust, are raised along with the air, hence making the whirlwind visible.

Wednesday, 25 August 1999   **Towards Antofagasta**

When the wind drops, the sun makes its presence felt. It gets very hot and any exposed skin burns rapidly so I cover up, even the backs of my hands. The world around me here is dead flat and wide open. To the left is a large range, the Sierra Nicuna McKenna. To my right, even further away, are the foothills of the Andes.

I've started to fill water bottles with pasta during the day so that all I have to do at night is bring it to the boil. It saves fuel, don't know why I didn't think of this before.

Saturday, 28 August – Wednesday, 15 September 1999   **Antofagasta**

I touch down around 15:00 dreaming of steak and ice cream at the Bavaria restaurant, which is two blocks from the post office. The restaurant staff agree to lock the Beast away for safe-keeping so I drag my stinking body around and collect my baggage from the bus station and some letters on foot.

I opt for a night on the beach, but am warned off by a local: 'Not a good idea, gringo, bad place, lots of drugs, prostitutes, people being murdered.' I get the message and try another bit of beach further on where a group of youngsters are also camping. I smell the dope they are smoking. The next morning, I call a friend of David's (the chap I stayed with in La Serena). He's Carlos Ramirez, an executive type with a company that distils sea-water. Although he's Chilean, he is, to all intents and purposes, North American because that's where he's spent most of his life.

His distinct air of authority marks him out. The longer I stay with him, the more he discloses. After national service in Chile, he was studying in the States when a friend's father, who was in 'intelligence', recruited him into, I guess, the CIA. Vietnam, Eastern Europe, Korea, Afghanistan, the Far East and Israel . . . the stories flow thick and fast.

After a week here, I feel a growing sense of isolation. Usually this is fixed with a pair of big brown eyes. In this town I'm clocked by girls who whistle and shout as I pass by – they even hang out of office windows. But sex is just a quick fix, a fast-acting pain-killer which does little for the real problem. I can't express my true emotions to anyone. I'm living a bizarre life; I've so much to say, so much to confide but none of this passes my lips. It's beginning to take its toll.

I've got thinner. Looking at myself in a full-length mirror confirms it. Shit, there's no doubt, I can see my ribs. I've always been slim and found it hard to put weight on but could lose it rapidly. I panic – how thin will I get? From now on, I'm on a 'get fat' crusade.

Friday, 17 September 1999   Michilla

A small mining town. Tomorrow is Independence Day so tonight it's party time and the flags are out in force. There's been a two-week build-up to this and for days cars have had pennants flying.

A café owner offers me a bed-space out back. I step over kids, chickens and turkeys only to be leapt on by a couple of reeking dogs.

I should have known – I'm shown to a decaying shed from which more fowl is booted. Maybe I should just kip on the roadside – being hit by a truck is swifter than dying slowly from some obscure disease. But these kind people have offered me the shed and I'm grateful. I will get used to the smell.

After dark, there's a 'do' in a cunningly converted barn and, at midnight, I check it out. Following the sounds of the music, I step through the barn door. It's poorly lit but I make out the wooden pallets that form the dance floor and a row of benches around the sides. All eyes are drawn to the strange gringo. They are Indians and the wives and kids are here too. Big hairy-arsed miners, most of them half-pissed, scan me with glazed eyes. It feels a real scary place. There's nothing else for it – I have to go into the 'drill'. Look as if you own the place – I've done it many times before. I stroll to the centre of the bar. Behind me there's silence and I can feel many pairs of eyes burning holes in my back.

'Chicha por favor,' I ask.

'Chicha' only comes in one-litre jugs. Bugger! This much will destroy me but there's no going back. I throw the money on the bar and find a seat. I am listening to an awful makeshift band comprising fat miners when a woman approaches. Dressed up to the nines, she looks well out of place here with a hairdo and get-up that reminds me of Maggie Thatcher.

Sylvia's a schoolteacher. I join her and her two daughters; one is twenty-nine and heavily pregnant and the other is a chubby fourteen-year-old girl. Sylvia offers me a place for the night. Thank you! That kicks the chicken shed into touch. It's not long before I'm under the influence of the devil's brew, but I manage not to show it and even finish the jug. Sylvia's house is tiny but very clean. I am given young Natalie's bed – she bunks up with her mum. I stay the weekend. Happily, Sylvia doesn't have a dog.

Friday, 24 September 1999   Tocopilla

Total distance to date: 2855 miles (4597 km)
There's no keeping up with worn-out tyres. I need another set in this larger mining town and it takes me three hours to find the scabby bike shop. The robbing bastard charges me ten mill for two new ones

(that's US$10 apiece). I spend a night on the beach before I telephone
an old chum, Sergio from Los Vilos, who insists I call on his sisters,
Laura and Maria.

I sniff them out in an old run-down house on the main street. I
was expecting two elderly ladies and, indeed, they look about eighty.
The first thing that hits me is the stench. It is horrendous. Cats and
dogs run amok. This place is gipping – cats and dogs are allowed to
crap where they feel like it and there is shit everywhere. Not surprisingly, a dog is ill – it's vomiting. The house is a biological
minefield and I can feel my health failing from the moment I step
inside. The old ladies are as nice as pie, but my mind is on other
things: fleas, typhoid, rabies, you name it.

The kitchen is gruesome. A fat dog growls at me from a corner.
'Feeling's mutual, pal,' I'm thinking. I am introduced to these creatures and know instantly that they can tell I hate them all. Maria, the
elder of the two, tends the sick dog, even though she herself is very
frail and can hardly walk. It has 'biohazard' scrawled all over it. I
glance towards the door and swear I can hear someone shouting:
'Run, Forest, run!'

Maria hugs the poor pup then leans towards me, urging me to
stroke it. I smile then wince and back off.

'Would you like some lunch,' she offers.

Say no, Karl, say no . . . I'm thinking.

'Why of course,' I reply. It just came out.

I take a seat at the old wooden table in the centre of the room. The
sick dog is left to join a group of kittens playing in another corner
but they aren't stupid – I see them do a swift 'bomb-burst' (military
slang for troops scattering in a contact with the enemy). Poor Maria
explains that they are out of medicine for the pup so would I fetch
some – yes, right away, I offer. The outside air is never so sweet.
Returning, I'm in time to see vegetables being prepared on the table
that is covered in matted cat fur and paw prints.

I'm offered a shower. Maria shows me to a dark, dingy back
room, its concrete walls green with lichen and mould, and points to
a square at one end where you stand under a cold-water pipe. I feel
I've entered the lair of something awful and sure enough, there it is
in the shadows. An ancient cat, lumps of fur missing, and covered in
battle scars, hisses at me. This is its territory and, to make sure I've

got the message, it has been using the shower place as a toilet. Maria chases it out with a broom and, spotting the cat crap, sweeps that into a convenient pile before shovelling it into a cardboard box that she leaves in one corner.

I can't see much daylight as I shower. Just one shaft of sunlight streaks through a crack above me. I feel a bit like a prisoner being processed before getting hurled into a grotty dungeon. The cat crap along the foot of the back wall has been here so long it's turning to soil. Christ, the smell. The drain at my feet is full. I glance at my toes, which are disappearing in a smelly, murky puddle of something.

I return in time to see Maria wiping the table with the 'cloth'. As she does so, she explains how they have four generations of cats and three of dogs living with them. The sick dog starts to vomit again. In Maria's loving arms, it is gathered up and brought to the table and its matted coat is wiped once again with, you've guessed it, the cloth, which is then returned to the table. Sniffing the air, the fat old dog waddles over and begins to lap up what the sick dog has just thrown up. The old girls laugh loudly at this. I try to.

Laura takes a set of dusty plates from a top shelf and places them on the table. I watch in terror, mouth wide open as she gives them a wipe with the cloth. Dinner is served but the smell is killing my appetite. The sick dog then throws up yet again, this time under my chair. On an empty chair, a cat sits watching me and I can see large fleas weaving their way through its grungy coat. I've got to get out of here.

Saturday, 25 September 1999   Tocopilla

Every now and again, you catch a glimpse of a girl you only thought existed in movies or in the pages of a fashion magazine. I'm reading a book in the town's plaza when she walks past. She moves through the square with the fluidity and power of a pyroclastic flow. She glides past without a glance. With such grace, I can only presume that she has stepped straight from a catwalk. She crosses the street, buys an ice cream and then takes a seat on a bench close to where I'm sitting. No contact is made but I can't get her out of my head.

Later tonight, I find myself alone on a balcony in a disco. I happen to glance to my left. I plunge into the depths of the most beautiful pair of deep-brown eyes staring back at me. It is 'her', the girl from the plaza. Looking down at the dancers, I play it cool, hopefully appearing unmoved by her presence. Inside, every nerve ending is screaming 'compose yourself'. I give myself a set of quick battle orders. We're going to go for this, we'll probably take a real stuffing and there'll be heavy casualties but this girl can wipe the floor with me. I won't care, it will be a pleasure trying . . . then she speaks to me in Spanish.

'You were the man reading in the plaza today?'

I respond with a blank stare. I've been surprised, I'm in trouble.

'Ah, you speak English. You were the man reading in the plaza,' she repeats.

'Err, yes,' I blather. Well done Bush, the old killer one-liners, that should do it.

The conversation flows smoothly. Tara oozes sophistication and I'm putty in her hands. She's perfect. She paints a picture of money, social status, fashion, rich friends and fast cars. We're worlds apart – get out Karl while you can. She says that she's a student but is taking time out for other things. I put her in her early twenties but in fact, she's seventeen. She urges me to be at the plaza tomorrow at midday. Why?

'Just be there,' she insists.

We dance the night away until 03:30 when she leaves, reminding me to be there at the plaza. Well, I could be washing my hair . . . but probably not. She has me by the nuts. Did she sing or dance – tomorrow is the town's centenary? Rabid dogs and flame-throwers wouldn't keep me away.

Sunday, 26 September 1999   Tocopilla

The plaza is sealed off. Crowds are kept to the sides as marching bands do their thing. Everyone is drawn towards a roped-off section in the middle of the square where rows of chairs and microphones are positioned. A series of smart cars pulls up and unloads what look like politicians, businessmen and military top brass in uniform . . . and Tara. Dressed in a white jacket and short skirt and sporting a crown and an embroidered sash, Miss Tocopilla – Tara – alights to a hail of wolf whistles. If her plan was to impress me, it's working.

She catches sight of me in the crowd and flashes me a broad smile. Two hours of speeches, presentations and singing pass in a haze as every now and again, she looks at me and grins. I am lost in a fantasy world and have mapped out the rest of our lives together . . . starting straight after this parade. She signals to me to wait. Like I was going somewhere.

But afterwards, she is surrounded by 'suits'. I can't get near her. Now and then, she catches sight of me but she's tied up. Crowds are dispersing. She waves and mouths the word 'Ciao' before she's whisked away. She's slipped through my fingers. I said I'd felt like I was falling . . . well, now I've crashed to earth.

I try to imagine I had been able to spend time with this girl and even formed a relationship. A few days, maybe a week, and then I would have had to walk. How bad would I have felt then? I pick up the Beast from the two ladies and decide to head for the desert. This is the only answer.

Monday, 27 September 1999   Beyond Tocopilla

This morning begins with a road tunnel that must be 700 metres long. It's unlit and very narrow, but luckily there's little traffic. In its centre, it is pitch black and I bounce off the walls, which is disconcerting. It's a hot day and I decide to make it a long one and add an extra ten kilometres. As a result, I'm knackered when I sit down to watch the sunset.

I unfold the map and trace my progress from the outset. I see all those place names and so many faces, all the way back south to Punta Arenas. I watch the moon rise over distant, snow-capped peaks. A single hummingbird flashes past in the dark undergrowth, its green, red and gold illuminated in a shaft of light that penetrates the trees I'm under. I recall many other things. There was the ten-kilometre wide valley in Patagonia and so many endless roads. I then picture myself parachuting from a C-130 and the long trail of worn, weathered faces of paratroopers as they tabbed for days through deserts during an exercise in Kenya. Then there were the tense, strained faces of other recruits as we watched and waited, like coiled springs, for the smoking thunder-flash to explode to start the log race on 'P Company' (selection course for paras). I think of family, friends, Belfast, Adam's birth . . . and Tara looking back at me through the crowd.

Friday, 1 October – Saturday, 2 October 1999   Iquipue

Total distance to date: 3080 miles (4960 km)

Rounding the last spur, I expect a city, but all I can see is fifteen to twenty kilometres of nothing . . . just a rocky landscape. Where's it gone? Gradually, my eyes adjust to the middle distance and what I thought are rocks begin to look a bit too square. I peer even harder and these regular shapes turn into tower blocks and streets as, bit by bit, Iquipue emerges from the grey clouds that camouflage it.

Although I'm tired and sore, I must dash to catch the Western Union office before it closes because I've no money. Pushing inside, I'm dripping with sweat, simmering, almost at boiling point, when the cashier on the counter spots me and flips the sign to 'closed'. I've no cash, no contacts, no change for the phone and have nowhere to sleep. Time to find the beach.

I'm introduced to a tribe of hippies. They live under a restaurant on stilts above the sand and I spend a couple of nights there. On the second night at 05:30, I wake to see some bloke kneeling beside my rucksack, trying to unstrap my equipment, which is tricky in the dark. After my bad experiences in Argentina, I always make sure everything is well secure, so I've time to collect my thoughts. Coiling up in my doss bag, I fire my left hand at his throat but only connect with his shirt collar. My other fist goes into the 'sustained fire role' and rains blows on the target. For a moment he's dazed, then tries to leg it but I'm not letting go. He stumbles away but I've still got hold of his collar and am being dragged along in my bag. He wriggles out of his shirt and makes a dash for the rucksack. He's after my machete, or perhaps my knife. I drag him off before he has chance and pull the machete from its sheaf. Then he's away so I give chase across the beach. I've woken several couples and must look a bit of a loony tearing about with a huge knife – I let him go before I get myself into serious bother. His losses – a nice Chilean footy shirt, bum bag, some blood and a loss of pride. Mine – a pin on my watch strap.

Friday, 22 October 1999   **Huara**

I'm on Route 5. It runs flat and straight for as far as the eye can see. To the east, I can just make out snow-capped peaks far away across the vast empty desert. The only movement is from dust devils moving south, like a herd of strange animals. There are hundreds of them, some very spectacular; huge monsters throwing up clouds of dust several hundred feet into the air. You know all about it when one of these thin, compacted columns of sand hits you.

Huara – just a village – is at my thirty-kilometre mark. The first thing I notice as I reach the outskirts is the smell of dead dogs carried on the wind. At least they're dead, I'm thinking. As I unmask – I'm wearing my shamag because of the dust – I'm approached by a smart-looking character who speaks good English. He's read about me in the Iquipue newspapers and buys me lunch at the restaurant across the road.

He gives me a guided tour of Huara, not that there's much of it to see. The highlight is the graveyard on the edge of town, which is enclosed by a white-washed stone wall. Inside, it's like a scene from a Hammer horror flick – it's full of half-exposed corpses that are making their way out of the sand. This is how they will be left. No one will bother to rebury them. And what makes it worse is that the heat and sand has, to some extent, preserved them. They look like pieces of dried fruit. Just imagine it – you're visiting old Grandpa's grave and there, more or less, is old Grandpa, much as you remembered him, staring up at you from the sand. Ugh. Where would you place your bunch of flowers – in his ribcage?

Friday, 29 October 1999   **Arica**

Arica's the last town in northern Chile and I try to hit the Bavaria restaurant as soon as I arrive. It's on a first floor so there's no secure place for the Beast. No matter, I just ask two waiters to help me struggle with it up the stairs. I take a seat and feel the stress drain from me. The restaurant is spotlessly clean and I'm caked in dust, filthy and stinking yet feeling pleasantly numb as, once again, the staff treat me like a celebrity.

The manager appears with a note.

'You know someone in Tocopilla . . . a Tamara?' he asks, reading his piece of paper which contains a number and a single name, Tamara.

I don't know a Tamara.

'She just called,' he insists.

Then it clicks. Tamara . . . it must be Tara.

Tara must have got my letter. I'd written her a note and had asked someone to post it in Tocopilla for me on their way south. I'd addressed it to 'Tara – Queen of Tocopilla', telling her she could contact me via the Bavaria restaurants. Sensing my urgency, the man lets me use his phone and I call her. I dial the number. She answers in her unmistakable soft voice. I tell her I'm coming back to see her.

Monday, 1 November – Monday, 8 November 1999   Tocopilla

I take the bus back south. The route retraces my steps and takes a gruelling nine hours, and it's strange to pass places I know so well yet had thought I'd never see again. I'm relieved when I'm dropped off opposite the plaza, where I find a phone box and call Tara. This was where I'd last seen her. She seems happy to hear my voice, and is soon strolling across the square towards me. I know why I'm here – and why I shouldn't be. Greeting me with a hug and a kiss, I'm invited to stay at her place, or rather her parents' place. We get into her car. In the streetlights, her eyes sparkle, and oh, her smile . . . I'm sentenced to death already.

Tara is full of surprises. I had assumed she'd had her fair share of boyfriends but I've got that wrong. She is, she admits, as pure as the driven snow, and intends to remain so until her wedding night. This won't be until she's at least thirty. Next year, she'll be a student in Santiago – I know lots of those. It will be interesting to see how long she hangs on: her sister is twenty-three, and a single mother, and is expecting a second child by a different boyfriend. Her brother is now divorced so Tara is her parents' last hope.

She warns me that ours is a 'hands-off' affair but as the week progresses, this rule is up for review. Her parents keep a keen eye on us and we are seldom alone. Our only chance is if we take her father's car at night. It isn't long before I realise that she means more to me than any other girls I've yet met, and it's physically painful to find there's a limit to how close we can get. The line is drawn in the sand. Our time together is a constant struggle for self-control, yet the days have never been warmer, the food tastier, times sweeter. One week, that's all I have.

Before I go, she gives me a small silver medallion to wear on my ID tag. It has the initials KB engraved on one side and a short message on the back: 'For Karl, never forget me, Tamara, 06.11.99'.

Tuesday, 9 November – Friday, 12 November 1999   Arica

Before I slipped down to see Tara, I'd met Karen in a disco. She's twenty-three, speaks no English and is a social worker. Blessed with a great sense of humour, we got on like a house on fire when we first met so when I get back to Arica, I give her some thought. To sit alone or to be with someone, that's what it boils down to. I call.

Next day, I hitch a lift eighteen kilometres to the border. Here, there's a problem. The officials won't let me leave, I have to be travelling in a vehicle.

'Oh, for Christ's sake, I'm alone, just thumbing a lift to Peru, what's up?' I plead.

'Can't do, must be part of a group or in your own car,' the man says.

Luckily for me, a group of Aussies overhear our argument and offer to take me across to the Peruvian checkpoint where I get my entry visa, then hitch a ride back to the Chilean border by bus.

'No, you can't come back in,' says another official.

'What,' I gasp.

'You've been in Chile too long – you must stay in Peru.'

'But my stuff's in Arica,' I plead.

'If you've a problem, better to try Chilean consulate in Tacna [Peru].'

Sweating, I get a lift to the Peruvian border then take a bus to Tacna where I wait three hours for the consulate to open after lunch. If the worst comes to the worst, I guess I can just slip back unnoticed. On one side, there's an international airport between the coast and the highway but nothing on the other. Well, nothing except a ten-metre minefield that's marked on my map, although I can't believe there are any live mines in the ground. In any case, having spent many years in the Assault Pioneer section in 3 Para, one thing I know how to do is to breach a minefield in the dark. Happily, I need not resort to such extremes. Consulate staff are very helpful and one rings the frontier post telling them to stop being such pricks, and to let me back in. Phew.

Monday, 15 November 1999   Arica

Karen finds all this highly amusing. Her cracking sense of humour reminds me of the lads back home and she constantly takes the piss. Once she has beer inside her, she's dangerous and we have a hilarious last weekend. She spent most of yesterday glued to a dictionary trying to translate a message into English. The end result is:

> 'To wish see happy with you credit
> to taste time but life the desire better
> much fate I to get a with perseverance won't
> to doubt to call necessity help remembrance
> Chile faithful good friendly'

I reach the border at 13:00. Armed with some press cuttings, this time I'm able to get through the Chilean post on foot. It's there I run into a Swiss lad, a cyclist I'd last seen 700 kilometres south of Santiago. He's heading for Ecuador and is planning to catch a bus from Tacna, and we arrive at the Peruvian post together. My Swiss friend speaks fluent Spanish so I take a back seat and let him do the talking. Paperwork is the problem. Everyone travelling in a vehicle has paperwork and we have nothing to show. The fact that he's cycling and I'm walking doesn't wash. It takes an hour but eventually they let us pass.

This just leaves the sentry post, the last inner barrier. A guard asks for 'transport' papers.

'No, you can't cross without your transport papers being stamped,' insists the guard. The Swiss turns demented.

'I'm on a bike! I'm on a bike! I'm on a fucking bike!'

He then sprints back to the checkpoint, leaving me smiling at the po-faced guard. I sympathise, he's just doing his job. A minute passes before the phone in the sentry box rings and we are allowed to proceed.

I feel a deep sadness at leaving Chile behind. It is a country that has felt like home, somewhere I know so well and have felt safe in. I feel as if I've lost a great many friends, as if a door has just been firmly shut. I've only gone a kilometre or so before a wheel spindle breaks. A cracking start to new adventures, I'm thinking.

I push on until I'm twenty-six kilometres from Arica before I camp for the night. Safe inside my 'green cave', lit by a single flickering candle, with only the spectre of loneliness for company, I look through the tent flap into the darkness. I can still make out the glistening lights of Arica. There is a two-hour time difference between the two countries and while it is 21:50 in Chile it's 23:50 in Peru. Tara feels so distant, Treiz a lifetime away. I stand transfixed by the distant lights, shivering in a cold wind for some time before zipping up and drinking a hot brew.

Chapter Three

PERU

Halfway across a main roundabout on the outskirts of Tacna, another wheel spindle snaps. As I'm sure you'll appreciate, finding yourself immobile slapbang in such a busy, swirling place isn't great. It's a familiar story. Horrendous traffic mixed with the very real fear that the wheel will collapse again. I'd hold my breath . . . if I had any. I intend to find a supermarket, then a post office before getting the hell out of here. Now, of course, I also need a bike shop. I try asking the locals – well, those who will talk to me. I am directed all over the place and, after an hour, rapidly lose my sense of humour. Eventually, I do find somewhere but they're clean out of wheel spindles. Because I'm clearly visibly distressed, the man in the shop takes pity on me and dismantles the only bicycle in the window and fixes me up with a freebie.

I need to find somewhere to sleep although I've already had enough of Tacna. Not far from the centre, I trace a path running beside a dark drainage ditch between two rows of buildings. There's no one about so I just pull into the shadows and decide to sleep in my sleeping bag liner. It's a warm night so I'll just bandage my head with a shamag to keep the bugs off.

As I lie there, I coin a new South American custom I've picked up on . . . I'm calling it 'Dog on the Roof Syndrome'. I first noticed it in Antofagasta but it's more widespread as I head further north. Sometimes, I see packs of dogs on a roof, always in a state of frantic euphoria screaming at anyone and anything below. They're stuck and

ECUADOR

Loja

Sullano

River Caiuas

PERU

Chicalayo

Trujillo

Pacific

Ocean

BRAZIL

A
n
d
e
s

Lima

BOLIVIA

Nazca

N

W · E

S

Arequipa

Lake Titicaca

| 0 | 100 | 200 | 300 miles |

Tacna

Arica

| 0 | 100 | 200 | 300 | 400 | 500 km |

can't get down. I now see the logic in the owners slinging them up there. The dogs love it; they're out of the way, they can't crap in the garden and no one steps in crap on the roof. Great idea. Tomorrow, I'll leave first thing. I can't wait to get back into the desert.

Sunday, 21 November 1999   Beyond Tacna

Yesterday, I was in a roadside snack bar when a coach pulled up. Two or three people got off. One was a girl and she looked sort of familiar: Poula, the mystery girl from the desert south of Antofagasta. Her mother had bought her an air ticket to Arica from Vina del Mar as a birthday present and I gather she'd been looking out for me for two days. What perfect timing – I needed cheering up.

This morning we had a lie-in. It is hot and windy when we stir and the air is filled with clouds of dust that covers everything, including our food and drinks, in a fine layer. We don't pack up until noon, when we're joined by a passing truck driver. He has a ton of food, which he shares with us. He also whips out his flute and starts to play – and sing – traditional Peruvian folk songs as we get stuck into rice, curry and some unidentifiable animal body parts.

Poula walks with me for five kilometres until we reach the next café. She doesn't say much – nor do I. This is where we must part and it's unlikely I'll see her again. We don't have long to wait as a coach soon appears. Poula stares at me as if she's waiting for me to say something deep and meaningful. The coach pulls over and she is hustled aboard by the driver and is gone. Goodbyes aren't getting any easier.

Saturday, 27 November 1999   Towards Arequipa

Six in the morning and, incredibly, the sun is already way above the horizon and the tent is heating up rapidly. I reach the top of the valley by around 11:30 and I'm pleased to see that the road flattens out and is dead straight until it disappears in a haze. Irritatingly, distances are marked every kilometre by a small concrete post – a real pain as it makes the days drag on. I'm constantly reminded how far it is to Arequipa, the next big city. Right now, it's exactly 150 kilometres away.

Behind me, an eighteen-wheeler swings into the road to overtake – it doesn't have to 'cos I'm on the hard shoulder. The driver hasn't looked in his mirror: had he done so, he'd have seen the coach that was trying to overtake him at the same time. The coach driver, who must have been bricking himself, sounded his horn and swerved to miss the truck, his wheels hitting the edge of the desert, kicking up a curtain of dust. Too late to jump, I freeze, clenching my teeth, fully expecting an impact and certain deaths. Then the dust clears and the truck and bus thunder on their way. They've missed each other and, more importantly, they've missed me.

A little further on, still shaking, I stop at a police checkpoint. Traffic cops ask the usual questions, look at my passport and ask about the trip. One has a play with my knives while another lectures on road safety and on how dangerous the Pan American is.

'Really, officer, I hadn't noticed,' I say, still shaking.

Thursday, 2 December 1999   Arequipa

Total distance to date: 3485 miles (5612 km)
By midday, I'm closing on the outskirts of Arequipa and the traffic on these narrow roads is a problem. There are trucks and coaches fighting for space and angry drivers hurl abuse at me for no particular reason. Since crossing into this country, the entire male population has an incredible urge to whistle and shout at me from passing vehicles. The favourite greeting is 'Hey mister, fuck you!' They shout it as if merely saying 'hello there' then laugh out loud afterwards. This is starting to wind me up. I've stomach pains – bound to be stress. I need to find an open space to pitch the tent in before I get any closer to the suburbs. Eventually, I find an old abandoned brick building with a patch of waste ground tucked away behind it. I am overlooking an irrigation ditch with a crop field beyond in which I can see some people working. This ought to do me – I don't think I'm in anyone's way.

But as I begin unpacking, a large Indian woman from the field has noticed me and is coming over. Worryingly, she is starting to scream and yell at me, which attracts the attention of the others who have now downed tools.

'This is my land, get out,' she bellows.

'Hello,' I begin, surprised at the offence I'm causing.

Her verbals increase as I try to reason with her.

'Would you mind if I just sleep here,' I ask, politely.

'No, this is all mine,' she continues.

'What, even this bit of waste land?' I wonder, pointing to the scrubby patch I was planning to park on.

'Yes, all mine, now get off.'

The hell it was, I'm thinking, but I tell her I'm going. Some in the crowd that is gathering begin to snigger and clearly find all this highly amusing. I can understand most of what they are saying: obviously, they don't think that I can so keep up the insults while the big woman gets louder and more aggressive. There was no need, I told her in Spanish, because, as I'd said, I was going.

Then Paps turns up. He comes stumbling across the field from somewhere and, get this, he's pissed out of his skull. He looks like he wants a bit of a scrap, and closes in, arms swinging everywhere. I simply push him firmly away whereupon he falls on his arse. Everyone laughs . . . except the big woman. Now reinforced by her elder daughters, she decides to throw bricks at me – which isn't a joke at such close range. Paps, meanwhile, is on his feet and launches a second attack. His arms flailing like a demented windmill, and so out of it he can scarcely see to hit me, he simply sways in front of me. Enough. I stick one squarely on his nose and he drops like a shot moose.

The big woman goes berserk and comes at me clawing, punching and screaming like a banshee. I can barely fend her off. Helped by a sea of kids, Paps counter-attacks again while the woman grabs a half-brick and tries belting me with it as if it was a hammer. Paps, his nose pissing blood, catches on and picks up another lump and comes at me from the other side. Time-out! I pull my machete from the side of my sack and brandish it. Silence. It is as if someone has shouted 'Cut' on a film set. Everyone freezes.

During this lull, I've a second or two to shove the tent in the Beast before the volley of bricks and stones resumes. Ducking, I make my way up the track and to the road. Unhappily for me, the big woman's aim is improving and she deals me a real dinger across the shoulders, which leaves a nasty mark. Arequipa . . . it's more like the Falls Road.

AREQUIPA

The second largest city in Peru, it has one million souls, is situated in the Desert Mountains and is 1000 kilometres south of the capital, Lima. A beautiful city, it is built almost completely of sillar, a kind of white volcanic stone, hence the city's other name, The White City. The city is surrounded by mountains: the volcano, El Misti, the even higher Chachani, and the smaller but curiously named Pichu Pichu. Once independent for just four days – the bullet holes in the cathedral clock underline this story – the locals are fiercely proud of this event and some even carry Arequipan passports.

Saturday, 4 December – Thursday, 16 December 1999   Arequipa

Arequipa has an impressive backdrop of five large snow-topped volcanoes and the River Chile runs through its centre. For the genuine tourist, there are lots of old Spanish churches and bridges and there's a magnificent cathedral in the main plaza. At such places, the Khaki Brigade (that's what I call the tourists who all wear khaki kit) are always out in force and where you find them, you always find beggars and locals hard-selling anything and everything. I'm constantly hassled. It's no good sitting in a café because they do the rounds in there too. From very young, snotty-nosed kids to very old cripples, all prey on your sense of pity. Some break your heart. In the shadow of the cathedral, I witness a badly crippled woman dressed in rags having to shove herself along on her backside wearing thick leather gloves to protect her hands as she slides along on a square of cardboard. Her legs and arms are badly deformed, all twisted into strange shapes. Three very young children walk alongside her looking equally pathetic in filthy clothes.

I can't think that I will stay much longer. I've no friends or contacts and I'm running out of cash. But then along comes Kumari, a Colombian girl I met in a bar. Kumari is another 'Child of the Moon', a wanderer, a hippy living in a world of tarot cards, magic, infusions and yoghurt . . . you might know the sort. For just US$1.50 a night, student friends of hers will put me up in their place just across the river.

The house is on the side of a hill. To reach it, you descend a series of narrow winding stairs and it seems rather an odd set-up. A real mix of rooms, there are balconies, outhouses and more stairs and it is run by an elderly lady, who is, not surprisingly, a touch eccentric. I find a bog-standard box room and there's hot water in the shower. The kitchen and communal dining room is fine but is in a shit state. I'll have to sort that out! At this price, I am happy with these close-knit, left-wing Bohemians who are all in the same rock band. It will be interesting if nothing else.

Things are also taking a surreal turn. I am apparently Kurt Cobain reincarnated. Even I'm starting to believe it. I'll explain. There's a bar I frequent – the Deja-vu. On the wall is a photograph of the late Nirvana frontman. I have to say, in this photo, it could be me. It has been hung above my favourite chair and now, every time I walk in the door, everyone points at me and at the photo and shouts 'It's him!'

I'm also asked to star in a charity fashion show. Why not – I agree to. I turn up at this club as ordered, and team up with four other male models and some stunning girls who are tall and slim – that's freaky for Peru. The outfits we wriggle into are all made from recycled materials created by some bonkers fashion graduate. I guess we look like real jerks but it's a great laugh striding down the runway. From the desert to the catwalk . . . mine is a strange life.

Saturday, 18 December 1999   Arequipa

I've been here for over two weeks now and I feel pent up. I find it hard to relax and I'm always looking over my shoulder every minute of the day. People tell me the same stories of gringos staggering into bars at night, bleeding from multiple stab wounds, or of those found unconscious the next morning, half-dead from beatings and robberies. I sense that trouble will eventually find me here. It does tonight.

Alone and on my way to a bar I know, I pass the old church in Plaza San Francisco. On the steps outside, a gang of older youths, around fifteen in all, are watching. I take a narrow street off the plaza, when, from nowhere, some big kid is swinging off me, trying to get me in a headlock. A split second later, the others are on me like wolves. This is scary. I am surrounded by a mob with punches and kicks coming from all sides. I could be fighting for my life – they may have knives. I'm like a baited bear, exploding into a whirlwind of aggression, so fast and furious that most of it is a blur. I remember focusing on different faces and hitting each very hard before moving on to the next target. I break free and instinctively, I leg it. I sprint fifty metres back into the plaza but my pursuers don't give chase. I slow to a walk and turn around. I feel a 'red mist' descend.

'C'mon,' I roar. 'I'll take on any one of you that thinks he's worthy, here and now! In fact, no, make it any two of you.'

I keep up the demand but no one wants to play. If gringo-baiting is the favourite local sport maybe they'll think twice the next time.

Thursday, 13 January 2000   Beyond Arequipa

It's a week since I left Arequipa. The Pan American is following the coastline again, in places, even overhanging the crashing waves below me. It's a grey, overcast morning, yet it's still very hot so the sweat pours off me. Close to midday, the road dips almost to sea level and I have the first chance of getting on to the shoreline, something I've never dared as it would have meant leaving the Beast unattended on the road. I have fish in mind – shellfish. It's a rocky piece of coast. I ought to find something because I can see fishermen down there. I strip down to shorts and boots, grab a sharp knife and a plastic bag and clamber down between the large rocks until I reach the water's edge. I feel sure I'll find something I can scoff.

The people fishing are a family of Indians from a town to the north. This is how they make their living, both collecting molluscs and catching fish on lines from the shore. They don't mind helping me get started; they show me where I may find the best shellfish and even how to prepare and cook them. I soon learn what is good and what I should avoid as the father leaps about the rocks in and out of the surf before letting me sample the pick of his catch.

There are a few common varieties, which I understand are edible, and I can see plenty of these. One is the Barquillo, a cross between a large woodlouse and a limpet. Another is the Lapa, which again looks like a limpet but has a distinct hole in its top and is more oval-shaped. This is great! Proper nosh again. I can also see some

Abalon. These are really terrific. Big ones live in deeper water, but at low tide, you can find them on the rocks. A good eat, the locals sell them for US$20 a kilo, so people make a living from collecting these alone. Getting to them is dicey. Taking your life in your hands, you dash out and cling to a rock like an iguana while prising them off with waves breaking all around you. It's about synchronising your run before the next incoming wave comes and knocks you over.

I'm told my best chance is tomorrow morning between 06:00 and 09:00 – this is low tide – so I will try again before I leave.

Sunday, 16 January 2000　　　Towards Tanaca

It is overcast today. This keeps the temperature down to a bearable 35° C rather than the killer 45° C and above that I have been walking in this week. By the late afternoon, I reach a long stretch of sandy beach and after some scrambling, I manage to get down an embankment and on to the sand. I can't get my kit off fast enough and leap into the sea. It is, to my surprise, icy cold and truly amazing.

This beach is alive with thousands of crabs with red shells – the ones they must hire for those natural history programmes. You have seen them . . . they have eyes on stalks that look like horns and they scuttle sideways between the holes they've dug in the sand. There are so many that the beach itself almost turns red – there must be thousands if not millions of the little blighters. I sit and watch them go about their business. Interesting little chaps – you can feed them as if they were pigeons.

Tuesday, 18 January 2000　　　　　　　Tanaca

Later in the day, the road descends steeply alongside a very flat stretch of beach in front of which is the small settlement of Tanaca. From a distance, it looks deserted – nothing but old mud-brick houses without doors or windows or any sign of the inhabitants. But as I get closer, I can see people moving about. Parked in the shade behind the houses, is a row of flash cars. Most odd. I stop outside the first house, and observe a group of old people drinking on the porch, dressed as if they are at the golf club. Greeting me with smiles and raised glasses, they hand me a glass of water.

Just about everyone here is from Lima. This is where they come for a month at a time during the holidays. For the rest of the year, it's a ghost village. It's easy to see why people come here. The beach is a belter and begins at the bottom of the street – it's a far cry from the madness of the capital, which is home to eight million souls.

As I reach the last house, I pass a chap and his son heading for the beach armed with a bat and ball. They stop to speak because they'd seen me on the road a few days ago. Genette Toutin Plaza grows olives on a farm in the next valley and exports them all over South and North America. They spend two months a year here, something of a family tradition, which means bringing everything they need and taking it all away again when they leave. This includes doors, windows and even the toilet. Anything overlooked would be removed.

I accept their offer of a bed and we talk long into the night. I learn much about Peru: its history, politics and stories of Shining Path, the group that once terrorised the country. I wash in water warmed by the day's sun then relax in a chair on the porch, drinking coffee . . . this family swamps me with kindness. Genette slips me US$40 and his wife makes a pile of soup cubes, sugar, two tins of tuna and some crackers. They also give me two rolls of colour film. Lovely people.

Sunday, 23 January 2000   Nazca

I begin the day just ten kilometres from Nazca, which is world-famous for the large-scale mystical drawings in the desert, or Nazca lines, as they are known. Along with drawings of birds, lizards and monkeys, there are, so I've read, 'runways' for alien spacecraft to land on.

On the road, I pass some tramp heading south. He is in rags with only the soles of his shoes remaining. Shuffling past me, I'd been about to offer him some water or something to eat but he didn't want to talk. He just looked at me with deeply sunken eyes from under a mass of black, matted hair and beard before continuing on his way. He looks almost European. Perhaps he began his journey twelve years ago and is walking the world the other way round.

There are a good number of tourists here, all here to see the 'lines'. Most take short flights in light aircraft as you can only really appreciate them from the air. I don't want to spend the night here so push on through. It becomes a race against time to get clear of the suburbs and into the desert again. Sod's Law – everyone I meet wants to talk, so it's well after sunset when I eventually pull over. Very dark it is too.

Monday, 24 January 2000   Beyond Nazca

The temperature is way off the scale in the high forties. As I intend to rest today, I attempt to charge the battery on my satellite phone so I can make a call. I'm camped in the pampas on a piece of rising ground, just a few hundred metres from a mud house with an old car rotting outside it. I hadn't noticed it last night. It isn't long before I get a visit from the whole family. The husband, with his glazed eyes and beer belly, and his plump wife, seem pleasant and invite me to come to their place for some food. I accept but I am just not sure and the fleet of skinny flea-ridden dogs that accompanies them reinforces my instincts. I promise to come over once I've sorted the phone.

The family home is the usual run-down squalor: dogs, hens, ducks, turkeys and even the odd mule running amok. It smells really grim. But again, I'm met with overwhelming kindness and handed a plate of pasta and rice with beans. I'm given a glass of crushed lemon and sugar in water and urged to move to the rear of the house where we eat under a tin roof. Besides us are four rotting cages each with a bird inside. Once the dogs have been beaten into a silence, the man explains that these birds are his fighting cocks. Cockfighting is very popular here and he insists on giving me a demonstration.

Two birds are lifted from their cages and what mean mothers they look too. I am handed one to hold as another is placed a few feet away. Even the dogs close in to watch.

'OK, let's go,' he barks.

My rather smelly bird leaps into the arena. There is a moment of silence as the pair freeze, eyeing each other up, standing tall, chests stuck out. Then suddenly one bird lets out a tremendous 'cock a doodle doo'. That's it. Beaks, spurs, feathers and dust are every-where as the two birds try to murder each other. My host lets this continue for a moment or two then pulls them apart – quite an effort in itself as the birds are still trying to get at each other as they are shoved back in their respective cages. They're absolute psychopaths, these creatures . . . born to kill.

I'm not keen on sleeping here. I wait until everyone gets stuck into the beer before saying goodbye and pushing out a brisk ten kilometres.

Thursday, 27 January 2000   Beyond Nazca

As I packed my kit this morning, a passing farmer came over to tell me about the long beans on the tree I'm sleeping under. They are edible. The bean hangs from the tree and is about ten to twenty centimetres long. It has a yellow shell, which is green when it is younger. You just bite off a lump. Inside the woody case is a thick goo with a sweet flavour like caramel. You simply chew until the goo disappears and spit out what's left. I take a bag full with me to chew along the way. I could get a taste for these.

Wednesday, 16 February 2000   Towards Lima

I spent last night at a Texaco station because I'm getting nearer to Lima and the way is totally urbanised. I dozed in a room at the rear while the Beast spent the night in a cafeteria under the protection of a guard, complete with body armour and Remington pump-action shotgun. It doesn't get much more secure.

It's raining this morning so freshens the day up. By 14:00 I succeed in tracking down the contact address for this evening. This is thanks to a couple I'd met a week ago. It's a rather nice place too, on an estate surrounded by greenery and with its own security guards at the main gate, called 'Vigilantes'. Clearly, it's home to those with money. It's the couple's daughter who lives here with her family and I am invited to camp in their garden and take a shower. It's great to have hot water. I lie in the grass for the rest of the afternoon and sleep.

When I stir, I begin to consider the best way to get myself into central Lima without getting squashed, murdered or robbed. I've two routes to choose from. I can take the longer coastal road then switch to a main route through the north of the city or stay on the Pan American, which is shorter but riskier. I also refer to my 'intelligence map' of Lima. It shows all the dodgy parts I've been warned about.

These are shaded in red. I've been working on this since I left Arequipa. By the look of it, the safest way in is along the coast but this route does finish in a red area, Rimac, where I have a contact.

LIMA

Peru's capital was the chief city of Spanish South America from its founding in 1535 until it became a republic in the early nineteenth century. It is situated in a valley fed by the Rimac River, and is in the middle of the country's desert Pacific coastline, and the Andes, whose spine is 160 kilometres away, send their foothills almost to the city gates. Mild in summer, it has very humid winters with no rain worth mentioning and, as a result, the sky is almost always overcast at this time of year. This is not helped by rising air pollution in the last decade, as there are no restrictions on the age or condition of vehicles. It is a magnet for struggling highland villagers and has a population that exceeds eight million.

Thursday, 17 February 2000   Lima

Total distance to date: 4060 miles (6358 km)

I choose the coast. The road traces the seafront and is separated from the city by high cliffs on which are built high-rise hotels, flats and restaurants. At last, I turn off and begin the steep climb into the city centre on a main drag that will take me very close to where I hope to stay. It's busy so I feel secure in one sense but the traffic isn't much fun. I'm spat and sworn at by drivers and my patience soon runs thin. I've eaten nothing and by mid-afternoon I'm feeling weak. With no phone numbers for my destination, no one is expecting me so it's going to be a bit hit and miss.

I finally arrive at a river bridge, which is on the edge of Rimac. Crossing to the far side, I pause for a swift map check because I can't be far from the address. Big mistake. Two 'smack heads' sidle over and are all smiles.

'Hey gringo,' they begin. This spells trouble and one puts his arm around my shoulders.

'Get off and go away,' I say firmly.

The next thing I know, the shorter one has come in from the other side and is swinging off my watch. Your first mistake of the day, mate, I say to myself. As he clings on to my arm, I rain a series of punches straight into his face. He drops to his knees and takes some serious blows as he does so. Four policewomen on the other side of the street have seen the commotion and are running our way. Just then, my assailant's friend steps in and suddenly I'm outnumbered. Still strapped into the Beast, I reach over my shoulder and unsheath my machete. As one man picks his friend off the floor, a crowd is gathering and I've a real fear I might get jumped and picked clean. I issue threats to anyone that moves.

Then I see my watch is missing so focus on the thieves who are still stumbling about just a few feet away. Frantically, I wrestle off my rucksack and, pointing to the Beast, scream 'Protect that,' at the first policewoman. Advancing, I have the offender in my sights and the red mist is down. Coming from behind, I grab him by the hair, drag him off his feet and fling him into the base of the bridge wall. Funny this, he does nothing to defend himself and just falls about as if he's pissed. I keep belting him and demand he hands over the watch.

It doesn't immediately occur to me that I would do better questioning him in Spanish. All I can extract are grunts and groans and even his friend is telling me that the man hasn't got my watch. A minute later, two male policeman arrive and ask me to desist with my interrogation. I go back and look over the ground in case the man has dropped it – by hook or by crook, I want it back.

Returning to the scene, the thief is being strip-searched by two members of the public under the direction of the police. Not thinking clearly, I storm in and land a real corker of a punch in the man's face as he is held arms apart by the two helpers. I get three more on before a policeman pulls me off and holds up my watch in an effort to calm me down.

A huge wave of relief sweeps over me. I have my watch and the police have the thief but I decline to go with them to make a statement. I've got my property back, that's all that matters, and I can't be hassled to drag the Beast anywhere. Besides, I don't want them to know my visa has expired. Back in my harness, I take deep breaths and look at my hands. My knuckles are split, bruised and bleeding, and my clothes are splattered with another's blood. Skin on my wrist where the watch had been is grazed and sore and I have to smile when, for a moment, I reflect on all the warnings I'd received about the city. Christ, welcome to Lima.

Friday, 18 February 2000   Lima

I'm staying with Ruth and Roberto who welcomed me with open arms. They were a contact I'd made through friends in Arequipa and live in a tiny, poky flat on an estate that reminds me of the homes in the Divis, Belfast. Their place is basic – there's no hot water – but at least it's safe.

This morning I track down our embassy, where I get a warm welcome. Waiting for me is a re-supply parcel from Dad; inside is a new pair of boots, a new Leatherman tool to replace the one I've lost, US$30, some new clothes, four pairs of socks and an adaptor to charge my sat-phone. This is a major morale booster. Back at the flat, I recharge the phone batteries but to my disappointment, I can't get any life out of the phone. The mains supply is 200 volts, more than sufficient, yet I'm getting nothing. Depression sets in and I feel a churning in my stomach as the distance between here and home increases tenfold. Communications are down and will stay down unless I can get a £4000 phone fixed out here. This will cost the earth and, on top of that, I need money for a new visa.

Friday, 25 February 2000   Lima

Lima is just too big, too expensive and too dangerous. Everything feels wrong here; I'm eating out and going to the wrong places, spending way too much and too quickly. In addition, I'm frustrated, snappy and ill-tempered. I took the sat-phone to an electrician but he decided it was well out of his league and wouldn't touch it. A second place asked me to leave it overnight – no fear.

Any visitor who spends any time here will take a trip on the 'combies', the small minibuses that flood the streets. It's like a ride at a very scary funfair. There are no rules – just cram as many people into your vehicle as possible. Red traffic lights mean nothing – you simply go if you think you'll make it. With no lane markings, it's chaos and twice I've been on a bus when it has hit a taxi. I've seen several fights between drivers. The other day, I saw a truck pull over after a shunt with a combie had dented it badly. The truck driver tried to drag the bus driver through his cab window, beating the living daylights out of him as he did so but a passenger came to his rescue and closed the window and locked the doors. In response, the truck driver returned to his vehicle and struck again with a pair of pliers, smashing all the combie's lights as it tried to drive off.

I am standing at a busy junction waiting to cross, when my precious watch is whipped away for the second time in a week, this time, with remarkable ease. How can I have been so stupid as to be wearing it? I barely felt it, I saw no one, just an ocean of faces as people flooded across the road. No obvious face stood out as my attacker, no eye contact or swift body movement to give them away. It had been so easy.

Sunday, 12 March 2000   Beyond Lima

Lima's suburbs are four days behind me and it's good to escape the urban sprawl and get back in my green cave with just a candle for company. I feel I can relax again and I can see the sea. Even so, at night I can still see the capital's massive electrical output illuminating the sky over 100 kilometres away. I never did extend the visa beyond seven days. I had been at the mercy of some fat guy official who just kept demanding more money. Stuff it, I thought, and decided to crack on and take whatever comes.

I find a tomato plant growing by the roadside. It's laden with ripe fruit, which really bucks me up. The valleys I've just passed through were green so there is much 'fresh' available and my current fad is raw tomato and boiled eggs. I also enjoy lemon and onion, which is served with seafood or as a salad. What I can't fathom is the complete absence of ice? The one thing that you would say was a big seller on these roads in these extreme temperatures would be ice-cold drinks, but I've never found any. Or am I just being fussy?

According to the map, I'm about to head into the last big stretch of desert as I move north towards Ecuador. Once I'm beyond that, the gaps between towns and villages look to be shorter, so it's going to be easier to find fresh rations and water to cook and wash up with.

Monday, 13 March 2000   **Towards Chimbote**

I'm frequently stopped by couples in smart 4 x 4's on their way to Ecuador. 'Look, it's you,' most seem to blurt, waving copies of *El Comercio*, which has a nice piece on the expedition and photos too. They always look more European, drive smart vehicles, speak English and wear expensive designer clothes and have a surfboard strapped to the roof. Today, a girl hands me a bottle of juice and a packet of nuts because they've read that I 'like nuts'.

I'm told that *El Comercio* is the thinking man's national daily so it's not widely read beyond the capital, which doesn't help my PR as much as I would have liked. As far as I can tell, the Indians of Peru, who work on farms, drive wrecks or ride bikes, read what I can only describe as something along the lines of our *Sunday Sport* – it's mainly pictures of fat naked local girls. It seems a very polarised society – just the haves and the have-nots, with nothing in between.

In these poor parts, trouble is never far away. Just before I find a gas station in the late afternoon, I have a close call with two big, ugly types who stop me in my tracks on the roadside. They want me to buy some cassettes but when I refuse, just expect me to give them some money anyway. I feel the tension rising and ease my waist buckle undone because this is, I sense, about to kick off. This unnerves them. Shrugging, they get the picture and let me pass. This was another close call – these two were built like brick shit-houses.

It's hard work living with your finger on the trigger. After the experiences in Lima, I'm constantly wondering where the next threat is coming from. I dare not take my eyes off the Beast, even for a moment. As I write, it's outside a café window at the gas station and a group of people are having a good look at it. They watch me watching them watching it. I'm a lone gringo . . . I must be a tempting target.

Saturday, 18 March 2000   **Towards Chimbote**

At my twenty-kilometre point, I break at a wayside restaurant. At precisely the same moment, a convoy of over forty police cars, yes forty, pulls in and parks up and all the drivers and passengers pile inside. This poor little restaurant is swamped with policemen, giving the owner a hard time because there's nowhere for them all to sit and he can't get the grub out fast enough. He'd probably only had two customers in two days. The poor owner, his wife and eight-year-old daughter are run off their feet with coppers yelling at them from all directions.

After they clear off, the owner shows me a notebook that contains short paragraphs written by other gringos, all of them bikers, needless to say. There are entries from Brits, French, Swedes and Canadians, North Americans and Japanese, most of whom are coming from or heading for Alaska or Punta Arenas. People have left photos, newspaper cuttings, expedition logos and other mementoes.

I'm amazed how many gringos have found this place in the middle of nowhere. Now here comes 'the walker'. Sure enough, I'm fed a bowl of soup, a plate of fish and rice and given a bottle of pop, all for free. He sends me off with a bottle of spring water and even slips me some money S10 (Peruvian Nuevo soles, about £2). What a guy.

Tuesday, 21 March 2000   **Chimbote**

Since leaving Lima, people have warned me about Chimbote . . . 'a place of thieves, not nice, somewhere you must be careful'. I arrive at midday, having moved through an industrial estate that runs along the coast, with factories filling the air with smog.

I find a grotty hotel for S10 (£2) a night. Although Mother's money – S338.57 – does swiftly arrive at Western Union, the fact that I'm moving too fast is giving her less time to raise funds back home so she is not sending as much as she had intended. This problem spirals. If I've little or no money, I tend to push on even faster as I can't afford to wait in towns, even cheap ones like Chimbote where – and this is quirky – you don't get a knife in a restaurant unless you ask for one. Like it or not, I must slow down to let my admin keep pace but I intend to leave on Sunday. This must be the smelliest town in the world – it reeks of bad eggs, which has to be the fish-processing factories.

Tuesday, 28 March 2000   **Beyond Chimbote**

Last night I slept in what probably resembles your granddad's garden shed, which, in this case, comprises the sleeping arrangement for five youths. Happily, I only had to bunk up with three but their behaviour still gave me the creeps. I know it's not my country nor any of my business but these lads would sit on each other's laps and stroke one another's hair.

The shed place had become filled with what appeared to be flying baseballs. Huge bugs came crashing in through the windows attracted by the light bulb and would bounce off the tables and walls – and off me. By the middle of the night, hundreds of bugs and moths the size of birds filled the place, yet no one minded and we continued eating. By midnight, everyone retired to bed, and I to the toilet with stabbing pains in my stomach. That's where I stayed all night, on the pan, as my insides disintegrated . . . here we go again, I thought.

Come morning, I'm wrecked. I've been bitten to the bone by mossies and feel a sick man. Somehow, I don't let on to my generous hosts and thank them for all they've done before hitting the road. I'm at my lowest of low ebbs and must sprint to the desert every two to three kilometres and drop my trousers. It's painful too. I'm taking Loperamide for the diarrhoea but as I'm passing nothing but acidic water, my backside is in rags. It feels as if I've razor blades up my bum, white hot ones at that. Normally, antiseptic cream does the trick, but I'm really suffering. By the evening, the drugs are kicking in and the turmoil in my stomach subsides. The only problem now is sitting down. Ouch.

Sunday, 2 April – Friday, 7 April 2000   Trujillo

Roberto Ramirez Otarola is someone I'd met near Viru, about sixty kilometres south of Trujillo. He'd urged me to call him when I got there. Trujillo is the third largest city in Peru. Arriving at midday, I dial his number and am invited to stay. It's not far and is in a very posh part of town. Roberto manages a plant for a large crop-producing company, Camposol, which exports goods all around South America. He and his wife, Anna, a sculptor, meet me in a car as I head for their place, a most beautiful house which is a distinct contrast to my last hideout. The Beast has its own corral in the walled garden and I even have a room with, get this, a warm shower en suite.

Over the next few days, I've the house to myself during the day so spend time studying my maps. How do I intend to cross Ecuador and Colombia? Should I stick to the lowlands or take to the Andes? The low plains are hot, wet and mosquito-infested. Malaria and yellow fever are prevalent here and both are carried by mosquitoes. Although I can take anti-malaria pills and my yellow fever vaccination is still current, there's little defence against getting bitten in the first place. Insect repellent, as any well-travelled soldier will tell you, is about as much good as a scary mask. Loose clothing offers the only real protection, but, in this heat, you don't wear very much.

Altitude could avoid much of that. Nights would be cool and the mosquitoes would disappear between 2000 to 2500 metres which makes taking to the Andes a much more attractive prospect. The big issue here is the workload because I couldn't take the Beast off-road – the answer, I believe, is a donkey. I pass them nearly every day in the valleys, always loaded up to the gunnels, and I'm told they can carry my kit no problem. A donkey will cost around US$100. Quite how I look after one or cross a border with one in tow is beyond me right now but I'm sure I'll deal with it when the time comes: the hills it is, although why I keep calling the Andes 'hills', I'm not quite sure.

Saturday, 8 April 2000   Chocope

The stomach pains return. I'm feeling rough and find it hard going after my wonderful recuperation in Trujillo. By midday, the pain is increasing and I stop for a break and wonder if I'll be able to walk any further today. I am bent double outside a café in a small place called Chocope, when some local girls start to worry when they see me this way in a bout of pain and clearly stressed. It gets worse. Some religious nut joins them and is standing over me, chanting prayers out loud, as if he's giving me the last rites.

'Oh, look, I'm feeling betterrrraaaarrrgghhh!' I groan, wracked by another bout of pain. The pains are so bad that I'm short of breath. I have saved my last four Loperamide capsules for emergencies and this feels like one now. I use the loo at the café , a stinking little room with a grotty old broken toilet. I look around for a bucket to pour water into the toilet – that's how you flush out here – but it is filled with what looks like evil pig swill. As I peer at it, a rat's head emerges from the grotty depths and with a 'phut', blows the crap from its nose. For a moment, I swear it is staring straight at me.

My mind is now made up, I'm pushing on. I plod on for another ten kilometres and go through a living hell. I'm bent double by the roadside every ten metres or so and each kilometre feels like a hundred. I can never recall a day quite so bad. Eventually I make it as far as Paijan and crash at a gas station. I take the last of my pills and, feeling sorry for me, the boss here makes me a cup of tea. I sit cross-legged and bolt upright, bracing myself for the next sharp stomach pain. It feels as if someone is ripping my guts out with a hook, but after an hour, the pains ease a little though leave me feeling very tired. I pitch the tent outside in a corner. I eat nothing.

Tuesday, 11 April 2000   Guadalupe

I can't face food this morning. I'm in rag order and in some serious pain when I walk into a small place called Guadalupe at about 14:00, having stuck it out for sixteen long kilometres. I'm as weak as a kitten and my head spins. I need to rest here, I can't go any further today and I'm relieved when I find a chemist that has both Loperamide and Plidan (for stomach pains).

After a few hours, my guts calm down – probably because I'm taking pills as if they're Smarties, something I hate doing, but I've no choice at the moment. Earlier, I'd asked for directions at the health centre and, passing the place again, the staff invite me to stay the night. It's an OAP care centre . . . just the place I need the way I'm feeling.

Wednesday, 12 April 2000   Beyond Guadalupe

Left town feeling much better. Stopped on the road by a TV crew – I'm not convinced they were actually looking for me but I did an interview . . . entirely in Spanish. To my amazement, this went without a hitch, it just seemed to flow and is a real milestone in my efforts to learn the language.

Later I pass an odd-bod tramp on the side of the road who does a little dance whenever a car appears. A few kilometres further on, I stop for the night behind a sand dune but groan when I see the same man making his way along the road in my direction. Once he is directly opposite, he suddenly halts, plonks his two plastic bags on the road and sits down. Hell, how long will he sit there? Has he seen me? I don't think so. After fifteen minutes, I'm pleased to see him get up and continue on his way.

Thursday, 13 April 2000   Mocupe

Passing through the town of Mocupe, I find our lunatic tramp beside the road again, this time masturbating vigorously in front of the oncoming traffic. I must say I think his dancing showed more style.

I stop here for a Coke. I'm soon surrounded by people who just keep on staring at me. I smile and try to ignore them. I listen to them discussing who they think I am. An old boy is the local know-it-all and does most of the talking. Initially, they grapple with the concept of walking.

'But he's on a bike,' insists one.

'It's not a bike,' argues another.

'It's a bike,' one huffs.

This goes on for some minutes. They clearly take it for granted that I can't speak Spanish.

'Where does he come from?' wonders one.

The old boy obviously knows.

'He comes from Cuzco,' he announces.

A safe guess as gringo tourists come from Cuzco before they pass through Lima.

'Why is he walking?'

'It's his hobby – all gringos have a hobby,' continues the old boy.

The sage inspects the Union flag stitched on my shirtsleeve and then pronounces with certainty.

'Ah, he's from France – he's French.'

'Ah, he's French,' the whole bunch repeat.

At this point I have to smile.

Friday, 14 April – Sunday, 30 April 2000   Chicalayo

Total distance to date: 4565 miles (7363 km)

Newspaper exposure is working. Mariano, another agricultural engineer, has read about me and stops me on the way into town. He offers me a room above the medical laboratory run by his wife, Celima, close to the main plaza. It's perfect; I strip the Beast down, hump it up stairs then have a shower and a bit of a sleep. I'm in good hands. Celima brings me some pills over the weekend and I suddenly find I've gained a new mother. On Monday, I'm given a free blood and urine test. Hepatitis and typhoid are around so I'm screened for these and a host of other possibilities.

After waiting, a little nervously I may add, the tests come back with negative results for all diseases. There are, however, some points to note. The main one being my haemoglobin count: it's very low at 11.4 gr/dl, when it should be 14. This means I'm anaemic. It's the equivalent of being short of a litre of blood, which is why I tire so quickly at the moment. I also have a high white blood cell count, an indication that my body is fighting an infection.

Loperamide seems to be losing its effect so Celima puts me on a special diet. When things still don't improve, a further stool test indicates an infection and the presence of a high blood count. The sample also shows fungus and yeast spores so she puts me on stronger drugs: Bactrim Forte, twice a day, Floratil for the fungus, Confer (an iron supplement) and Buscapina for the pain. I take double doses for the first few days – they put me to sleep for the entire day. In fact, I do little else this week.

As to my appetite, I find the amounts of rice that the 'Doc' wants me to eat is a struggle. It's the staple here and I now hate the stuff. Everything comes with rice and I find it hard to hold it down. Worse still, as soon as my plate is empty, Mariano or Celima always notices.

'More rice for the gringo,' they shout.

'Oh, crikey, no thanks, I'm stuffed,' I always reply.

'Nonsense, you need it and, as we've *invited* you to eat with us . . . go on, more rice.'

'Oh, yes, of course . . . thanks guys,' I mutter.

Celima, unbeknown to me, has been shopping around, trying to buy me a new top for walking in as mine has had it – it's in rags. But as I've found, it's irreplaceable, so she has paid a seamstress to make two versions of the original. God bless her. I go with her for a fitting. They're perfect – now I have two extra-long tops with reinforced shoulders. I'm eating well again and feeling much stronger. Tomorrow is Sunday and Mariano's birthday lunch. I must leave on

Monday. I know I will never be able to thank this couple enough for all they've done.

Monday, 1 May 2000   Mochumi

It's 17:00 when I walk into Mochumi. I'd hoped to park up well before I got there but found the route boxed in by irrigation channels so, inevitably, found myself drawn to the town centre. I find a restaurant that's next to an open area where it looks like I might be able to hide the Beast. Seated at the tables, groups of wild-eyed lads look to be getting pissed. This, I gather, is a farmers' town and this lot are as rough as guts. It is, I find, best if you can meet these types on their level, which means playing it macho. I try and pretend that I own the place and heigh-ho, they ask me to join them for a beer. It only takes the copy of a newspaper to give me international hero status – I'm one of the boys, I'm offered free drinks, food and a bed.

Tonight is the town party and this restaurant is where they are holding the disco. It doesn't kick off until 23:00 and, after I've eaten, I'm still being treated royally. The newspaper cuttings are even read out over a loudspeaker and I find myself seated with the local big boys who are getting stuck into a home-brew made – I think – from pisco and soft drinks. Not that I can understand them. For some time now, I perceive a strange phenomenon when talking to males in Peru – I can't fathom a word they say. Funny thing is, I have no problem understanding the women.

Despite trying not to get drunk, it just isn't happening and it's not long before the town wants to see the gringo dance. The lads grab some poor girl who has little choice in the matter. She looks more scared than I am. I do my level best: the crowd seems impressed but that's not hard here.

The end is inevitable. Extremely pissed, I stumble off to some couple's house. House? It is a room in a mud-brick building divided with sheets hanging from the ceiling and mattresses on the bare earth.

Sunday, 7 May 2000   Beyond Mochumi

The world is greening up. Thick vegetation smothers the landscape and the roadside is blanketed by creepers and vines as, day by day, the desert turns to something else. It's not looked like this since I was in southern Chile. For as far as the eye can see, all the mountain ranges are swathed in lush foliage and the air is heavy and humid. Farm animals seem to wander around as they please. Pigs, goats, cows, chickens and turkeys as well as donkeys just do their own thing. This is campesino country and donkeys are the main form of transport; trains of them pass me all day hauling firewood, plastic drums of water and are usually led by boys as young as six.

What really strikes me is the unbelievable numbers of insects. If you stand still and listen, the whole world seems to hum. Today there are millions of butterflies, dragonflies, grasshoppers and black wasps as big as your little finger. I also skirt around dead snakes and scorpions by the bucketload and have seen the biggest centipede on the road, but I've yet to find one in the bush.

I also see a lot of foxes. They tend to look more like jackals and coyotes rather than what we're used to back home. Earlier, I came across a really odd group walking down the road towards me: two donkeys and a fox. The three eased to the other side of the road as they passed me but they still stayed together. A second fox appears a little later and begins walking the road a few hundred metres in front of me. He is there, tottering along for an hour, five kilometres or more. Every now and then he hops into the bush for a minute or two before he reappears, halts and stares at me until I get a bit closer. He then pushes on again but, alas, this ends in tears. A large bus coming our way spooks him. Mistiming his dash to safety, he disappears under the wheels and becomes messy food for the vultures.

Tuesday, 16 May 2000   Sullana

It's very hot when I trundle into town. Sullana is a medium size place set beside the largest river I've seen in Peru. It's in the most beautiful valley. If there's a Western Union, I'll email home for some more money so I can buy this beast that will get me across the mountains. Locals I meet on the road swear that I'll find a donkey here for as little as S200 (about £40). I check my email and discover one from my mum informing me that Treiz arrives in Piura, about forty kilometres away, by plane tomorrow. Lordy. I'd called Treiz from

Chicalayo and we'd talked about the possibility of her coming to see me. Now she's inbound.

I take a breather in a restaurant and one of the staff – a girl – offers to take me after work to the market where donkeys are sold. At 18:00 I find a safe place to leave the Beast and we take a taxi to the market. A good size animal could be had for S200, possibly less if I haggle hard, she tells me. She points to one that looks in good nick and I decide I want it so long as the seller will hang on to it for a few days. Until this point, she has been doing all the chat but then the seller realises that it is a gringo who wants it. That's different – the price ratchets up. In the end, we persuade the man to hang on to it until Thursday when we will try and do a deal.

Wednesday, 17 May – Wednesday, 24 May 2000   Sullana

I'm looking forward to seeing Treiz again. It's a year since I watched my friend climb aboard a bus near La Serena and fade into the heat haze. Crazily, she doesn't know if I'm even expecting her so she's taking a chance. She had merely left a message on my mum's answerphone, said she was coming to look for me and decided to go for it.

She is flying to Piura so I take a bus there in the late afternoon. Waiting at the airport, I watch two aircraft land: Treiz steps from the second plane. I recognise her from her walk as she totters across the tarmac and gives a huge wave when she sees me. It's so good to see her. It has taken her five hours to fly the same distance it took me a year to walk.

We're back in Sullana at 23:00. This is Treiz's first time in Peru and she already finds it very different from Chile. She has come with a bag of money so, although we're in a cheap hotel tonight, we can upgrade in the morning and live like tourists. In truth, we'll never be able to spend it all – I've never seen so much cash since I arrived in South America.

This week is a chill-out. We sample all the restaurants until we find a favourite and we eat like kings. I guess we're having the best of times but Treiz can't get over how many more beggars there are here. It's heart-rending; they come at you from every corner, even poking their hands through restaurant windows.

I buy the donkey and leave it under the watchful eye of some locals

on the river bank. The problem is, I won't be able to carry as much as
I had hoped so will have to leave some things behind. What if the
donkey idea fails? Then what will I do? Come hell or high water,
animal transport has got to be made to work. Once I leave without the
trailer, I will be donkey-bound and – except for the Darien Gap – will
rely on one to lug my kit, possibly as far as Mexico.

Treiz puts on a brave face at the airport. It feels just like La Serena
all over again as I watch her board the aircraft. It taxies, gets air-
borne and then fades into the distance before vanishing. I watch
forlornly, just as I'd watched her coach blend into the southbound
traffic from La Serena. It all happens so quickly – one minute she's
here, the next she's gone and I'm alone again.

Friday, 26 May 2000   **Beyond Sullana**

I was very nervous yesterday as my new friend and I set forth
together for the first time. It was plain to anyone watching that I've
had no previous experience at donkey loading and I was still in the
backstreets when I had to re-stow everything because it was slipping
sideways. Once on the way again, I soon realised just how slow this
donkey is. I also pick up on the fact that he has an aggressive streak
in him and is not lacking in the vocal department . . . he has the most
ear-splitting hee-haw.

When I unsaddle for the night, I find I've already given him a
couple of sore places on his back. I can't be having this. I then realise
I've no water bucket. Instead, I dig a hole and line it with a bit of
plastic but after all this, he isn't thirsty.

This morning, he doesn't want to play and is resisting. To try and
help, I strip the load again because it is still lopsided and decide to
sling some of my kit. I think I'm overloading him so bin my cold-
weather clothing and Lands End waterproof suit. I hope it makes a
difference. The thing is, if one side is even slightly heavier than the
other, even just a tiny bit, the load always moves.

As I'm sifting through the pile there is some commotion. My
donkey has trotted down the track and is attempting to mate with
two younger, tethered donkeys, much to the horror of the young boy
in charge of them. I can see I'm going to have a keep a close eye on
this beast.

Saturday, 27 May 2000   **Towards Los Lomas**

By midday, I'm truly pissed off with pulling this beast and I'm getting blisters on my hands. I decide it's time to sort him out. I want to get him walking without me having to drag him along by his rope. It takes some time but I think he's got the message. I walk just a fraction behind him and if he gets at all necky and won't play, or tries to do a runner, I give him a whack with a stick I've cut from the wayside. This works, but he doesn't really go any faster.

The cart track we're following narrows then breaks into a choice of uncertain-looking footpaths. We've lost the proper road somewhere – I can't think where – so I ask anyone I meet if I'm 'right' for Los Lomas. They always say 'yes'. I'm not sure so I just set a compass bearing due east and set off across country because, according to the map, I'll eventually hit a marked road running north–south. Then I'll know where I am.

Finding water is a problem. Right now, I'm down to two litres of very dodgy canal water. It doesn't look like I'll find running water near here because everywhere is bone dry so I'm relieved when, later in the afternoon, I find a water-pump beside an old church which runs clear and cool. I camp close to here because the donkey has been grabbing at stuff along the way; I think he's hungry. I've still come barely thirty kilometres from Sullana and find the pace soul-destroying. At this rate, I won't be in Los Lomas for two more days . . . I think I'll try and upgrade the donkey for a horse when I get there.

Monday, 29 May – Tuesday, 30 May 2000   **Los Lomas**

For some reason, the donkey is fired up this morning. Twice he freaks out, once when we meet a pig walking towards us on the track, and when we pass a hole in the ground, where he bolts and loses his load. What's wrong with him? I wonder if he has been eating hallucinogenic plants in the night? Sadly, his high soon wears off and we resume our familiar plod, which finds us in Los Lomas at noon.

We're moving eastwards again, and on tarmac, into the foothills of the Andes. For the next two days, I'll follow a river valley until the real climbing begins at a place called Ayabaca, some eighty kilometres from here. Were I to cross into Ecuador via Macara, I could be there in two days, but now I'm resigned to the fact that it will be another eight because I'm sticking to the steep scenic route. It's a 146-kilometre detour but, as I don't have a current visa, it will be better for me if I can give border police and customs a miss.

Wednesday, 31 May 2000   Towards Ayabaca

At 04:00 the distant braying of a donkey a long way down the valley wakes me up. This is answered by other donkeys, one over here, another couple over there until it is the turn of the one that is scuffling and farting outside my tent.

Eeeeee . . . eeeeeeeehahhhhh . . . hawwww . . . hawww . . . hawww!'

In truth, there's been a slight improvement in the performance of my beast; he seems to be picking up the routine – eat, drink, sleep and walk – and we made better progress yesterday. I still want to sell him though.

The chance soon comes. Mid-morning I spot three chaps ahead of me on fine-looking animals, big burly sorts of horses. When they halt, I'm soon popping the question. One man looks at me and then at another.

'Yes, sell him yours,' he says.

The man, a campesino, ponders for a moment. I'm willing him . . . yes, go on, sell it.

'How much are you offering?' he wonders.

'Eighty dollars, and this fine animal,' I reply.

The three talk among themselves and seem to like the deal. Then they dismount, hand their horses to a boy and walk up the track to a nearby house and talk with an older man. Minutes later, they return, complete with kids and a wife, carrying a notebook and pen. It's a deal. Nice one! I now have myself a good-looking dark-brown horse. Off comes his horse's saddle and harness and I strip down my donkey – goodbye fatso. The donkey is possibly the happiest of all.

When I get under way, I only manage a few hundred metres before, as with my donkey, the load slips to one side. This time, it's more catastrophic. The horse panics and bucks himself inside out, scattering my possessions all over the road. It takes all my strength to bring him to a halt and when he does, what's left of the harness is hanging upside down under his belly. When he's calmed down, I tack him up again and, this time, make a better job of it.

The way begins to climb and drop very steeply, the tarmac giving way to dirt track as we push on up the valley. Passing through a village, I have to fill a water bag as I find I lost two bottles when the animal went berserk. I also fear that my chap is getting hungry and is desperate to scoff whatever is growing at the roadside. Keeping him well fed could be tricky as I'm not carrying any proper hard food for him – I'm hoping he'll survive on grass. This might be a problem – there's plenty to eat in the valley bottoms but not in the high places.

I camp close to a water tap in a field. Tethering the horse, he roots around and picks on what he can find, which isn't much, and I decide I'll have to take time out to find him a place to graze in the morning. After I've eaten and I'm sitting just inside the tent, a man walks past and drinks from the tap without taking his eyes off me, which isn't unusual. I busy myself for a while longer and then step outside as the shadows lengthen. The horse . . . he's gone.

I rummage in the gloom and find the tether with no horse on the end of it. Dread twists in my stomach. The man at the tap, he must have nicked my fucking horse! Now it's my turn to run amok. I sprint on to the track and run down the hill, along the winding road but find no trace of them. I'm pretty frantic. I'm in a rage, and can't believe I've lost my horse after only half a day. I'm snapping. The thief could have taken him anywhere and I'll never find them. Local people know these hills like the backs of their hands. I sprint back up the hill but still nothing.

Further on, I can just make out a farm in the low light. It's just above me up a short track and in the yard in front of it stands a large brown horse. I run past four men sitting on the veranda and look the horse over. It's not mine. Had it been, I might have picked up the nearest object and set about all four of them. I sit down next to them. By now, others are appearing, all staring at me with wide eyes, wondering who the hell this lunatic is.

'What do you want?' one man asks nervously.

With my head in my hands, I explain. They all exchange glances as I mutter away to myself.

'How the hell did he do it, how did he get past me, how could I have been so switched off?'

I come to. I apologise profusely for my intrusion and head back for the tent, running through all possible scenarios. If this had happened in a few days' time, I would have been doubly stuffed. I would have had to bin nearly all my kit. At least now, I can get a lift back to Piura or Sullana with my stuff and start afresh. This is awful, and of course, I've blown US$80. I sit with my head in my hands, how did he do it?

Then I hear a crashing in the bushes. There is my horse staring rather gormlessly at me. He hadn't gone *anywhere*, he'd merely slipped his halter and gone off to find something nice to eat. I'm a prick . . . what am I?

Thursday, 1 June 2000   Towards Jillili

It starts off hot and very humid but soon cools as we begin to climb. By midday we're in the cloud-base, where we rest near some houses. When I explain to a local how hungry my horse is, he cuts him some sugar cane, which he seems to really like. I'll remember that. Being so wet, it's soon chilly if you're not on the move so we don't hang around. It's also desperate underfoot; it's very muddy and the path is deteriorating.

On the far side of the next village, we're faced with a short, steep uphill section that is all boulders and mud. Looking from the bottom, I don't believe it's possible to get a horse up there and I wouldn't be attempting it were it not for all the other hoof-marks. Mine does his best. Stumbling and wrenching his way upwards, there is one fifty-metre section that is such hard work I'm amazed that he is still on his feet. He's blowing really hard so we need a breather when we make the top.

We camp early. It feels very 'jungly' here – everything is dripping wet and while I get the tent up, I keep the rain off my kit with banana leaves. I've found a nice sheltered place off the track where there's plenty of sugar cane and grass to pick at. I hack down a fair supply of cane for the horse so he's soon in heaven. He loves it, the stuff's rocket fuel.

Friday, 2 June 2000   Jillili

This morning I've got guests: a group of lads are sitting watching me as I stir. After a while, one plucks up courage and comes over and, very politely – almost apologetically – asks if I would stop my horse eating his coffee beans.

The small bushes dotted about my camp area are young coffee plants and, in my ignorance, I hadn't realised last night. The plants have been decimated, just laid to waste. The horse has eaten everything that he could reach including three young banana plants that are now nothing more than stumps. I apologise, and move him to a fresh patch of grass, which he immediately gets to work on.

Once I get going the tracks are hellish; deep mud hides ankle-twisting rocks that you can't see and I ford many streams, almost knee-deep in fast-flowing water, that turn to waterfalls on the downward slopes. At midday we reach a vantage point on a peak and then descend towards a settlement called Jillili. The track is nothing more than a tightly winding corkscrew. Although the village looked just ten minutes away from the top, the reality is a two-and-a-half-hour tortuous slog.

I cause a real stir. Everyone pours out of the houses to see me. Children come from all directions and a great crowd marches with me as I head to the village square and park up. It's almost scary. I buy some pasta, tinned milk and some matches, then sit outside the little shop. The children close in, wide-eyed in amazement. I ask one boy his age. He's thirteen. I ask if he's ever seen a gringo before. He shakes his head so I assume this is the case for most of the younger children. I speak to some of the adults and build up an intelligence picture of how I might cross into Ecuador. I learn I'm just a day away from the border, and leave with a useful sketch map showing a cracking short cut.

The track is turning into a real horror story. A bit further on I come to a steep uphill gully, just wide enough for me to touch the sides if I outstretch both my arms. It's tight and very rocky and I do wonder if it is possible with a horse. It's steep enough for a man with a heavy rucksack and I'm amazed at how well my partner is performing. Several times he loses his footing and nearly rears over backwards before he slips sideways.

We reach a fork. The right looks bad so we take the left and descend for fifteen minutes. It's the wrong way, confirm two men I run into. I'm tired and frustrated. Quite what the horse must think of me when I turn him round and make him head back up again, I don't know. Twice the load slips and I have to re-saddle him. Once back at the fork, we descend again and I decide to camp for the night in the first decent place I can find as it's getting late. The poor horse must eat and rest, so we sneak inside someone's fence and hope no one notices.

Saturday, 3 June 2000   Cucuyas

The track descends rapidly to the valley floor. It's still hell and we're taking it very slowly so we don't fall and injure ourselves. At the bottom it enters a fast-flowing river and exits, where it continues, on the far side. The riverbed is full of large boulders the size of cars, so weaving across with the horse is a challenge. Still, I know that it is a well-used route because, a few minutes ago, I met two kids on a horse on the way up the track. I guess they are off to school. Both couldn't have been more than six, perched up there like kids on a school bus.

The track continues to undulate and crosses several other tributaries before we come to a bridge-crossing. Unfortunately, the bridge has collapsed at one end and has been repaired with a few trunks of bamboo, which doesn't look safe enough to risk the horse. I untie his halter and watch as he crosses the riverbed and makes it to the far bank. The trouble then is that the bank is sheer and I can't get him out. We stay in the river and head downstream for 200 metres until we manage to scramble out and take a very swampy track that's very hard going.

We're soon in a real state, both of us plastered in mud and wet through. After another hour, we pick up a thin track that begins to climb steeply and, according to my sketch, we're still right. As we begin to climb, the load slips and it takes me fifteen minutes to strip him down and re-saddle him. We set off again but after only a few paces, it is slipping backwards again. By now I'm tired; it's hot, the flies are biting and the horse is also having a hard time of it. There are blisters on my hands through having to pull him.

This is not a nice place. We're in a very dark, narrow gully; high walls of ferns, moss and lianas seal us in. It feels forbidding and the forest canopy completely blocks out the sunlight. You hear nothing above the sound of rushing water as it pours past from all angles.

The kit slips a third time. I have a serious rethink and the solution is, in fact, very simple. I just need to run a rope around the front of the horse's chest and connect it to the baggage to stop it slipping backwards – how can I have been so stupid not to try this before?

The narrow trail winds and contours up the left-hand side of the valley. It's wide enough for the horse – just – but, as we get higher, the drop on our right side is sheer and I don't like to look down. Eventually, this valley runs into a larger one dissecting our direction of travel. It must be the River Caiuas, the frontier between Peru and Ecuador.

The question is, where do we try to get across? I'm still very high and the valley sides to my front are desperately steep and heavily forested. So we keep contouring west. At midday it's very hot so I stop and dry out much of the kit, including my sleeping bag that also got wet. I want to cross before I reach the village of Cucuyas, which has an official crossing point where, no doubt, I'd get into difficulties with police and customs. It may well be that such a small outpost wouldn't trouble me but I haven't struggled these last few days just to get tied up with red tape when I'm almost there.

Close to Cucuyas, some lads start following me. Taking my chance, I stop and talk to them. They know a place where I can cross and agree to show me. Picking up another steep, pack-animal track, we stumble our way down the valley side, which is very hard going for the horse, until we blunder on to the river's edge. We're not alone. A small group of men are using an inflated tractor tyre to ferry empty beer bottles across from Ecuador. After chatting them up, they say they'll do the same with all my clobber, so I unload. This leaves the horse and me to do our own thing. It's chest-deep and very fast flowing but we both make it. Just.

Mission accomplished . . . I'm in Ecuador.

Chapter Four

ECUADOR AND SOUTHERN COLOMBIA

Tuesday, 6 June 2000   **Towards Cariamanga**

I've a horrible feeling that my walking-with-an-animal experiment is doomed to failure. For one thing, this horse isn't shod – he should have been but what do I know about horses? Where would I find a blacksmith and how could I pay him? Many of the tracks are very stony and he's now foot-sore and finding it hard going since we crossed the border three days ago. I could swear he's looking thinner. His eyelids droop and he yawns a lot. It's bad news. I intend to jettison him tomorrow when I reach Cariamanga, the first small town on my route.

Without him I guess I'll just have to move my excess kit on buses as far as Loja (120 kilometres), just as I did in Chile between Antofagasta and Iquipue. If I can sell the horse, I should have enough to shift the kit and buy supplies. I'll take only essentials and carry them all in a rucksack.

Wednesday, 7 June 2000   **Cariamanga**

'Gringo! gringo!' The cries of children in the street ring out like church bells warning of imminent invasion. People appear from their houses and are soon lining the street as we enter town, which looks a run-down hovel. I pause to ask a chap to take a picture of me with my camera but he can't grasp how it works so I end up taking one of him frozen to attention. After an extended camera course, he does eventually depress the shutter but I'm sure he'll have cut my head off. (Actually, it turns out to be the best snap on the roll.)

The horse has a cold and the rasping sound coming from his nostrils isn't helping my sales pitch. I ask one old boy for US$30 but he scoffs.

'You'll be lucky,' he mutters.

Shit, I thought that was a steal. He offers me US $10 less, but I'm sure I can probably get more.

'C'mon, thirty,' I repeat.

'It's old,' says someone else.

Is it, I wonder? The horse is standing motionless, its head hung low, eyes half-closed and fluid dripping from its nose.

'It's sick,' someone comments.

I explain that it's 'just tired'. It has been walking for seven days and is a bit hungry. No matter, the few customers lose interest and move away. Bollocks. I sense I won't get much more than what they're offering if I'm looking for a quick sale. Anyway, I don't need that much money to move my kit so I could take less.

I find a hotel room. I swear it's the smallest room I've ever slept in – there is just room for a bed but none to stand next to it. I manage to arrange for a bus company to move my baggage, which is only going to cost US$2. A little relieved, I make friends with a hairdresser and spend time hanging out at his salon and talking to his customers. I'm still the owner of a horse, who's currently grazing on high ground overlooking the town, when a family arrives for a haircut.

'I'll give you fifteen dollars,' says the wife.

'He's yours,' I blurt.

Saturday, 10 June – Sunday, 25 June 2000   Loja

Absolutely knackered, I arrive in Loja at 20:00. It's a major city, is very large, yet most of it seems to be hidden in dead ground. I collapse into a fast-food restaurant feeling as if I could eat a horse . . . now there's a thing. I've walked an unbelievable fifty kilometres today, which means I'm faster than I was pulling the trailer. Funny this, but covering extreme distances is kind of addictive – it gives me a real buzz.

One of the first things I notice about Ecuador is the lack of begging; those that insist don't seem to hound you. You don't get hassled by taxis either and I spend the next week finding what I need, picking up money from home and going through the mail. I don't seem able to get a visa here which means that I'll have to return to the border – at Macara – at some stage. It's a six-hour bus ride.

I bump into James, a Canadian I'd met in Peru, and he's a serious pick-me-up. Inviting me to join him and two friends, Justin and Nathan – who are with the US Peace Corps – we spend a few days in Vilcabamba, a small place south of here, which is a real tourist spot and packed with gringos. We're not staying in the little town, but out in the wilds at another friend's place – an Argentine girl named Gabriel, who has a three-year-old son – in her small mud-brick cottage. This is where I discover the real purpose behind our visit – we are looking for the San Pedro cactus; when prepared in a certain way, a potent hallucinogen.

I know that preparing the cactus is a lengthy affair. You strip the outer layer of waxy skin to reveal a darker green flesh, then the whiter core. It's the green layer we're after and we spend an age separating it, before it is placed in a huge cooking pot to simmer. It has to cook away for eight hours. The next day Justin strains the resulting green gloop and there's a debate as to where and when we should try it.

Nathan is peering into the pot in the late afternoon. There's a lot of 'Well, what d'you think?' going on, which, frankly, I've had enough of. Grabbing a cup from Nathan, I scoop up some of the mixture and down it in one. It tastes, no surprises here, like crap and I have trouble keeping my second serving down. It's vile. James has used some old recipe used by the ancients. How long will it be before it takes effect, we ask. He just grins at us.

By 20:00 I know something is afoot. We're in a pub. Justin and I are starting to giggle but Nathan is still calm. I feel intensely happy. I find that I can stand and move around without falling about. By 21:00, the world is a different place; I feel hot and my hands are glowing, as if my body is accelerating the blood-flow. Nathan is still strangely quiet and wears an expression like a rabbit caught in a car's headlights.

Walking back to the cottage in the dark, things really begin to alter. Inanimate objects I focus on come alive and begin to move, even plants and rocks. The track itself turns into a tunnel of trees that shrinks and then expands . . . yet you still feel as if you are in control. It's not as if I am pissed – there is no stumbling or falling over. Without knowing it, we keep very quiet – no one shouts or even raises their voice. Looking into bushes, they move as if they're alive. Branches twist and turn and even curl. We pick up rocks and watch them change shape; they turn into a mouse, a face or even a skull.

By 03:00 we're all ready for a sleep. Just as we're about to get our heads down, Gabriel's son wakes and comes to join us, sitting with his mother. He looks just like Adam when he was this age and I'm reminded of the times he would wake and stumble into his parents' bedroom. Memories flood back. With them, tears roll down my cheeks.

'Missing your son?' asks Justin.

'I guess so,' I reply, as Gabriel gives my hand a squeeze.

All in all, an oddly illuminating experience. I was fine next morning. I didn't have a trace of a hangover.

SAN PEDRO CACTUS

One of the oldest known psycho-active plants, the San Pedro cactus (*trichocereus pachanoi)* grows wild at 2000 to 3000 metres in the highlands of Ecuador and Peru. It is a large columnar cactus that grows up to heights of six metres. It contains mescaline – a naturally occurring psychedelic – that is concentrated in the skin, which can be peeled, sliced and boiled for a few hours, and then cooled before the resulting liquid is ready to drink. Once ingested, it will allow you to explore your inner fantasy world. A trip, which will take two to three hours to peak, induces colourful visions, feelings of inner tranquillity, heightened awareness and rapid thought-flow.

Monday, 26 June 2000   **Beyond Loja**

I meet lots of locals on the road today, all dressed in black. The indigenous population are Saragurd Indians who you'll have seen in the tourist brochures; the women wear black shawls, long black dresses and trilby hats and the men, knee-length black shorts or trousers, a black jacket and, again, a trilby. And, in these conditions, welly boots. All the men have long black hair braided into a ponytail, and even the youngsters are mini-versions of their parents. I pass them all day, herding cattle, leading donkeys loaded with firewood, or in little groups with baskets slung across their backs.

In these cloud-covered hills it seems to be drizzling permanently. It's much wetter and cooler at this altitude, the vegetation has changed and there are no bugs. Roads wind east then west, zigzagging their way and this adds to the length of my journey. Making matters worse, the surfaces are so bad that it's sometimes unbearable to walk on them as you stumble on loose stones and twist ankles in the many potholes. This and, of course, the constant climbs would have made life impossible if I'd still been hauling the Beast.

I'm also hard up. In the cheapest country in the world, I'm going hungry because my visa cost me so much. [*Karl had to get the bus to Macara, just over the Peruvian border, to obtain a fresh visa for Ecuador.*] I'm at 3000 metres, my waterproofing is starting to fail and I'm surviving on bananas at 500 Ecuadorian sucre a go. Nice scenery though.

Friday, 30 June 2000   Combe

The small town of Combe is not much of a place and, once I find a restaurant, it's obvious they don't see many gringos around here. A young boy of about three years old toddles out of the kitchen and comes towards me. I just know that he hasn't seen me yet, as do all the women running the place, who are watching with knowing grins on their faces. This always happens. He walks right up to me then casually glances upwards. He leaps backwards with surprise and stumbles away, his eyes as wide as table tops until he eventually bumps into the wall. The women are in stitches. The poor child gropes his way along the wall until he finds the kitchen door. He scuttles inside, safe at last from the horrible white-haired monster with the blue eyes.

Friday, 21 July 2000   Towards Cotopaxi

It's 04:00 and, strangely, I'm awake. I can hear the sound of tearing grass right outside my tent flaps. I listen for a moment, thinking it could be an animal eating, but the sound is too rhythmical. I unzip my tent and peer out into the darkness . . . can't see a damn thing. I look up on to the bank above me and just make out the silhouettes of three hats against the night sky . . . Indians! They pick up on my movement and peer back down from the darkness at my tent. I'm left thinking, 'It's four o'clock in the morning, what in the name of Christ are you doing?' After just another moment the three heads disappear into the gloom with their supply of grass, off to feed the animals, I imagine.

I get off to an early start. It's a wet morning, with a chill in the air. I'm carrying a fair few blisters that always sting like mad until I get into my stride. The day sees me covering just short of forty kilometres and by the end of it I've Cotopaxi in sight, so I should make Quito in a few days' time. Cotopaxi is the world's highest active volcano. Extremely impressive, it's an almost perfect pyramid covered in snow and dominates the whole landscape.

Sunday, 23 July – Wednesday, 30 August 2000   Quito

Total distance to date: 5245 miles (8446 km)
The last push for Quito. It's cold and I'm feeling weak, nauseous and just plain hungry. Quito is only over the range of hills to my front but it'll be a long haul because the city stretches for thirty kilometres. I won't even touch the southern outskirts until 11:00. I look down on the cityscape that fills the long valley. Snow-capped mountains, including Pichincha, a 4794-metre active volcano, are a stunning backdrop to the swirling hustle and bustle of the capital. A few years ago, this volcano erupted and blew a spectacular H-bomb-style mushroom cloud over the city, covering every building in ash.

Since yesterday I've been mentally preparing myself for entering the built-up areas and I'm feeling like a coiled spring. The outskirts look rough and my heart is thumping on a number of occasions. I have a pre-arranged contact address but I'm not sure where it is exactly. Nor are policemen or bus drivers when I stop and ask them. By 16:00 I'm in the north of the city and beginning to lose my cool. The address isn't in Quito at all, it's San Antonio, a town bang on the equator and another twenty kilometres north. As it's Sunday, I can't collect any money because the Western Union people are closed. I sit outside a café, my head in my hands, wondering what to do.

A family walks past. Moments later, the son returns and starts to talk, giving me the opportunity to slip the fact I've nowhere to stay into the conversation. It's put to the vote and the family agrees to help. I shove my kit in the boot of their car and hop in. Within minutes I'm fast asleep.

When I wake, I see we're still moving.

'Where are we?' I ask, trying to get my bearings.

'We know where your friends live so are taking you there – they're going to meet us in San Antonio,' says the father.

It's no use trying to explain about the 'walking' thing. I'll just have to put that right later on by doubling back.

Jack and Marina, although we've never met, treat me like a long-lost son with hugs and kisses all round. [*Karl's cousin, who works on a cruise ship, is married to the couple's eldest daughter, Carolin.*] As I'm feeling really cold, because I haven't been eating enough, I'm happy to be hustled away to their place where I'm given my own room and a shower, loo, TV and video and, oh boy, a double bed. Fantastic. I crash and that's that for the day. For the next few days, I'm pampered like a big fluffy cat, which is really difficult to cope with after what I've been used to. I feel awkward because Jack is a university lecturer and, owing to Ecuador's crisis-hit economy hasn't been paid for several months. I feel bad because I'm staying here and can't – as yet – contribute, because the money that I was expecting to find in my Western Union account hasn't arrived yet.

San Antonio straddles the equator. A huge monument marks the line and it's strange that the northern hemisphere is just two blocks from here. It had been a firm arrangement that I would have a long stay here but quite how long I'm not certain. Colombia is beginning to weigh on my mind. I can't cross the Darien Gap until January at the earliest – the start of the dry season – so, at present, I'm running a bit early.

There's much to consider, what with the drugs trade, the kidnappings, murders and war between the government and the left-wing revolutionary guerrilla army (who basically want to turn Colombia into a larger version of Castro's Cuba), which is around 15,000 strong and currently holding large parts of the country. Right now, the US government is heavily involved and is pumping millions of dollars into the country to help it deal with the problem. Violence seems to be on the upsurge and news is all bad – recently, twenty-three people were killed on one day and bombs regularly explode in the larger cities.

This has been one of the most comfortable places I've stayed in, if not *the* most comfortable. It has become a home . . . unfortunately. This is part of my problem. I had a home, with a wife and son a long time ago. At least it seems a long time ago now. During our five years together as a family there were good and bad times and it filled an inner need in ways that little else will ever come close to. Such feelings and emotions can be pushed into the background but never completely buried, and they will reappear to trouble me given half a chance.

My son, Adam, is almost unknown to me now and I to him. To me he is still three or four years old, as that's how I remember him best, but in reality he's nearly ten. At present there is no contact with him and not even my mother knows where he is. His mother – my ex-wife, Angela – has moved back to Northern Ireland – she's from Belfast – so it's up to her to let me know where. I can only be patient and wait. My last letter to Adam is still with my mother, as she has no forwarding address.

Adam was born in Belfast. I was on yet another tour of duty with 3 Para at the time and Angela was living at her mother's there for that period. I saw them whenever I could but it was 'unofficial'. I was present at Adam's birth in the Royal Victoria Hospital on the Falls Road, the Catholic heartland of the city.

Being there, as I was a serving British soldier on a tour of duty, was completely forbidden, of course. I clearly recall the night Angela was admitted. It was three in the morning and I was sitting in the waiting room with her mother. Sharing the room was another man whose wife had also gone into labour at around the same time. Something about this man had caught my attention and, by chance, his wife ended up in the bed next to Angela so I took note of the name at the foot of the bed. Back in the unit, I traced the name. This man was a former commanding officer of the Provisional IRA's Belfast Brigade.

*

Purely by coincidence, I have a phone conversation with my father after my rucksack is finally packed. We talk about wills. Who did I want to leave my belongings to (as few as they are), were I to 'cop it' at some stage. Father guesses correctly. Everything must go to Adam, including all the diaries.

I'm about ready to move on now. Giving up on my broken satellite phone, I send it back to the UK and arrange to bus my unnecessary kit to Tulcan, the last big place before the Colombian frontier. Taking the bus back into Quito, I complete the walk from there to San Antonio – the bit I skipped when I arrived – and it takes just three hours to cover the twenty-two kilometres without equipment. Now the north of Ecuador awaits me – more deserts – which is a stark contrast to the wet lushness of the south.

QUITO

Circled by high mountains, Ecuador's capital is located 2800 metres (9186 ft) above sea level and stands in a hollow at the base of Pichincha volcano. Founded in 1534, it is 245 kilometres (152 miles) from the Colombian border and 750 kilometres (466 miles) from northern Peru. Although it is just 25 kilometres from the equator, it is high enough to make its climate feel spring-like with warm days and cool nights. Most travellers to Ecuador arrive here first and, although it is a large city, those who come here find its small-town feel very appealing. Its 'Old Town', once the capital of the northern Incan Empire, is now a World Heritage site. It has a population of just over one million.

Saturday, 2 September 2000   **Otavalo**

I've covered seventy kilometres since Quito. Each time I glance over my shoulder, there's Cotopaxi and Pichincha still standing boldly behind me in the far distance, their snowy peaks crystal clear in the white rays of the early morning sun. By 15:00, I'm in Otavalo. It's a tourist town – there is a famous market selling handicrafts and woollens – so it still has Quito hotel prices. Where you find tourists, you find restaurants serving western food, which is what I can do with right now; fish and chips, steak, apple pie, ice cream, that sort of stuff. I'm glad to say my monster appetite has returned. I think that the secret to a good appetite is not necessarily good food, but food that you like. Luckily, I've some money right now so will please myself.

South American food is, I find, incredibly dull, tasteless and bland. Nothing but rice, potatoes and beans. Here, in the mountains, people tend to eat the largest meal of the day at lunch-time and have a snack in the evening. This is, I gather, something to do with the altitude and their digestion. If you ask for a set lunch in a restaurant – this is the most economical ploy – you'll get soup, which comes with vegetables, boiled potatoes and odd things I can't identify. The main course is a mountain of rice, more boiled spuds, more veg and a scrap of meat. It's all very wholesome and dirt cheap. It's probably quite good for you but when you're forced to eat it day in day out, you can have enough of it.

Wednesday, 6 September 2000   El Angel

I pass through the town of El Angel around midday and stop to eat. Looking at the map, I decide I should be in Tulcan at the same time tomorrow, as it only looks about forty-eight kilometres from here. How wrong I am.

Looking for a track that will serve as a short cut, I see storm clouds coming over the mountains and there's a chill in the air. The muddy trail I set off on is ascending and the air is getting thinner. Soon I'm being bombarded with hailstones, so put my Gore-Tex jacket on. In answer to this, the downpour merely increases. Now it's a mix of sleet and rain, and I'm soon wet and extremely chilled – my poor old coat isn't up to the job.

I'm still climbing. The map didn't indicate this dramatic height gain, which certainly isn't welcome. It's thundering now and the farmland has turned to bare tundra, while my track becomes an ankle-deep stream of freezing water. All feeling in my fingers has been lost – this isn't good – as the route leads ever higher, towards peaks that are topped with a sprinkling of snow.

By 15:00 I reach the summit. I'm exhausted, frozen to the core, soaked to the skin and utterly miserable with it. A few hours ago I'd cooked breakfast under a burning sun and now here I am above the snowline. I'm shaking violently as the downpour continues. I've got to lose height. Trouble is, I'm not about to descend the other side as I find I'm on a plateau, which rather reminds me of some places in the Brecon Beacons.

I push on as fast as I can, stumbling through mud and over rocks and stones. By now, my face, as well as my hands, is numb with cold. It's lucky there's no wind – if there was, I'd be in real trouble. I have to keep cracking on and hope I'll run out of the storm and that the track will descend soon. I need to get out of the rain but can't stop to stick the tent up as the inner would be soaked before I could cover it with the fly sheet.

It's 17:30 when I spy an abandoned farmhouse on a hilltop. As I close in, I can see it doesn't have much of a roof left, so hope of shelter dwindles. However, all's not lost – there are just a few slates left in one corner to offer protection if I can get my tent up underneath. Despite having kept moving for five hours, I'm still frozen stiff. Just how cold it is, I can't say. It may not even be all that cold. The fact is that for two years I've enjoyed an eternal summer, so this is bound to feel extreme.

I don't sleep much. Having got things sorted, I even light a candle in the tent to try and raise the temperature a little. It works and I grab an hour or two before sunrise.

Thursday, 7 September 2000   Tulcan

At last I make it back on to the Pan American, which means I'm only eight kilometres from Tulcan. The sun has returned and I'm burning again. I must get it together. I want to appear fit and healthy because a sickly looking creature is easy prey and every town has its slums and dangerous outskirts. Tulcan is the highest town in Ecuador. I'm not sure how high but it's very cold when there's no sun. It's woolly hats, scarves and gloves here, and always very cold at night. Nowhere sells coffee.

'Christ, the border with Colombia is just seven kilometres away . . . what do you mean you've no coffee,' I splutter, in a restaurant.

While inside, I speak to some girls. They have friends with a car and we manage to arrange that they will drive my spare gear that was waiting for me here, over the border to the small town of Ipiales. From there, I can send it on again by bus to the next stop. This excursion goes swimmingly well. Crossing into Colombia is the slickest and easiest crossing so far, when I'd imagined that it would be the most stringent. On our return leg we were just waved straight through without so much as the need for an entry or exit stamp.

Tuesday, 12 September – Sunday, 17 September 2000   Pasto

Total distance to date: 5410 miles (8712 km)

I'm still in fairly safe territory at the moment, but once north of Pasto – my present location – I'll be in bandit country where the FARC and ELN are making their presence felt. Pasto is bigger than I'd thought it was going to be; the suburbs certainly gave me the heebie-jeebies and I've had a lot of attention, most of it unwelcome. 'Gringos get out of Colombia' is a common enough slogan, this time on the walls of buildings. 'Burn gringos' is daubed on the rear of a passing truck. It reminds me of Belfast, except it's harder to blend in.

Prices are higher here. Your average shitty hotel is US$3 – that's as cheap as it gets – and food prices are also two to three times more expensive than in Ecuador. I don't think I can stay in this town too long, again because of the costs, but I really have to try and slow my progress or I'll find myself in Medellin, the jumping off point for the Darien crossing, in early November. That would be a mistake. I won't be able to afford to live there for months on end.

City living is hard when you're striving not to spend money. I try to plot my route between where the Pan Am Highway ends in Colombia and begins again in Panama. One fact that is becoming apparent is the need to cross some very wide rivers . . . a bit of a problem because I can't take a boat. Other than this, I'm growing bored and impatient, as there's little else to do. Worse still, the fleas are at me again and I'm covered in red bumps. How I hate these pits. I'll stand it until Sunday.

Monday, 18 September 2000   Beyond Pasto

I'm back in the hills but seem to be descending more than I'm climbing and there are some splendid views. The downside – I'm in bandit country. Yesterday's newspapers were full of news of the latest military operations underway in the south, part of 'Plan Colombia', using new equipment supplied by the US. The TV news is full of accounts of a recent ELN kidnapping – people seem to be taken when they're stopped in cars. There's footage of troops on patrol in the mountains north of here and of captured ELN members. Also, there's news of an operation near Cali, in which forty were killed in a firefight between troops and the FARC. I'm not sure which side the casualties were on.

I need to find somewhere to pitch my tent. In the middle distance, I can see the perimeter fence of what looks like an airfield. Closer is a construction site with a large house not yet completed although it's next to two others that look occupied. Just across the road looks more promising. I can see a raised piece of waste ground with a hollow in the centre which could give me cover from view, although those upstairs in the houses may be able to see the top of the tent. It'll have to do.

I struggle up the bank, find a place to camp and begin to get myself sorted. I think I'm probably all right when a torch light appears. Someone is out there. There's movement . . . it's a group, possibly four people. The torch is switched off and a figure is silhouetted against the skyline. He's got a rifle, it looks like an old carbine, probably an M1. He's dressed in civvies so I don't yet know who I'm dealing with. A second figure joins him and now they're just yards from my tent flaps. They can see the tent but not me. The one with the gun brings the weapon into the aim, hails me and orders me outside.

Day one in bandit country and I'm already at gunpoint.

The second figure, who turns out to be a woman, is also armed and repeats her partner's command. Showing my empty hands, I tell them not to worry, to keep calm and that I'm just some camping gringo.

'Hands on head,' they bark.

'Sure, who are you?' I reply.

'Police. Who else is in the tent?'

'I'm alone,' I say.

'Come forward,' orders the woman, and keeps the drop on me as the man nervously creeps forward and shines his torch into the tent.

'Who are you and what are you doing,' they continue.

'I'm English, I'm just passing through and want to sleep here tonight. I can show you my passport.'

'Where's your rucksack?' one demands.

I reach for my passport and hand it over to one of them. By now, five other armed men have appeared in the gloom, all of them in combat fatigues with webbing and rifles. Very soon, I'm the centre of attention for a fifteen-strong unit. Torches are flashing everywhere and dogs are starting to howl . . . isn't this just dandy. In truth, they're as relieved as I am and now are finding this whole incident rather amusing. They leave me to it.

COLOMBIAN TERRORIST FACTIONS

The FARC (Revolutionary Armed Forces of Colombia) was formed in the 1960s by the Colombian Communist Party to defend what were then autonomous Communist-controlled rural areas. It is South America's oldest, largest and best-equipped Marxist insurgency and is organised along military lines. It carries out bombings, murder, mortar attacks, narcotrafficking, kidnapping, extortion and hijacking as well as conventional military attacks against the Colombian military. It has 9000 to 12,000 armed combatants and makes its presence felt in the Darien.

The ELN is a Marxist insurgent group formed in 1965 by urban intellectuals inspired by Fidel Castro and Che Guevara. It engages in kidnappings for ransom, often targeting foreign nationals and derives some income from the narcotics industry. It has 3000 to 5000 armed combatants and, like the FARC, is active in the Darien.

The AUC (United Self-Defence Force) – also known as the 'Paramilitaries' – is an umbrella organisation for right-wing groups fighting the FARC and ELN. Formed in the 1980s, the authorities had viewed them as a counterweight to the left-wing factions and they received arms and training from the Colombian army. In 1989, they were outlawed as the abuse and atrocities committed by them mounted. They number between 5000 and 7000 fighters.

Taking a break in the desert. Southern Peru, 11 January 2000.

Writing up the day's notes. Beyond Lima, Peru, 8 March 2000.

The donkey with a full load. Northern Peru, 26 May 2000.

A sugar cane stop for both me and the horse. Northern Peru, 1 June 2000.

En route to Loja, Ecuador, 9 June 2000.

An Andean valley, Ecuador, 11 July 2000.

In Colombia, with Catty, January 2001.

Disguised as a scruffy itinerant, ready to set off from Medellin, 14 January 2001.

Drinking from a coconut while crossing the Darien Gap. A good source of clean liquid.

A view of the river and jungle from Paya, Panama.

In the cell at Boca de Cupe, Panama, February 2001.

Leon, with Beast II, July 2001.

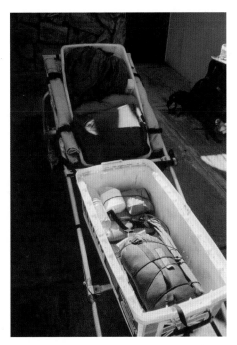

Equipment packed into both sides
(top and bottom) of BII's box.

Costa Rica, April–May 2001.

Mexico,
22 March 2002.

A tarantula spider,
found lurking under
my tent in Mexico.

With some
Mexican soldiers
on the Mexican/US
border, April 2002.

USA, May 2002.

Going over the Raynolds Pass, Idaho into Montana, 3 November 2002.

Bassano, Alberta on the Trans Canada Highway. Re-equipped and now ready to face the cold, 9 March 2003.

On the edge of Alaska, January 2006.

Tuesday, 19 September 2000   Towards Remolino

By 09:00 I've already covered sixteen kilometres, so chill out for a while in a culvert under the road. I feel safer here than I have for days; it's a pleasant spot with a cool breeze. Sitting dangling my legs on the downhill side is just like being in the doorway of a military aircraft before a parachute jump – the world just seems to fall away beneath me in a sheer wall of rock for hundreds of metres.

I push on, all the time descending a winding mountain road until the afternoon when, inevitably, there is a long hard climb again, always a killer when I'm looking for a campsite. As usual when I want to stop, the roadside is littered with tiny huts and poor people – every patch is occupied by someone. Often they stare as I pass and their dogs will snarl at me. I'm almost giving up on finding somewhere to sleep when I notice a bridge with room for a tent underneath and decide this is for me. I have an amazing view from here and make sure I don't show any lights. But it's all in vain. Just as the sun dips over the horizon, some shagging farmer appears and sticks his fat ugly head under the bridge.

'Hey look! There's someone camping under here!' he bellows.

Give me strength.

Wednesday, 20 September 2000   Remolino

The heat today is an absolute killer. It's 35° C. I develop a massive thirst, so that by the time I reach the small town of Remolino, I'm fit to drop when I take a restaurant break. It's some cesspit and I cringe when I hear the 'chefs' coughing their lungs up behind a screen.

'And what would sir like?' I imagine the waiter asking.

'Oh, I'll have the fried fish . . . the one so ill-prepared and under-cooked it's possibly lethal if you try and eat it . . . and a smattering of TB if you'd be so kind,' I'd reply.

'Certainly sir . . . and to drink?'

'Coffee please . . . if you have any. That would be with milk, the stuff with lumps of yoghurt in it that's been fermenting in your fly-ridden, cockroach-infested kitchen-from-hell for a week in these soaring temperatures.'

'An excellent choice sir . . . we'll only be two hours while we attend to drunken relations, change a few nappies and anything else we can think of while we forget all about you.'

'Fine.' I put my feet up and savour the stench of village life on this sweltering day. I even smile to myself as I notice the blood-gorged mosquito on the back of my hand.

'You little rascal, shoo, shoo. Off you go now.'

Perhaps I've had too much sun?

Wednesday, 27 September 2000   Towards Cali

I must spend the next eight days in the field because I can't enter Cali before 5 October, the earliest some more money will arrive. Unfortunately, I can only afford to feed myself for three more days so I'm going to get hungrier than I am already. Bananas are cheap and are my main source of food – I'm virtually living on them.

I feel as if I'm under surveillance every damn second of the day. When I pass a house or through a village, everyone I see is watching me intently. There's no let-up. Perhaps they think I must be flush, that I have so much money in my pockets, because I'm travelling the world rather than working. It would be very easy for them to ambush me and kill me. Who would know? It's paranoia, perhaps, but I think I probably have far less to fear from the paramilitaries than from the common bandits and cut-throats that give Colombia one of the highest murder rates in the world.

Friday, 29 September 2000   Towards Cali

I'm on the move by 07:30. I soon stop for water at a small store where an old TV set shows the national news. This time the army has something to cheer about. It has found a hidden construction plant used to build ten kilometres of road that the FARC was using as a clandestine supply route. The ELN has also released some hostages that have been held for several weeks.

With fifteen kilometres behind me, I stop at a café and buy five bananas, but they do little to stave off my hunger. I'm now forty-five kilometres from Cali and still have time to kill. I've just 6000 pesos left. It's precious little when you consider that one proper meal will cost me 4000. Living off the land is not an option as there are too many people about, too many dogs and just the one conspicuous gringo. I can make the money last a little longer but I'll be in for three to four days of suffering with nothing at all. This could get interesting.

I spend the rest of the day sitting in this café watching the world go by. Christ, I'm hungry. Having been forced to watch people eating all morning, I cave in and spend 800 pesos on a litre of milk. A passing army patrol calls in and is followed by six policemen who take an interest in me. They want to know what I'm doing and I show them my passport. One of them laughs as though he doesn't believe a word of it and walks away.

'Pah! He is carrying far too much to have walked so far,' he scoffs.

At 16:00 I push on. As I leave the edge of town, I bump into the group of soldiers that had called at the café. A pretty ragged-looking bunch, they've slung their hammocks in a disused building so I stop to ask if it's possible to crash with them tonight. A little wary of my presence, they say I can sleep just over the road in an old concrete roadside stall. It's grotty but I'm happy so move in.

One soldier comes over for a chat, asks the usual questions, then returns to his boss to fill him in on my story. Their minds at rest, some of the soldiers come over for a chat and there's even an offer of food, which I gratefully accept. They're just like soldiers in any army. I'm welcome to stay tomorrow and they appear willing to feed me, so that's another day taken care of. It turns out that my den is a night sentry post so I can sleep knowing I have my own personal armed guard a few feet away.

Monday, 2 October 2000   Towards Cali

With my foot, I rummage through a huge pile of crushed, rotting bananas on the side of the road. I'm in luck. I unearth two that are in relatively good nick so this is supper for tonight. Close by, I stop and ask for water at a house and notice a likely campsite behind a cemetery just across the road. Graveyards are becoming quite a favourite of mine when it comes to finding somewhere to sleep. As you would guess, few people wander around there at night so, generally, I'm not disturbed.

But this one takes the biscuit. Looking for a space, I can't fail to notice that there's some disturbing debris lying around. As well as broken headstones, there are piles of resurrected coffins, most with their lids open, and some with human remains still inside. I can see bones, skin, hair and even pools of gloop – what sort of a cemetery is this?

Trying not to dwell on this, I decide that it's spot-on for tonight because I'll be in Cali by midday tomorrow. I do find it a bit creepy, but I know that no God-fearing person is likely to be hanging around here after dark, so I ought to sleep soundly.

Tuesday, 3 October 2000   Cali

As I make my way into the centre of this large city, I hope to find a 'residencial' and persuade the owner that I'll pay when the money arrives, which, fingers crossed, it will tomorrow. It's almost 17:00 when I do find one – the Hotel Residencial Canaveral. It's 6000 pesos a night and I manage to buy some bread next door for 1000 pesos so I don't starve. The next morning, following a street map, I find the Western Union office and pray that Mother has put something into the account. She has – I'm saved.

The hotel is on a street full of restaurants and discos so, by night, is crowded with people, neon light and noise. It is always warm here, even at night, in this valley. Everything is open-plan and spills into the streets where, like in so many other places I've seen, there's an odd mix of the very wealthy and the very poor. Begging is rife and I'm a prime target, being the only gringo in town. It's common for someone to rush to your restaurant table when you have finished to see if there is anything left, be it a sachet of sugar or a few crumbs. It saddens me to see so many hungry people.

I spend a week here. During this time, the city is rocked by four bomb attacks, two of which I hear yet don't realise what they are above the noise of the streets. I also read that thirteen people were shot dead in a small town south of here and one I'd passed through on my way.

Karl spends three days in the town of Pereira and leaves early in the morning of 26 October.

Friday, 27 October 2000   **Pereira**

Before I left Pereira yesterday, I managed to get on to the Internet. Father has had an email from some ex-colleagues in Bogotá, who wished me well, but advise that things are not looking good on the main highway between Pereira and Medellin as guerrillas have been setting up roadblocks. This has been in the press – I've seen pictures of masked men setting fire to trucks. I've got about 230 kilometres and seven days to keep myself out of trouble before I reach Medellin.

Last night I was restless and uncomfortable. I am on the road by 07:50, but feeling totally bunged up with a bad head and a sore throat. As usual, it's hot and the winding roads climb and fall, when I come across my first coffee plantation – I was beginning to wonder if I'd ever see one. I've two road maps of the same area but they are far from identical, which makes life very confusing. For most of the day, I'm walking along what could be one of three roads marked on the map, so I'm far from sure where I am. The roads themselves make me nervous; they're very quiet, and there's a blind bend every few hundred metres – you never know what's around the corner.

Not long after I find a place to camp, the heavens open. Once I've eaten, I doze in the tent until I wake in the small hours feeling lousy. I'm lying in a pool of cold water. I must have pitched in a hollow and now the tent has filled with water that has got in through the leaks in the ground sheet. My sleeping bag is below the waterline and, still lying there, know I can do little about it at this stage. What the hell . . . it's not too cold. There's nothing I can do but chuckle to myself in despair. I'll dry out tomorrow.

Tuesday, 31 October 2000   **Towards Medellin**

Fifty-four kilometres to Medellin. I have to burn some time off as I'm still running early. But that's not hard because I have a heap of kit to dry out and more holes to stitch up on my rucksack cover. I'm still climbing and suffering from sore hips, which I've had for as long as I can remember. Since I've been in this country, they've opened up and won't heal. They're friction rubs from where my rucksack waist-belt sits on my hips. Right now, they're smarting like hell and in places my skin is red raw.

I run into some soldiers this morning and they insist on seeing my passport. I know they'll only look at the photograph page so I don't need to bluff them with some barely credible story. I hand it over and, as I expect, they glance at it and hand it straight back to me. It's a different story when I'm stopped by the police; I hand them the photocopy I'm carrying and I give them the bullshit story of how my jacket had been stolen, along with my passport – a ploy in case someone tries to confiscate it. Like the soldiers, these guys are armed to the teeth, their combat vests chocka with bullets and grenades.

Wednesday, 1 November 2000 – Monday, 1 January 2001   Medellin

Total distance to date: 5890 miles (9485 km)

Progress is swift this morning – too much so. There I am bumbling along a deep cutting running through a hillside, when suddenly I raise my head at the end of it. My jaw drops . . . before me is a vista of skyscrapers in a large valley. It's like finding a lost civilisation. It's Medellin – home of Colombia's cocaine industry. With a population of two million, this is the country's second largest city and the last I shall pass through in South America. I stand and gaze on it for a while. For so long at the back of my mind, it was still a distant focal point all the same. I have heard so much about it. I can barely believe that it is here right in front of me. Loved and feared, either way I'll know soon.

MEDELLIN

This is a well laid out industrial city – the second largest in Colombia – and is the main city in Antioquia Province. Situated in the Aburra Valley at an altitude of 1487 metres, it faces forbidding mountain barriers in all directions and has a pleasant all year round English summer climate of 21° C. It is a seething, vibrant place. It is said that this city created Colombia's 'arepa' – a bread and corn patty stuffed with cheese, chicken or beef. It was also home to the world's richest and most brutal drug trafficker, Pablo Escobar, leader of the infamous Medellin Cartel. After escaping from prison in 1992, he was killed by Colombian forces in 1993.

With just a few coins left, I need to stay somewhere that doesn't mind if I don't cough up until Friday. Sure enough, there are loads of cheap places to crash, some as little as 4000 pesos, yet those at this price are death traps, places I wouldn't stay even if they were free. Absolutely stinking, with beggars sleeping on the hall floor, they have doors that don't even close, never mind lock. I find somewhere before dark for 6000 pesos a night. Striking a deal, the sweat-stained, greasy, fat owner shakes my hand on it and agrees to wait until my cash arrives. That said, he still ambushes me next morning, rubbing his fingers together, as I leave to find the Western Union office.

Trying to transfer money was a test because once again I don't have a valid visa. The girl at the desk takes my passport and starts thumbing through it . . . bugger! Stopping at the visa stamp, she notices that it's one month out of date. I then begin my rehearsed explanation with plenty of smiles. She smiles back.

'No. You can't have your money without a valid passport,' she smiles again, which catches me out.

I too keep smiling and ask to see her boss. Another woman appears wearing a fixed smile.

'No!'

'But'

'No!'

'Bu . . .'

'No!'

'. . . t.'

'NO!'

I try everything but she won't budge. I exhaust all means, including all my press cuttings . . . they don't even look at them. I decide to go because I know there's another office, way off across town. It's my only chance though it takes an hour to walk there by which time I'm feeling a little desperate. This has to work. The staff is mostly female so I turn on all the devious charm I can muster. Ultimately, the boss says that she'll have to ask Central Immigration for permission . . . bollocks. I now have an hour to stew until Immigration reopens after lunch.

I flirt with everyone, trying to get anyone who will listen on my side and soon I feel that the atmosphere is changing. By chance, during this hour, my father has also put some more money into the account so I'm rich . . . if only. I give it one last shot with the boss. If she manages to speak to Immigration, I suspect that I'll get stiffed for the cost of a visa extension. I want to avoid that as I don't even need one for what I'm planning. She read my cuttings and knows my situation although I can see that she finds bending the rules difficult. Then she cracks and gives me my money. She even gives me a wink. The sense of relief is enormous. I can eat, pay the fat hotelier and, as it's Friday night, can get out there and start making friends.

I opt for El Pub, a rock bar, which comes well recommended. I'm leaning on the bar when I notice a chap with a blonde girl standing next to me. At first I pay them no attention but then the girl and I lock eyes and she stares at me for a few seconds. Soon she moves closer still and, placing her left hand next to mine, crosses her little finger over my little finger while I just stare straight ahead trying not to look too surprised.

Covertly, I print my name and hotel room number on a piece of paper, which I slip into her hand. We don't look at each other or give the friend any signs that this game is taking place and, indeed, she keeps up her conversation with him. She nips to the loo and on her return slips me a note: 'I'd love to know you, Adriana (Ade).' Later, we strike up a conversation and I don't know why we've been playing these silly games. Her friend is, in fact, just a friend. It's an effort to communicate because they both speak no English and they don't understand much of my Spanish. I have her number so will call her tomorrow.

I meet Ade on Saturday night outside the cathedral in Plaza Bolivar. When I get there, my eyes are on stalks. It is a sea of people: skinheads, hippies, New Age types, punks, rockers, jugglers and fire-eaters, all mixed in among a number of small food stalls. Half-naked people covered in body paint and other weird kit . . . a seething mass of humanity dancing to the music in this extraordinary city. Bloody hell, it's like no other place I've ever seen. From this mayhem a girl yells my name, a girl in tight leather trousers, wearing cool shades and her hair in what look like blonde 'dreads'.

I've no idea it's Ade until she introduces herself and another friend, Willy. Straight away, we leave this scene behind and take off in a jeep to pick up both their sisters. Things are looking up when we arrive at Willy's home in the east of the city. His family is really great and they immediately offer me a room in the house for as long as I care to stay in town. Christmas if needs be. Wow! How about this – it's more than I could have dreamed of.

The night cracks on, as they tend to do in Medellin. It gets crazy; we drink loads and dance in a club until we drop. Ade is a wild one. In another rock bar, a large bunch of longhaired rockers in Iron Maiden T-shirts are crashing into each other. Catching my eye, she grabs my hand and runs straight into the thick of it. She's spectacular to watch, a mere slip of a girl giving it all she's got and only giving over when she nearly has her jaw broken.

I move into my new home, extremely glad to be shot of the hotel. Not that I've much opportunity to relax: tonight, we're back out again. It's a continual blitzkrieg and, by Monday morning, my body is just weeping for a chance to recover. But that night, Willy insists we're out again. This time, something significant happens. We bump into two more friends of his. One is Catalina Estrada, 'Catty', as she's known. She seems to click instantly with me, and added to this, we can communicate easily. She's twenty-eight and a civil engineer, overseeing projects in the city, so is seriously smart . . . and has one helluva body. I guess she kicks Ade into touch and I soon find that I'm seeing her every night. Life slows down – thank God.

I weigh seventy kilograms. The last time I remember noticing my weight was in 1998 when I was seventy-seven kilograms. Not bad, I guess, given what I've put my body through. Gradually, I'm trying to increase my food intake rather than hitting my normal calorie tidal wave, which can't be good for me. I'm fed well by my new family, and on top of that, am using their blender to concoct something I'm calling banana soup to which I add concentrated milk powder and Brazil nuts. This gives me 1300 calories so I should be able to put on some weight given the time I expect to be here.

Willy has friends with knowledge of the Darien Gap. I meet a cousin of his, who has apparently walked the Gap, and an old boy who used to own a farm in the northern Darien, as well as his two sons, who know the area. Just how much they know, I am eager to learn. At first they all express how dangerous my idea of walking the Gap is, that it is ridiculous . . . and that it can't be done. This goes on for some time and they have the impression that I haven't a clue or I wouldn't be proposing such a crazy scheme. Their solution is to take a boat from Turbo (in Colombia) to Panama.

'No, I can't. No boats,' I tell them.

'Don't be silly, you have to.'

They insist that the guerrillas are my main problem because nothing and no one moves in the Darien without them knowing about it. There are no police or army except for the 150 held in FARC prison camps as bargaining chips.

'They take what they want, when they want,' Willy's cousin says. 'As a result, the tracks you are talking about using have disappeared because no one is using them anymore. You can't do this . . . you'll die.'

I go through my possible routes, discussing what information I already have but all he concludes is that the crossing cannot be done on foot.

'If you try, you'll die,' insists the old boy.

I almost feel foolish, trying once again to convince him that I can do it. Willy and I then leave.

'So what now?' he asks, as we make our way to his car.

'I'm going to cross the Darien on foot . . . they are *wrong* . . . I know they are,' I affirm, and, despite the negative vibes, I did extract some useful bits of information and some more contact addresses.

Next day, I find the Instituto Geográfico Agustín Codazzi where I study maps. Although not detailed, they confirm there's an unbroken route that leads off from the main road to Turbo from where it heads fifty kilometres west to the River Atrato. This area had been causing me big worries; it was looking like fifty kilometres of swamp until snippets of information had begun to hint that there was some sort of track. Now I'm sure that it exists. It looks as if it runs to the village of Port Libre on the Atrato, which, according to Willy's friends, is the guerrilla's heartland.

It appears that I have, essentially, three routes to choose from:

1 Red route. This uses a network of paths that would take me north-west through a chain of villages running alongside the rivers to Yaviza in Panama. This route is usually taken by people on foot, and as a result is preyed upon by bandits, cut-throats and guerrillas. My local friends believe that to take it would result in certain death.

2 Blue route. This goes north along the east coast. It's easier
   in that there are tracks to use, and good ones at that. But I
   will have to travel alone on routes controlled by the FARC
   and further north by the paramilitaries, right-wing groups
   engaged in a war of attrition against the FARC. According
   to Willy's old farmer friend, it is basically a war zone
   interspersed with cocaine plantations and drug-processing
   factories. But I must be aware that these people spin a
   good yarn, and consequently it's hard to gain a realistic
   idea of the situation. Once I'm across the border into
   Panama, the tracks end, though, and I'm faced with
   seventy kilometres of jungle and rivers before I can rejoin
   the road running north from Yaviza to Panama City.

3 Black route. I received an email from my father, who is not
   struck by either the Red or Blue option, and suggests I
   should avoid all tracks and civilisation altogether. A lively
   email dialogue has ensued, in which he has constantly
   reiterated that I should consider the possibility of taking
   the west coast. Until now, I've never considered that for a
   number of reasons: firstly, there's nothing there but a vast
   wilderness – one of the world's most virgin rainforests;
   secondly, I also have to weigh up the relationship between
   energy input and energy output. This is affected by how
   long I'm on the ground, the nature of the terrain and
   humidity levels. I would also have to carry a lot of extra
   weight in food. Not only is the Black route longer than the
   other two but apparently the west coast is in a perpetual
   rainy season. On top of which, there's the problem of
   navigation in this wilderness. Taking everything into
   consideration, Father's idea sucks. But it's got me thinking.

The Gap is, of course, not the only major obstacle on this next leg.
There's the route from Medellin where I leave the road to head west,
which is just south of the town of Chigorodo. It's barely a road and
soon becomes a dirt track, along which I'll pass towns and villages . . . and much more guerrilla activity. Unfortunately, I won't
find much of a military presence so I'll be on my own for the two
weeks I estimate it will take me.

Being tall, blond and blue-eyed with a rucksack full of goodies is as good as a death warrant so I've a very special plan in mind. For a long time I've taken a curious interest in the homeless drop-outs and, sometimes, the plain nutcases that I've seen tramping the road-sides of South America. It's interesting how they survive on the very edge. I watch them closely – after all, one day the sky might fall in on me and I could end up joining them. Lord knows, at times I feel as if I might. The reason these types appear to live in another world is simply because they do. No one interacts with them, or even looks at them, not even the police. And in this part of the world there are lots of them. Perfect.

When I leave Medellin, it will be as a filthy hobo, a worthless man of no interest to anyone . . . I hope. A great theory – but will this work? Transforming myself is going to be tricky. Whatever I come up with has to be able to get me as far as the point where I leave the road, but once I begin my approach to the Gap itself any disguise will lose its effectiveness. Even if you're dressed as Coco the Clown, anyone moving in this area is of interest to someone, so there it becomes an escape and evasion exercise, where the fewer people who see me the better. This will not prove easy, and on the Red and Blue routes, would be near impossible. If I chose the Black route, I'd have a lower profile but I'd be carrying a skip-load more food and it could take me two months to cover the 110 kilometres.

I'm given the contact details for Major Castillo at the HQ of the 4th Counter Guerrilla Brigade. He ought to know more. The major, it turns out, is a huge, burly chap with a clean-shaven head, well-chiselled face and a set of US Army Para wings on his tunic. He has served in the Gap and now works in operational planning, which is perfect as far as I'm concerned.

Despite a few language difficulties, I am able to glean much from him. His main worry as far as the expedition is concerned is the section of road northwards from Medellin to Turbo. It is FARC-infested and, basically, I'll run into them at some stage. They operate in groups of six to ten, a mix of both sexes, and most of them are youngsters aged fourteen to fifteen years old. How bad is that? Castillo agrees. What could be worse than a bunch of gun-toting, trigger-happy teens.

'I don't know how best to advise you,' he says. 'If you're recog-nised as a gringo, they'd pick you off on this road like a tick.' He, like others before him, reminds me of a Russian cyclist who was stopped and shot on the same road.

'You won't make it down this road. In disguise, you may get so far but sooner or later, they'll want to know who you are,' he warns.

It's looking bleak. Everything now seems to point to the Black route, which would avoid me seeing people. Thing is, I've got to get to the start of the Darien area first and there's only one way to do that . . . go down the road. Then there's the River Atrato to consider. It's a kilometre across so I'll have to start way upstream if I'm to drift over with the currents. Then something strikes me. If I'm thinking of drifting for a few hours, why not make it a few days and miss out much of the road in FARC-occupied territory. I wouldn't be using a boat so will not be compromising the expedition's concept, and it just might keep me alive. It has the glimmer of a chance. I can feel a plan beginning to form.

Monday, 1 January 2001   Medellin

Medellin is a city of lights. It also has the only Metro in the country, which is extremely modern and clean, and means that I can be in the city centre in five minutes from where I'm staying. I like the people and I've seen less trouble here than in any other city since I began my expedition. I'm making great friends and the girls are mind-blowing, quite the most beautiful in South America.

Catty and I spend a lot of time together – she's almost my personal assistant. She shares an apartment with her mother and a cousin and it isn't long before I am allowed a sleepover there – and in the same bed as Catty – which is very unusual in South America. She's as much in love with my dream as I am and the thought of just going for it gives her the same buzz. Since we met, I've shown no interest in other girls. She is the only real sidetrack from the plan for the Darien.

Weighing up my options, I decide on the Red route after all. It may be right under the nose of the FARC but it's shorter and more direct – I'll be carrying less in my rucksack – and the route-finding is probably easier than the Blue or Black options, which will involve too much thrashing about in the *ulu* (jungle). Also, two Brits, who had been thought long dead, have just turned up alive, after having spent nine months in the hands of the FARC. I guess that the group is beginning to think about PR so the release of these men is encouraging. Perhaps I can survive a contact. Maybe they'll even bump into me and just let me pass without a problem. It's not much to base a plan upon but I'm taking it as a good sign.

I concentrate on preparing my disguise. This is hard work. Father is right when he says 'I'm the wrong shape' but I can't do much about that. I'm going to darken my complexion and hide my kit. I'm not trying to look like a local – that's not feasible – but don't want to be taken for a gringo who might look as if he has some cash or kit worth pinching. There are many people in Colombia with western features but not many look like homeless bums.

Turning myself into a tramp proves testing. Darkening my skin is the biggest problem – it won't. We try everything from felt-tip marker pens and food colouring to clothes dye and bronzing cream but I'm still lily-white. Then Catty finds a fake tan that seems to work. I dye my hair and apply layer upon layer of fake tan until I begin to look like a Tandoori chicken. I tone the colour down a touch with a little dirt – carbon deposits from my cooker seem to work a treat. The kit I'm carrying is heavier than it has ever been, most of it food, but it will lessen as time wears on.

My GPS (a small, hand-held global positioning system that uses satellites to tell you exactly where you are, and enables you to key in 'way points' to aid navigation) arrives. Unfortunately, I must pay US$50 to import it so I'm back in the red. But it's here. The green light is now on.

Chapter Five

THE DARIEN GAP

Sunday, 14 January 2001   **Medellin**

I wake at 08:00. Lying here, curled up warm and safe beside Catty, thoughts of what may lie ahead are unwelcome now. Before we stir, we talk. Outside, it's just another normal sunny day in Medellin, but it feels far from normal to me. Gloria, Catty's mother, has made breakfast. This consists of *arapea*, a kind of pancake made from corn and scrambled eggs, which is what every Colombian starts the day with. Having eaten without speaking, we drive to Willy's place where my kit is ready and waiting. I mess around for a while making finishing touches to the packing or, as I suspect, subconsciously delaying the start.

Time to leave. Catty doesn't have to say a word – it's written all over her face. I don't know which one of us is saddest. We troop outside for photographs, for thanks, well-wishing and hugs – and more kisses from Catty – before I begin the long haul out of town. I am sad and apprehensive as I leave the street I've come to know. Never, never, at any point in my journey have I felt so alone. Or that I am leaving so much behind.

It is Sunday, so the streets are full of people. I wonder if I will draw the usual attention. In South America, strangers have the habit of staring directly into your eyes, but I notice that today they avoid my gaze. My downbeat appearance must be working. On the edge of town, the way steepens. This is how it will be for the rest of the day – an uphill haul that promises to almost wipe me out.

Just before 16:00, I come across a camping place that is too good

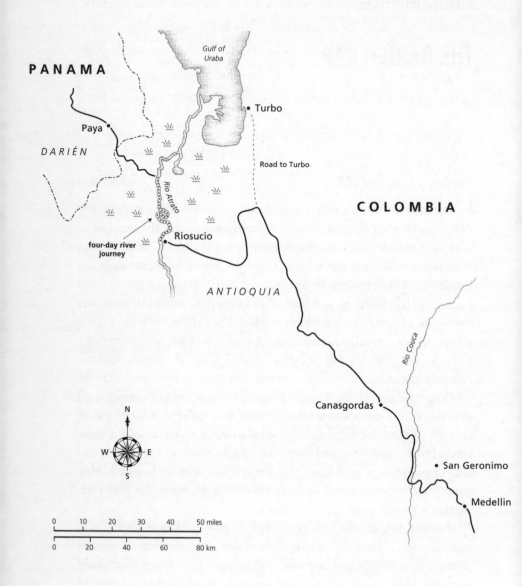

to miss. My hammock and I are not the best of friends; in fact, rigging it is a complete pain in the arse and takes a damn sight longer than pitching a tent. I have a grim and depressing night. Far below, but still pretty close, the lights of Medellin twinkle at me in the dark. I sit staring at them for a couple of hours. I miss Catty big time.

DARIEN GAP

The Darien is a 26,000 square kilometre swathe of jungle in Panama and includes the border with Colombia. Known as Panama's 'Bermuda Triangle' it is considered a place where 'things seem to go wrong more often than elsewhere'. Having swallowed explorers for centuries, today guerrillas, drug-runners, poachers and jaguars rule this vast no-man's land which, due to the volatile political situation, is rarely visited by travellers (as kidnapping and murder are rife). Impassable by road, those who decide to come through here take detours by sea or air. It is home to 100,000 people, half Afro-Caribbean, half native Panamanian, and these are concentrated in a number of villages.

Monday, 15 January 2001   Beyond Medellin

I have blisters. It's self-inflicted, of course, as I'm now wearing old boots, cut down and modified to look like shoes as part of my cunning disguise as a local vagrant. Trouble is, I have been breaking in some new ones for the last two months in the city – ones I'd been sent from home. Now, I'm finding it really hard to readjust to my old pair again because the heels have worn unevenly and they're crippling me. I try to level them with my knife, but it doesn't help much.

The way is uphill all morning until midday, when the climbing is over. Relieved, I begin to descend the road into the valley of the Rio Cauca, but by late afternoon I am, I have to admit, in a crap state. Two months off the road and I've gone soft, particularly my feet. In truth, they and the rest of me are in rag order. I find every step a strain. I feel in my shoulders as if I have been strung up by my wrists for a week.

I am about fit to drop when I spot a small store about a kilometre below on a bend in the road. Unfortunately, there's little to eat. I have to make do with four small cakes for tonight's meal, although I do manage to refill my water bottles. As I sit resting here for a while, I can make out San Geronimo far below me. It's been a long, hard day and it's getting late. I must find somewhere to lie up before I lose the daylight. By chance, there's a likely looking place just a few hundred metres away. It's a small gully just off the road, so I grab my kit and trudge off to investigate.

From a distance, this place looked encouraging but, on closer examination, it isn't. It is rough, steep ground and I can barely stand up on the loose scree as I search for two trees to sling the hammock between. I am so knackered I can hardly be bothered, but I must focus for a bit longer. Wrestling with the hammock, I have one cord around a decent tree and have caught the end between my teeth when I lose my footing. I skitter backwards in a flurry of sliding scree and mud with the cord still in my mouth, and plough sideways into the base of another trunk, shuddering to a painful halt. I lie still, stunned, the wind knocked out of me. As I cough and splutter, trying to get my breath, I taste the blood in my mouth where, thanks to the nylon cord, I have all but removed a front tooth. Feeling for it with my gritty fingers, I find it dangling by a slither. Instinctively, I wiggle it back into the socket and hope it will stay put.

I struggle back up the slope and try again. On very uneven ground, I finally fix my hammock but, in the half-light, I see that it's then too high to climb inside because I've managed to position it above the bed of a small stream and the ground falls away in the centre. I fly into a rage – how could I be so stupid? I drag some rocks over, pile them up and, after some gymnastics, I collapse inside. I lie there feeling as if someone has given me a good kicking. And this is only day one.

But it's not over yet. Moments later, there is a rustling in the undergrowth which, I guess, is probably some creature. Then I make out the beam of a flickering torch in the darkness. Someone must have seen me come up here. Presently, the beam falls on my sleeping place, so I call out, 'Who is it?'

No answer.

I try again: 'Who is it?'

Worryingly, I get no response. Damn it.

Annoyed, I struggle out of the hammock in my stocking feet before I am caught full in the faint beam. I duck behind a tree for cover, avoiding looking directly at the light so as not to lose my night vision. Then, at last, the silence is broken. It's just some old campesino chuntering away in Spanish – not that I understand a word of it. But I get the picture; he wants me to pack up and shove off. I begin to remonstrate. Surely, I offer, there's no problem with my staying here if I move off early next morning? This doesn't wash. It's his land and I must leave now.

I don't want trouble, so I decide to comply. Just as I'm beginning to move, the old boy whips out his machete and threatens to cut down the hammock. Now I *am* pissed off and seriously consider slinging him down the hill. Jumping between him and my swinging bed, I point at the weapon and, rather forthrightly, shout in wobbly Spanish, 'Put that away right now!' I guess I'm slightly losing it at this stage. I'm certainly losing my grip on Spanish as, in the gloom, he slashes wildly, shouting at me not to come any closer.

'Fuck it, OK, OK, I'm off,' I yell back at him, in English. 'Just put that thing away.'

He does so, only to reach into his satchel and pull out a shotgun. It's 'broken' at this point and, as it's about an inch from my nose, I catch hold of the barrel end just as he snaps it closed. Now, I don't think there's a shell in there but, hey, I'm holding the wrong end to find out.

'OK,' I hiss, taking a step backwards and flinging my arms high in the air as if in surrender, 'Let's just calm down', as the man, his voice faltering, continues to scream at me. With the gun still pointed at my nose, I strip down the hammock, bundle my kit into a pile and, using my own torch, gather everything up in my arms and stumble down the slope to the roadside.

I home in on the lights from the store I left an hour ago. In the yellow glow emanating from it I can make out three more campesinos. I drag myself over to them and dump my kit in a heap. I'm in a real bad way; I've been ripped to bits by thorns and will need some time to sort my stuff out. The three men stare at me in silence. I flop down next to them as I get my breath back. They look like simple folk. One of them grins at me, so I grin back. Hmm, I think to myself – these guys are psychos. Funnily enough, the one who grins gets up and moves a little further away to another chair, so perhaps the feeling is mutual.

It isn't long before I realise that all three are, in fact, not psychopaths, they're just deaf and dumb. After a while, they stand up, throw their sacks over their backs and head off into the night, leaving me alone again. It takes an hour or more to repair the tears in my hammock and to re-stow everything. Now what? Where am I to spend the rest of the night? I have no chance of finding anywhere else off the road in darkness so this is as far as I'm heading. Moving to one side the tree stumps the men have just been occupying, I decide to crash out here and now in the shadows.

It's a hot night. My tooth hurts surprisingly little, but I'm worried that the wound to my gum is going to be a problem. Trucks pass now and again and, as they do so, I'm coated in another fine layer of dust. I wish I was in a bed. How I wish I was with Catty.

Tuesday, 16 January 2001   Near San Geronimo

Restless night. Didn't get any sleep until 04:00, but was on the road two hours later. I find it so hard to get back into the swing of things and I'm suffering something awful. I must re-acclimatise. I've grown used to the higher, cooler altitudes of Medellin, so this sudden change in temperature and workload is wreaking havoc. In the foothills around San Geronimo, the barometer is through the roof and, although I stop for a breather every kilometre, each muscle and bone begs for mercy. My pace feels incredibly slow; even when resting, I pant like a dog. I cannot get enough water down me but, though I'm hungry, I cannot eat. My head is spinning. The bronzing cream isn't working, either – I sweat so much that it simply washes off as soon as I slap it on. I also managed to lose my hat last night, so I'm suffering under this bitch of a sun. The day's end can't come quickly enough.

Wednesday, 17 January 2001   Antioquia

I stop for breakfast at a roadside café at 07:30. When an old man and a girl sitting beside me ask where I am heading, I mutter, 'North.' The girl then spurts out: 'You're the man walking around the world and crossing the Darien!' Bloody marvellous. So much for my cover story.

Crossing the Rio Cauca and into Antioquia, it's hot again and I'm feeling rotten. It is uphill all the way as I begin to attack a second mountain range. After just a few hundred metres, I am destroyed and must rest every half-kilometre or so. I want another meal around midday but there is nowhere to go. It was too early to eat in Antioquia and, as always, I must watch how much money I spend. The landscape has changed to desert now – dry rocks and sand, with sparse tree cover – and is very different to the lush, cultivated surroundings of Medellin. I seriously worry how I will cope. I could be in for a long slog with little food or water to spare. My pee looks like Guinness – has done since yesterday. I am a sick man and feel awful.

I find a camping spot after 16:00. I've come a pathetic distance, but I'm done for. With little enough water, I eat nuts and lie like a zombie in my sack. Tired as I am, sleep never comes. I don't know why . . . maybe it's the nuts? Around 22:00, a snaking column of troops passes by along the road, followed over the next four hours by yet more platoon-sized groups. I hear them talking loudly before I see them, but now and then I can see their silhouettes in staggered file in the lights of passing cars. I presume it's the army; unlikely to be the FARC this far south. I lie awake until sunrise, going out of my mind.

Thursday, 18 January 2001   Beyond Antioquia

At 13:30, as the steep road at last flattens out, I arrive at a small store that sells only Coke. It appears those inside were half-expecting me. They have heard that a gringo is coming, so even in this get-up I'm still news. I press on. Later, I camp in what is becoming my normal squat – another steep ravine, thick with undergrowth with a stream bed running through it. I will be cold tonight because I threw away my sleeping bag this morning to lessen the weight of my load. I'd hoped to lose height again but haven't, so, by 20:00, I'm freezing my nuts off. Four hours like this and I've really had enough; I drag together some dry wood, light a fire and warm my frozen bones. I spend the next three hours hugging the fire and sewing up rips in my mosquito net. Back in the hammock, it's a long wait for dawn.

Friday 19, January 2001   Canasgordas

It's becoming very hard keeping up my disguise since everyone I meet refers to me as 'mono' or 'gringo'. Is it worth it, I wonder? Things are looking up, though, because I'm making better time now and covering the ground; on top of that, I'm eating well. But my feet are bad and getting worse. I eventually lose my temper with the ill-fitting old boots I've used as part of my disguise and change into some new ones. I toss the old pair into the valley bottom. Have I done the right thing?

I soon reach the next town, Canasgordas, which marks the edge of what I have earmarked as a hot spot. The road between here and Mutata is, basically, the front line in the conflict that has been raging between the right-wing government and the FARC since the 1960s. I want to keep a low profile, so I avoid the centre. There's only one bridge over the Rio Sucio, on the other side of town, where I am noticed by a small group of men seated outside a row of buildings on the far bank. Rising from their chairs, they seem ready to intercept me.

I feel uneasy. Making a snap decision, I head into a café, order a Coke and sit down in order to give myself a moment to think this over. The barman glances at me, then into the street, then back at me. Something is about to happen. Sure enough, the men appear in the doorway: the first two are a touch on the fat side but tall with it and look as mean as hell – one has a badly scarred face. Both walk over to my table and stare at me, not saying a word. Behind them, five more – these in their late teens – appear and begin pulling down the café's metal shutters. I'm trapped. My mind is racing, but there's nothing I can do. I sit back in my chair and smile.

'Give me your papers,' requests one of the big guys.

'Yeah, sure, but why do you want to see them?' I smile as I hand him my passport, then I ask him straight out, 'Who are you?'

From my three years on the road, I've learnt that, in such circumstances, you must play it cool; you cannot show fear or they'll feed on it. You don't get upset; you don't shout about your 'rights' or how you'll call the police, you don't even say 'no'. You just keep it friendly but do as they say.

'We're United Self-Defence [AUC],' one announces. Phew, they're the good guys, local forces sponsored by the Colombian government.

I flick my eyes around the group trying to read each face in turn. Is this a bluff? Are they FARC and just testing my reaction? Given the area, they probably are AUC. And nothing in their eyes tells me that they are anything other than who they say they are.

'Well, thank God for that, fellas. For a moment I thought you were FARC and I don't want to meet *them*. But you guys, that's cool with me. Rather you than them. Those guerrillas are a big problem for you, and me, in fact, for everyone, and if you're here, they're not! So pleased to meet you. My name's Karl,' I blather, offering my hand to one of them. He shakes it without smiling.

They ask questions. Where do I come from? Why am I here? And why am I dressed like that? I give them answers and whip out my press cuttings to back me up. They all gather round. One mobster is keen to show off a revolver tucked between his belt and rolls of fat. The atmosphere grows less tense: they're impressed and the interrogation turns to genuine interest in the expedition.

The younger ones are keen on my cuttings and, after a few smiles and jokes, the two fat gangsters drop their act and nod in agreement. They open the shutters – Christ, this feels good – and I am allowed to keep all my kit as we talk about the town ahead and who runs what. I finally get my Coke – I guess the barman didn't see any point in handing it to me before now. My new friends aren't that keen on answering too many of my questions, so I drink up, wish them well with the 'fight' and depart, almost forgetting to pay for my Coke.

'No! No problem, it's on us,' they say.

'Aw, you guys!' I bellow, as I set off at a fair pace.

Well, I guess this incident confirms that this *is* a hot spot.

Saturday, 20 January 2001   Pital

I bin the disguise. It's difficult to maintain, it slows me down and, hey, it isn't even working. I also ditch anything I won't need in the jungle. The next stop, Uramita, is twenty-five kilometres away and the road runs along the Rio Sucio valley. Give it another two days and I will be out of the Andes. The hills are smaller now and I am losing altitude.

Around noon, I stop for a Coke in the village of Pital, where I get into a conversation with some locals. The children hide and the adults seem nervous until they realise I'm a gringo.

'You must change your clothing, you're wearing the uniform of the FARC,' one urges. It seems my jungle greens are indeed in the same shade as the FARC's. It might cause a problem but I'm kind of running low on options right now. When I ask about the FARC or AUC, they are reticent, although one villager spells out the danger I am in. Beyond Uramita is El Boton, where there are lots of guerrillas; they also occupy Taparales and Santa Teresa, places I must pass before reaching Mutata.

'Don't walk at night,' they warn. 'Be careful from now on.'

Just six kilometres from Uramita, two guys on a motorbike approach from the direction of the village and screech to a halt in front of me. Stern-faced, tall and well-built, they demand to know what I'm up to and insist on going through my equipment.

'And you are?' I ask, not that I need to.

'United Self-Defence Force,' says one, continuing to ask questions as he rummages through my rucksack while his chum watches the road. It feels very routine, like police at a checkpoint, and they aren't aggressive. Once they are happy that I am who I say I am, one asks why I'm wearing FARC uniform.

'To scare the shit out of you guys, of course,' I answer, before they climb back on the motorbike, the pillion rider first adjusting the pistol tucked into the small of his back under a shirt. They must have come out to meet me – information is being passed on whenever I'm seen on the road.

Uramita is just a row of 'shop' houses straggling alongside the road. Talking to a café owner and his regulars, the conversation has a familiar ring: remarks on my rebel uniform; warnings about walking at night and where I intend to sleep. I had planned to find a spot to camp on the outside of town but its inhabitants have other ideas.

'No! No! Not there! We have a place, a room for you where you can get cleaned up. It will be a lot safer. Don't go down that road tonight. It's likely you will run into guerrillas.' I get pally with this lot, and again, they feed me. Later, the AUC chaps on the motorbike drop by. They give me a high-five when they see me.

Sunday, 21 January 2001   Dabeiba

Before I go, last night's hosts warn that this next stretch is very dangerous. 'If anybody points a gun at you, put your hands up!' says one, who also advises carrying a white flag to wave if I meet any bad guys.

'Er, thanks, I'll try and remember,' I reply.

I am advised to take the 'old road', a track that runs alongside the river, rather than the main road through El Boton, a dangerous town that I should avoid. Taking the 'old road' means keeping away from a known guerrilla hold-out, but following poorly marked tracks which in these parts could prove tricky. I find it, but soon drop on to the shale bank on the water's edge since it offers good cover.

A bad move. Soon, the shale runs out and the old track has vanished – it has climbed away from the river. Up an overgrown sheer slope, I have the devil's own job finding it again and lose the best part of a day.

I reach Dabeiba at 15:30. Again, I'm the talk of the town, mobbed by both children and adults, some claiming never to have seen a gringo here before. The police and also the army show up. I explain that my passport was stolen in Medellin – a lie – and show them a photocopy.

'Ha! That's what all you gringos say,' one barks.

This place has been overrun three times by the FARC. Last time, there was a two-day battle; they mortared the town with bombs made from gas cylinders but withdrew when reinforcements arrived in the shape of helicopter gunships. Right now, there's a strong military presence. This is good news. With garrisons in Mutata, El Tigre and Chigorodo, the way to Barranquilla is looking much safer. In bypassing El Boton, locals tell me, I have avoided the worst.

Monday, 22 January 2001   Beyond Dabeiba

The road traces a deep gorge on the Rio Sucio, the walls of which are thick with tropical forest. It's kind of creepy really, with only the sounds of the jungle for company. I feel like I'm a lonely cowboy in 'Injun country'. It's all *so* still. Out there, somewhere, the guerrillas are hiding.

I meet some campesinos – three men and a boy – in the road, who seem friendly enough and beckon me over. As well as asking where I'm going, they want to see my papers, which is rather a surprising request from such a motley crew.

'Who wants to know?' I begin.

'FARC,' sniggers one, showing me an old revolver tucked into his trouser belt. I feel uneasy, not sure how this one might go. But it stays friendly. I use my 'poor Spanish' to pretend I can't understand. I make out I'm impressed, using lines like, 'Hey, that gun looks good on you', which works a treat. I depart with three soft drinks.

Minutes later, I pass a group of huts covered in FARC slogans, unit names and numbers. 'BCG 26th Inf FARC.' Those within let me pass when the fellows I've just met roll up. Whether they're FARC or not, I can't say. Maybe they are just locals who've been given guns and told to watch the road on the guerrillas' behalf: who knows? They seem too slack to be participants in a vicious war.

I press on. The undulating road continues to descend as the humidity rises. Water runs down the sides of the gorge, naturally filtered through the moss. Food, however, is scarce, and there are no settlements until Mutata. Villages are shown on the map but these look like they've been worked over by a squadron of B52s when I pass through them. I manage thirty kilometres and camp on a small hill. In the half-light I string up my hammock, but the tree at one end gives way without warning. I manage to make some sort of repair just as it throws it down with rain and get wet through, and in the night I slide against the mossie net. I'm eaten alive.

Tuesday, 23 January 2001   Mutata

This morning, I find a papaya tree laden with ripe fruit, which is a treat as the locals have usually got there first. I use a long stick to spear one and sit eating it in a culvert before continuing.

Around 14:30 the road flattens out and I can see uniformed troops in the distance. They are wearing wellies like the FARC, but then so does the army sometimes. Closing in, I see that they are carrying

Galil assault rifles, not AK-47s, so this *is* the army. I've arrived in Mutata. Again, my kit gets searched. The town is small yet full of troops – a good sign. I can afford to stay in a grotty hotel, where I clean up and sort my feet out. I give Catty a call and she emails England to say all is well. Hell, it's good to hear her voice.

Wednesday, 24 January – Thursday, 25 January 2001   Beyond Mutata

The way flattens out and I make good progress over two days; there is much fruit to eat, mainly ganavarna – a common local fruit – and coconut, which is very refreshing. I see many colourful birds: toucans, hornbills and lots I don't recognise. On the night of 24 January, I camp out. Although the nights are warmer, I am still cold. The plastic hammock seems to absorb my body heat and I freeze. I spend the next night in El Tigre, a cluster of huts on a junction where, next morning, I must take the track for Barranquilla. I catch my last glimpse of the northernmost tip of the Andes, which for so, so long have been my guide.

Friday, 26 January 2001   Barranquilla

By 06:00, I'm on my way, even though it's quite dark. It's still early when I pass through Barranquilla. I breakfast in a shack that sells drinks and some greasy roast chicken, which I guess was cooked about four days ago and left on the counter. I also eat a large, cold boiled potato.

The track I'm following is long, flat and dusty, with a farm about every kilometre. It carries a surprising amount of traffic, most of which wants to give me a lift. I am also watched by many poor-looking locals along the way. Much to my disappointment, this track does not go all the way to the River Atrato, which I must cross in order to continue my journey. At Casa 40 (House 40) it just stops, and so do I.

Saturday, 27 January 2001   Bajira

Next morning, I climb a nearby hill to look at the ground. As the crow flies, the river is just fifteen kilometres away. Surely there's a way through. But from the summit looking west, I see nothing but waterlogged swamps and no signs of any ridges that I could use. My heart sinks. That's me knackered. Reaching the river is impossible from here.

The only way to get there, the locals advise, is from the village of Riosucio, and the only way to get there is to retrace my steps to Barranquilla, then walk for two more days using another route. This is a problem as, without much money for food, I am relying on locals to keep me alive with handouts of bread and rice. I don't want to break into my jungle rations yet, so the longer I spend on this side of the river, the hungrier I will get.

I thumb a lift back the way I've come with some lads from the AUC in their pick-up and, before Barranquilla, they drop me on the track junction I must take. The heat is nothing short of terrible. The first place I stagger into is a small village, New Orient, where the locals are very encouraging.

'No one ever uses that track anymore,' says one, when he learns of my intentions. 'The guerrillas will kill anyone they catch. Don't even think about it. There's fighting and Riosucio is surrounded by guerrillas. If you go down that track, you won't come out.' These people mean every word they say and insist I take another route. I am in a fix because there is no alternative. I begin to wonder if it is all possible.

When I reach the next village of Bajira, I am weak, almost fit to drop. Nearby is the track that heads west to Riosucio. The local AUC do nothing for my confidence. They say it would be a grave mistake to walk the track. The guerrillas are, they insist, the most ferocious of all. They call themselves the 'Dragon of Uraba' – the dragon in question being a dreadful beast if the graffiti daubed all over the houses is much to go by.

I'm half-scared out of my wits listening to this lot. They live here, they know the area, are they right? Who am I to walk in from the other side of the world and tell them otherwise? Decision time. I always said I'd put my life on the line, but now it doesn't seem so easy. I still hope that they are wrong and that I can pull this off. But the prospect of dying is real. At no time in the journey – or in my life, for that matter – have I been so scared.

As I stand motionless on the dusty track staring at my feet, the locals, equally still, wait for me to make up my mind. Heck, why I am dithering, of course I'm taking that track. I was always going to. And if I survive, there will be other decisions to make, other tracks to take later on in my journey and in life.

I nod to the men. They raise their eyebrows and I am led to see their 'boss'. A sober, strait-laced man, he does not attempt to dissuade me further, except to say that it is my choice. One of his men is ordered to show me where the track begins. By the time I reach the edge of town, it is late afternoon, so I need to find a place to sleep and something to eat. I come across some troops encamped on the outskirts, who start to question me.

'Going where?'

'Are you insane?' they demand.

Obviously, I am. They take me to meet their commanding officer. I find the lieutenant sitting with his radio operator on the porch of a house they are occupying. After the usual questions, I am fed rice and meat in a mess tin and am invited to spend the night here. My dice is rolling. What might happen tomorrow doesn't matter any more.

Sunday, 28 January 2001   Bajira

The best sleep I've had in ages. I wake early, pack up all my kit and sit on the porch watching the sunrise. Everything feels rather surreal and quite strange. An odd calm has come over me – or maybe I just don't know how I should be reacting at a time like this? The soldiers hand me a canteen of warm chocolate and a flat fried *agape*. Hardly a meal but a lot better than nothing.

The officer and his first sergeant try one last time to change my mind but once they recognise my resolve, they desist. From his pocket, the lieutenant pulls a dictaphone to record my decision so that they won't suffer any comebacks when I turn up dead. The sergeant reconfirms the dangers I will face in a loud, clear voice and gives me a brief run-down of the political situation in Colombia. Because of 'Plan Colombia', the major US initiative to help fund the Colombian government, I will – as a gringo – be seen as an enemy by the FARC.

'You understand all I've said?' says the officer.

'Yes,' I reply.

PLAN COLOMBIA

In 2001, the Government of Colombia developed Plan Colombia, an integrated strategy to meet the most pressing challenges confronting the country. Its aim is to promote the peace process, combat the narcotics industry, revive the economy and strengthen the pillars of Colombian society. The US$7.5 billion programme includes $1.3 billion from the US, which incorporates training and equipping counter-narcotics battalions with UH-60 Blackhawk and Huey II helicopters.

'We have given you all the information we can, so it is your choice?'

'Yes. I understand completely.'

He then composes an official memo, stating the time, date, place and the people involved, which he and the sergeant sign while a soldier is despatched to photocopy my passport. This backs up the tape recording and absolves them of any responsibility.

I am almost physically sick with fear. This could be the last day of my life. I pen a short letter to be forwarded to Catty, explaining my predicament – the time, the date and where I am – which can be passed to my family in England. I hand it to the lieutenant to post.

After much handshaking, dumbstruck young soldiers stand and watch me leave: one sends a radio message to troops in Riosucio to confirm that I am setting off. Passing the last defensive positions, I convince myself that this is *not* as bad as it might seem. Sure, I'm frightened, but I must keep the faith. I must keep the faith. 'Fortune favours the brave,' wrote my father in his last email to me in Medellin, ending with 'Who dares wins'. Nice mottos, but I'd sooner have a bullet-proof vest right now.

I head west along a dusty track for ten to fifteen kilometres. I pass a few occupied farms but these soon change to abandoned ones that have been overrun by the encroaching jungle. The day is hot and hard. Water quickly becomes a problem; I am losing it in sweat faster than I can replace it. I pass small stagnant ponds of stinking swamp water which, unless I get desperate, I will leave well alone. Coconuts are the answer. They grow around the deserted farms and their milk is a fantastic source of clean refreshment. I keep my water bottles topped up.

Jungle life is prolific. There are strange birds, reptiles, huge insects, leaf-cutters and inconceivable numbers of ants, all kinds of nasty little bastards. I pitch camp before it starts to get dark. I make sure I am zipped up in my hammock before the mosquitoes do their stuff. Believe me, you don't want to be on the outside when they come. I've seen nothing like them. Here, one mossie – the locals call it the *zancudo* – is suicidally voracious at last light. Unlike the ones I'm used to that buzz around taking care to find a spot on you to feed from, ones which will avoid your swipes, the *zancudo* just hits you like a bullet, drills into you and sucks as soon as it makes contact. It can bite through your clothes; nothing stops it. You think you're wiping raindrops or sweat from your face when, in fact, it's your own blood. I have so many bites right now. Some are looking dodgy and may turn septic. I've seen the locals sit out in shorts and T-shirts at night just slapping the bugs away. Christ knows how they do it.

I have chosen a good spot to camp. It's just far enough off the track, about three metres, on raised ground, with a nice bit of cover between myself and anyone who happens to be passing. In the half-light I lie watching small lizards jumping a metre or more between leaves and stems around me, chasing each other and puffing up their red throat sacks like the displaying frogs I've seen.

Then, just before total darkness, I hear movement. Jungles are full of noises at night, but these are unnatural. Wide-eyed and with my heart thumping, I lie perfectly still. Someone is approaching along the track, maybe on horseback. It's faint, but they're getting closer. Then it is as if it all happens in slow motion. The top half of a figure appears and then another, walking in file, silhouetted against the night sky. Men with equipment and, very distinctively, the clunk of metal. Is it the Dragon? I can make out heads and shoulders as around twenty of them snake past me in silence and disappear. I almost daren't breathe. Like me, they are heading west. Will they also lie up nearby and bump into me in the morning? They cannot be the military as I know they don't patrol here – they must be FARC.

I don't get much sleep after this, twitching at the slightest sound.

Monday, 29 January 2001   **Riosucio**

A very early start. I set off at a good pace, just hoping that the patrol in the night has pushed on and is out of my way, not encamped a kilometre in front of me. I guess my camp is about halfway to Riosucio, so I should be able to make it there today, all being well. My route is more overgrown and also noisier – when I disturb any birds, they screech in alarm. Oh, for fuck's sake, do shut up! The racket is relentless; it tears at my already taught nerves.

The sky is a clear blue and the sun takes its toll. My clothes, designed for the jungle, are hell when I'm not under the forest canopy and absorb the heat. I grow dizzy. Were it not for the coconuts, I would not have enough to drink. Worse still, the track is petering out. As I enter a large open plain, chest-high with thick reed-like grass, it disappears completely. 'Nooo! Don't lose it now,' I blurt out to myself. I thrash around a bit, backwards and forwards, in sweeping searches. I make out faint signs of a trail, but keep losing it in the thick grass. Every step I take has to be forced, kicking hard at the undergrowth. It's exhausting. I worry I might lose the track for keeps. I could end up lost in a maze of swamps, bogs and dense foliage.

I find a tree and climb it. There! Beneath me, I can make out the subdued impression of a trail heading north-west. However, once I'm on the ground again, it's almost impossible to find. There begins an infuriating game of hide and seek; one minute I have it, the next it disappears again. It is a desperate fight. The GPS is an absolute god-send. Having 'set' Riosucio as a way point, it will guide me very easily on a direct route, but I need firm ground to walk on.

Presently, farm buildings come into view and the track improves. They are clearly occupied and I can see livestock, so I must be close to the village. The worst must be over. Next I come across a group of cowboys on horseback who look a little bemused to see me, a sweating gringo puffing and panting in the direction they are heading.

'Where are you going, gringo?' one asks.

I want to say 'Pluto, for Christ's sake!' but refrain.

'Riosucio, where is it?' I reply.

'Um, about one and a half hour's walk,' he says. Since they are heading there, why don't I join them?

'You need water?' says another.

Dead right. My head is spinning. I've no energy left and I'm fit to drop. I set off behind them at a fair clip.

'What about guerrillas? Any about?' I manage to blurt.

'No, they're back there. You won't find them around here.'

I smile inwardly. I've done it. I'm alive.

I stride out behind the horses but when we stop for a drink I just collapse flat on my back. The cowboys give me some coconut milk and I lie there in the shade for forty-five minutes. The town is close now, so I press on. My dried clothes are white with salty, sweaty stains, but I am soaked again in no time. The open, dusty track picks its way through swamps, crossed by wooden walkways, until, in the near distance, I spot a figure, rifle slung over his shoulder with hands in pockets – a soldier. He is a sentry and he greets me with a huge smile.

'Ha, gringo, you made it!' he barks.

I collapse behind a sandbagged wall – the outer defences of Riosucio, which look like the set of a Vietnam war movie – and soldiers gather around, offering me a canteen of water. Ragged and, as usual, soaked through, I am also extremely happy. They knew I was coming and are impressed that it took me just two days. My newly found friends invite me to eat and rest with them. I am given my own private shack to crash in. I'm soon asleep.

Tuesday, 30 January 2001   Riosucio

Up early and straight into my admin. The troops wash in the Rio Sucio which, having been white water when I first found it, is now almost motionless – hence its name, which translated means 'dirty river'. Still, when in Rome. I get a good bath and wash all my clobber.

Breakfast is a wafer-thin disc of fried cornflower washed down by a cup of tepid chocolate. At midday I am served a plate of rice and beans and in the evening, more rice and beans with some fish. This village is virtually under siege and running low on supplies, so fish is the staple diet.

Around evening I take a look at the main river, the Atrato, into which the Sucio flows. It is bursting with fish. Trouble is, this river is not as wide as I'd hoped it would be. Also, it is slow-flowing, which is worrying. Nowhere near the three to four metres per second I'd been told it would be. With no tracks on either bank, my plan had been to float downstream for fifty kilometres or more until I reached a place where I could leave the river and head west. At this speed, I could be in the water for four days, which is longer than I'd bargained for ration-wise.

As is the norm, everyone thinks it is a crazy idea and bang on about crocodiles and man-eating fish. I cannot listen. I *have* to use the river.

Wednesday, 31 January 2001   The River Atrato

I test my kit in the river. Well-wrapped in layers of bin liners and the proper army-issue waterproof bags my father sent me, I slide my bundle of belongings into the rucksack and slip four empty two-litre plastic bottles down the sides and at both ends. I also secure two more under my waistcoat and four smaller ones in my other pockets for my own flotation. It works perfectly, keeping my head and the top of my shoulders just out of the water. A captain and his soldiers who have been watching my odd behaviour with interest appear greatly amused by my efforts.

I spend my last Colombian pennies on toilet paper and a Coke. Now I've only dollars left and I will need them. I don't have enough supplies. Already I've dipped into my jungle rations. I wasn't expecting to spend as long in the river as I'm now going to have to. I will need any cash I have to buy food from villages en route, which had not been my intention.

Sunset comes, and so do the mosquitoes. Clouds of them. They even find a way inside my net. Fate, of course, intervenes and I keep on having to get up in the night with diarrhoea. I'm convinced they are waiting in ambush. Within two seconds of my undoing my belt, mosquitoes are hanging from every inch of exposed skin like tiny red Christmas tree decorations. I sleep badly.

Thursday, 1 February 2001   The River Atrato

I had intended to slip away at first light before anyone stirred. Fat chance. By 06:00 it's like Waterloo Station in the morning rush hour here. Even though I'd asked the army to keep my plans under their hat, everyone seems to know what I'm up to. Out of the town and down to the river bank, I pick up a large following. I camouflage my equipment, pose for photographs, then wade into the water. I'm away – albeit very slowly – connected to my gear by a length of nylon cord.

The water isn't that cold, but after thirty minutes I begin to shiver. I can still see the spot where I entered. Christ, this is slow. After about an hour, I decide to try a stately, measured breaststroke in order to speed myself up and keep warm. Drifting painfully slowly, I pass clumps of floating mangrove strung out along the river, moving from side to side where the current flows the fastest. I pluck bits off to improve my camouflage.

The banks are thick with mangroves and a few scattered trees. I can see groups of reddish brown apes in the larger bows. I've heard them before, howling their eerie growl, but I've never actually seen any. There are masses of fish, and from time to time I see an eagle or osprey dive and rise from the flow with one in its talons.

At around 15:30, I strike out towards the shore to find a place to sleep. It's a struggle and I must kick hard to cut across the current. In truth, it takes almost an hour to reach the bank, just north of a place where I've seen a hut marked on a map. I'd always had this spot in mind. It has been a long, hard, cold day. Also, my plumbing is giving me grief again. Relieving myself midstream and keeping clean is relatively easy but I am in real pain again.

I string up my hammock and don't have to wait long for the mossies to show up. Before I know it, I'm under a buzzing blanket of them, so thick I can hardly see through the mosquito net. Something is wrong. I use my torch to look for a hole, but can't find one. Then the batteries fade, so I dig out two new ones. I then find a concentration of insects forcing themselves inside the net along an opening in a seam where it attaches to my shelter sheet. It's like a horror movie – hundreds of insects are fighting their way in, head first. I massacre those I can, then smear insect repellent along the seam, which seems to do the trick.

Unable to sleep, I am gripped in the early hours by a sudden pain in my guts that means only one thing. Outside, the flying hordes await. The pains grow sharper as I fight my way out of the sleeping bag liner, in the process of which the hammock starts to swing violently. I tense up instinctively. It goes horribly wrong. I lose control of my bowels and what feels like a bucket of sewage covers my body, my clothes and the inside of my hammock. I just want to lie there and weep. But I need to sleep, please let me sleep. I try to clean up from the inside but it's impossible. This never happened to Indiana Jones, the bastard.

Friday, 2 February 2001   La Honda

I scrub my body and soiled kit at the water's edge, then prepare for more floating. I double-dose with antibiotics, hoping to give them a kick-start, and also swallow some Immodium capsules to control the diarrhoea. I am making ten kilometres a day, or thereabouts, so I might get beyond La Honda today. I hadn't taken into account the intense sun and its reflection on the water. The whole of my face is sunburnt, and particularly my lips. I cut a length of material and tie it around my brow as a sort of improvised sunshade.

All goes well until the afternoon. As I inch my way past a cluster of cabins on the bank, one of the plastic bottles launches itself from my combat vest and floats out of reach. Bollocks! It has upset my buoyancy and I almost lose a second one trying to catch the escaping bottle. This hasty movement is spotted by the eagle-eyed children on the river bank. I've been clocked. Children and adults are running along the water's edge yelling. Three boats are 'scrambled' and make towards me. I'm blown. Now what? I remember my father's warnings about how easy it is to create a peachy target floating midstream when swimming rivers. No way can I make it to the other bank in time. Three boats are powering towards me and I can see boathooks being readied to fish me out as they close in. I should have more faith in the people of South America. When they pull alongside, the boats' passengers express only concern for a man in need of a rescue. A confusing exchange takes place.

'No, please, don't worry, I'm fine. Thanks anyway,' I say, as they warn me of man-eating fish and crocodiles. They look at me disbelievingly. A gringo has fallen into the water but he doesn't want to be rescued? They'll be talking about this one for years.

By the late afternoon, I am closing on La Honda and decide to crawl ashore well before I reach the village. As I move between float-ing mangroves, I find myself face to face with a two-metre-long crocodile that is hitching a lift on a clump of vegetation. As croco-diles go, this one is relatively tidy but, hey, he's bigger than me. His jaws are only an arm's length away. I don't know if he intends eating all of me, or just part of me, or, maybe, none of me at all. But I do know that just one bite will cause me so much infection that I'll be well out of the game.

He remains dead still – but that's what crocodiles do, don't they? His eyes look kind of blank. Is he asleep? I know that they have two sets of eyelids, including one transparent set they use underwater. Are both sets closed? Hardly daring to breath, I reverse away and detour around him to a different bit of bank.

La Honda, a single row of grotty-looking shacks, is in sight and I'm closer than I had planned to be. I make camp and string up my hammock, but it is only a couple of hours before the villagers, natu-rally concerned that someone is skulking about, come looking for me. They call out so I guess the best thing I can do is go and meet them – I'm not well hidden, so they are relieved that I'm 'just some gringo' and invite me back to theirs.

These guys are black African-looking South Americans and have muscles as though they spend their lives in the gym. As poor as they clearly are, they can't do enough to help and a plate of *plantano* (a variety of banana) and some fish is fed to me. They offer me water but I say, 'No thanks, got my own', because they drink straight from the Atrato and I'm not ready for that. Yet.

Saturday, 3 February 2001   La Honda

Rounding the first bend of the river, I enter a long, straight section and there, way off in the hazy blue distance, is my first glimpse of the hills and peaks that mark the border with Panama. 'Land ahoy,' I say to myself. It's so close and yet so far.

A large grey heron stands on a log and watches as I pass just yards from it. Big fish . . . best left alone, is what I imagine it is thinking. Miniature monkeys with black and white faces leap about the trees and mangroves chattering among themselves, paying me absolutely no attention at all.

I drift near the bank, where I am better camouflaged. Boats pass all the time, sometimes coming quite close, but I am not spotted. It is windy at times and the water becomes choppy, which does not help my progress. Now and then I hear a loud 'splash' as something enters the water and I'm left looking about, trying to see what it is. I am constantly on the lookout for crocodiles. Normally it's just a large iguana.

Just after 15:00, I crawl out on to the bank and start to hack a bit of a clearing in a dry place when, suddenly – Argh! What the fuck? Ants, falling from the trees. Red ants, with bites like bee stings. Back into the water, I think. I move further downstream before trying again. This time, I smear Vaseline on the hammock's guidelines and ties to fend off any further ant attacks.

My drinking water now has to come straight from the Atrato but I double-dose it with chlorine tablets. I'm also eating my lightweight, dehydrated jungle rations – mostly pasta, rice and dried fruit. From the map it looks as if tomorrow ought to be my last day in the river. I can make out the first, smaller hills ahead of me so, as soon as I can, I will make a break for them.

Sunday, 4 February 2001   Travisa

Around midday I reach Travisa, which consists of a row of three huts on the river's western bank. I need to know where I should start walking from, so I speak to three black guys who have been catching crocodiles. In front of them, a string of dead ones are hanging on a line and some skins have been laid out to dry. They are not much help with overland routes but keep offering me a lift. No matter how often I explain that I don't want one, they insist I go with them – I think they smell money. Not mine, I'm afraid. I float off again.

Just as I pass the confluence with another river, four army patrol boats skim down from the north with .50 calibre machine guns mounted on their prows. Later, a larger, camouflaged boat passes, followed by four more fast boats, probably some sort of border patrol.

I pitch on the bank with the hills to west. I'm done with the river and will start walking next morning.

Monday, 5 February – Wednesday, 7 February 2001   Beyond Travisa

I strike west. Monday I spend cutting through impenetrable low-lying mangroves trying to find higher ground. The mangrove cuts easily but it is desperately tiring work and I retrace my steps several times when faced with standing water and uncrossable mud. I make two to three kilometres by nightfall.

In the morning, I feel I am gaining height and the vegetation changes to secondary jungle where, with no canopy above, the scrub is still thick on the ground. The jungle remains 'in your face' and it is a case of machete blow after machete blow before another step forward. I'm eaten alive by bugs of all description, wet through and resting every ten minutes. I climb for a moment only for the ground to fall away again. Jungle lore says, 'Don't cut your way, manoeuvre around', yet I can't move a yard unless I chop and slash. At times, I just stand there cutting at a vine and nothing happens. Tracks, I need tracks.

The following day, Wednesday, the canopy becomes higher and there is less undergrowth, so I speed up. That said, I am now negotiating fallen trees. The thick material of my jungle-clothing comes into its own, but still I am being cut to ribbons by hook-like thorns that remove chunks of skin as I pass. At night, I remove ticks the size of fingernails.

Thursday, 8 February 2001   Towards Paya

This morning I stumble across a clearing; in fact it's a man-made strip running north to south. I pause. What's this? A track! I do a swift recce to make sure it's going somewhere. Yes, it seems like it could wind north-west. I set off along it. It's not much of a track – it's easy to wander off it – but at least I can move easily now. Good. When I can see some sky, I will get GPS readings so I know exactly where I am, as I'm no longer sticking to a compass bearing and will be going slightly off course.

I come to a junction. Perhaps I have found the track shown on my map running between Bijao and Cristales? If I head back the way I've come, I should arrive in a place called Cacarlo, which the crocodile fishermen had talked about. Of course, I'm not sure, but if I take the fresh track north, it may lead to Bijao. Worth a shot. This proves a costly decision. It becomes hard to follow the track and I keep losing it. When it heads west then eventually south, up and down some really steep spurs and re-entrants, I admit that it is not for me and I retrace my steps.

Friday, 9 February 2001   Towards Paya

I must get a grip. Last night I felt a claustrophobic anxiety/panic bubbling just below the surface. I put this down to 'terrain shock', if you like. But thinking logically, I tell myself that things are, in truth, going rather well. I'm moving – generally in the right direction – and I'm not using any villages. I may be extremely tired, covered in cuts and full of thorns but, hey, what else was I expecting? So far, I haven't met a soul on this phase, which is just the way I want it.

Once across the border, it is around ten kilometres to my next destination, the frontier settlement of Paya. By then, all my jungle rations will have run out. As I haven't intercepted any tracks that might head north or north-west, I set a direct bearing for the border and head back into the jungle. I might be looking at a four to five day slog. The way is steep and as hard as before but I seem to be finding my 'jungle legs'. I pace myself, I don't need so many rests and I don't burn myself out. To my surprise, I walk into a large river that, according to the map, should be well east of here.

It's Eden. A wide, open stretch of water strewn with flat rocks and large crystal clear pools. The sound of running water is music to my ears and, best of all, there are no mosquitoes. It's off with the kit and straight in. The river is teeming with fish. Easily caught, they supplement my meagre rations. I overnight here.

Saturday, 10 February – Monday, 12 February 2001   Towards Paya

I keep heading west for the ridge that must be on the Panama border. It's more of the same: up-and-down terrain swathed in thick jungle. I am learning which vines and creepers will part with a single swipe and which the machete just bounces off, wasting precious energy. I make another river camp at night where I recover and clean my scratches. I fall asleep to the distant sounds of 'deadfall' – dead trees that eventually fall, crashing through the surrounding jungle.

Making good progress I spend a third night on another river where I catch more fish on night-lines. I cook them on a decent fire; there is plenty of dry wood as it hasn't rained in days. I'm putting away eight to nine litres of water a day, more than I was drinking in the desert, so it's lucky I keep coming across these rivers.

I am now very close to the Panamanian frontier. I find more tracks, follow them for a bit before abandoning them again. I'm very tired, almost to my limit. From the map and GPS, I know there is a river three kilometres from here and Paya is on that. I struggle on. Late in the afternoon, I camp just short of my target. Tomorrow, having spent a month crossing the Darien Gap, I hope to announce myself in Panama.

Tuesday, 13 February 2001   **Towards Paya**

The track continues and I follow. I must be in Panama by now, I think to myself. I cross a small bridge made of cut logs and make out more footprints. Possibly two or three people – only a small group and too small to be a patrol of any kind. I lose a little confidence in the track because it is running too far north and does not tally with my map, although I am not sure that this is all that accurate. I stick with it in the hope that it will swing west again.

Eureka. I reach a junction and take the fork that heads due west. After half an hour, I stumble into a clearing in some rising ground. Scrambling to the highest point, I see there beneath me the river and, on the far bank, the little village of Paya.

I take a breather. I sit there watching the village going about its business just to give me an idea of who is about. It looks quiet enough, so I descend the slope and wade across the river and wander into the settlement. The first thing that strikes me is how clean and neat it is. With its well-manicured 'lawns', it's like a Village of the Year entry.

When I plonk down on some grass, the locals seem happy to see me, but not as happy as I am to be here. In the early afternoon sunshine, it feels, if only for a moment, that the weight of the world has just been lifted from my shoulders. I lie on my back staring at the sky. Welcome to Panama, welcome to Central America, I murmur to myself.

Chapter Six

CENTRAL AMERICA

A few kilometres from Boca. I am looking for a track to take me there when some guy in a dugout canoe puts me right. Leaving the river, I trace the faint path cutting along the bank next to a plantation. I can hear music up ahead, and after about fifteen minutes stumble into a clearing and some huts. Just for a moment I think I'm looking at sand-bagged positions. I must try and shake Colombia from my mind. Then I realise I *am* looking at a defensive position, and at a 7.62mm belt-fed machine gun. I sidle around the back totally unchallenged and walk up to a chap in a dark-green uniform, carrying an AK-47. There's a moment of tension.

'Who are you?' he asks, very surprised by my arrival.

'Who are you?' I reply, equally ruffled.

'No, you first?' he says.

I try to establish their identity. The US-style Kevlar helmets sitting on the sandbags and 'Police National' T-shirts hanging from the washing line tell me they are friendly forces and not insurgents.

'I'm a British walker, on my way to Panama City, and you are?'

'Police. Now show us your papers.' I'm searched and questioned then taken to see the boss in a small concrete police station, where I explain all. Because I don't have a visa this makes me an illegal immigrant, and I'm asked to stay until they talk with a higher formation. There seems to be some confusion as to what to do with me, so I get a cell to sleep in. I'm to be held here until a police chopper can lift me, initially to Meteti and then to La Palma, where there is an immigration office.

This would maroon me up north and I would have to spend time and money coming back south again. I need to speak to our embassy in Panama City to ask them to confirm my identity and sort this out. But it's Friday evening and the embassy's closed until Monday so I'll have to wait here.

'No problem,' says the officer in charge. 'You can eat here and relax.' I'm shown to my cell and the door is closed behind me and a padlock applied. Just before they do that, I'm asked to hand over my money, US$21, which they count and note all the serial numbers of before giving it back to me. What's all this about, I start to wonder. What have I just walked into?

That evening the captain explains why there is such a heavy presence here. This is the first village with a reasonable food stock and small medical centre. A few years ago the FARC raided the village for food and medicine, killing several policemen. Last year they tried again, but this time the police were ready and counter-attacked, killing nine guerrillas. Panama, I learn, has no standing army, only a police force that does an army's job here on the border.

The helicopter doesn't materialise which gives Karl time to call Andy Newlands, the British vice-consul in Panama City. His father has spoken to this helpful official several times and he has been following Karl's progress on the website. Newlands tells Karl 'not to worry' and that he'll speak to 'some people'. Meanwhile, his hosts also relieve him of his machete, Leatherman tool, passport and cuttings. All he can do is sit tight.

Tuesday, 20 February 2001   Boca de Cupe

At about 10:30 a 'Huey' arrives and I'm shoved on board. On the way we pick up two Colombian illegal immigrants trying to sneak through to Costa Rica. Then the old rust-bucket springs a leak and we're forced to land at Yaviza, where we walk to the police station. This just gets better. For four hours, we're made to sit on the floor – we can't move or stand up but at least we're fed so I can't complain. I don't know what the embassy told these people, but I'm beginning to wish I hadn't spent US$3.50 on a shagging phone card.

I'm searched yet again. This time they go through my kit with a fine-tooth comb, taking all sorts. My pills, medical kit, safety pins, maps and GPS all go into a sealed bag. As I am now an illegal immigrant I'm treated accordingly. We're then escorted out and put into a pick-up truck, transferring to another on the outskirts of town, before rattling off to Meteti. An hour and a half later, and some fifty kilometres north, I'm standing in line outside another police station before being questioned by two cops.

Why had I entered Panama illegally? they want to know.

'For Christ's sake, read my newspaper cuttings,' I answer. Once again, I explain what I'm up to.

'Why have you got a machete of this type?' they continue.

'What?'

'What's this?' and they open a folded sheet of paper, inside of which are paraffin blocks I use to light fires.

'Look, it says here what they are on the packet!' (One of the policemen sniffs at them.)

'Why are you travelling with two Colombians?'

'Because you put me in the truck with them.'

'You're not travelling together?'

'No!'

He scribbles out a passage where he's already noted that I'm travelling with two Colombians. Oh, Christ! He's writing my answers before he even asks the questions . . . this is all going tits up! I tell them to just read the newspaper clippings and then they'd understand. They do and things improve . . . a bit.

Back with my Colombian comrades, we're fed again, put on to a second truck and driven to another nick. In the guardroom, we're searched yet again and more items are removed, including my bootlaces. We're then shoved into a stinking cell; four bare walls and a toilet overflowing with human waste, it is humming. There's one guy already in here, a Peruvian illegal caught on his way to the US. I can't believe this is happening to me.

Wednesday, 21 February 2001   Meteti

I sleep on a stinking urine-stained sheet of foam. It beats sleeping on a concrete floor, I guess. I've now been in custody for six days. The impression I get is that there's some confusion among the staff here as to why they have a Brit in their cell. I ask again if I may phone the embassy.

'No, not until our captain speaks to you.'

'Where's he then?'

'He's not here, he is in El Real. He's back later.'

The police interview me again only this time they take a statement, writing down all I say as I go over my story for the tenth time. I still get the feeling it's going in one ear and out the other.

Back in the cell, I do some push-ups and sit-ups as the boredom begins to bite. The captain does not show and I'm told again that I can't ring the embassy. When they eventually change their mind and allow me to call, it's closed.

Thursday, 22 February 2001   Meteti

At least the food's not bad – we get a slice of ham and a piece of fried bread for breakfast. This morning, I do get through to the embassy and they reassure me that they're doing all they can. There's no hope I'll move today as it's the start of four days of carnival in Panama. One of my cellmates tells me that some guys are stuck here for a year so I can expect to be stuck in this hell-hole for at least a week

We are now six in our cell. The latest is a local lad. I'm not sure what he's in for. Then someone I haven't seen before speaks to me through the bars in the cell door, explaining that I just need to be patient. He says it won't be long now. He says I'm in here because the frontier with Colombia is closed to everyone. I should never have been allowed to cross it, as you're only allowed to enter via the sea or airports.

This 'someone' is the Captain Eric Estrada of the D.I.I.P. (something similar to the Directorate of Information and Investigative Police), the chaps that last interviewed me. I guess he's read the case notes and is after any useful information because we sit down and he asks me to go over my complete route. He's very interested in the GPS and where and when I used it. He knows I'm an ex-soldier and can tell from my notes when I've seen things, marked maps, defensive positions, troop movements . . . you name it. I've absorbed what I've seen. I spent time with the Colombian army, and met the paramilitaries in various places so am quite an intelligence asset when it comes to what's coming and going around the border with Colombia.

He gets quite excited. I'm given a drink of Coke and some biscuits while I draw maps and explain in great detail what I've learned about military and police movements and positions. I even mark his maps. I tell him all I know about the AUC and the guerrillas. He's now my 'best mate'.

PANAMANIAN JUSTICE

Panama's judicial system is inefficient, corrupt and non-transparent. Impossibly hard to understand – for nationals as well as non-nationals – it is also highly susceptible to manipulation. Its shortcomings have become increasingly prominent, seizing the attention of the public in headlines and editorials denouncing its systematic snail's pace and its inefficiency. Its criminal justice system continues to suffer serious, systematic weaknesses that have resulted in delayed, flawed and legally incorrect decisions. Consequently, there are increasing backlogs in cases to be heard and a prison population in which 65 per cent of those held in preventative detention have never appeared before a judge.

Friday, 23 February 2001   **Meteti**

I'm going to prison in La Palma by boat. It's a very pleasant and scenic route, with wide, open waterways in which sea lions and dolphins play. But enough of that.

Soon I find myself being searched, processed and then thrown into a prison compound with about a hundred jailed Latinos, in for a mixture of offences from armed robbery and theft to Lord knows what else. It's a bit of a nightmare.

I'm met with wolf whistles and all sorts of comments.

'Look, it's Chuck Norris! . . . No, no . . . it's Rambo!'

Dressed in my green 'uniform' (as far as everyone here is concerned), with my rucksack, combat vest, headband, and having not shaved for months I am indeed looking like some one-man army from a Hollywood movie. Faced with this mix of very large black-

African South Americans, Latinos and Indians, some of whom have been here for years, I'm one very lonely honky. I've got to get this right from the start. I must stick my neck out and show some bottle. Here goes.

'Well . . . you're one bunch of ugly fuckers!' I begin, smiling all the same.

'And you're one pretty piece of arse!' comes a reply, but followed by laughter.

Funnily enough, word soon spreads. 'It's the walker' . . . 'two years, ten more to go'. I begin to make some friends. Ricky, a large mean-looking guy with a heart of gold, seems to like Brits and gives me his food bowl as it is bigger than mine.

'You need it more than me!' he grunts. 'Fill up,' and he passes me a huge bowl of rice. He later gives me a roll of foam to sleep on as well. Ricky is Costa Rican and serving five years for armed robbery. He explains how he's turned to religion and that's why he felt obliged to help. I'm touched. Having been in here some time he knows the ropes and is the kind of friend you need.

Five in the afternoon is feeding time. When I join the queue, a fat guard directs me to bring my food so that I can eat it outside the compound. I've just spotted Estrada so this must have something to do with him. I'm let out into the main yard and told to sit and eat in the canteen where the guards eat.

While I'm tucking into some rice, an immigration official comes in, puffing and panting, having been chased out of wherever he's been hiding. The man starts to explain very apologetically how there was little he could do now as everything is closed for the next four or five days, and how he would need to speak to my embassy first.

'No, no . . . you don't need to speak to my embassy again, they've spoken to you twice and told you everything. Let's just do the paper-work!'

'OK, but it's Friday, there is nothing I can do now,' he whines, flicking through my passport, again apologetically and in a flustered manner. I think Estrada has been kicking arse. The fellow sees the captain and has a word. I can see Estrada shaking his head and talk-ing into a radio as the immigration official holds his hands in the air as if to say 'what can I do?' I'm called over and Estrada dials the number for the embassy and hands me his cellphone.

'Ask them to call us as soon as possible,' he says.

An answering machine says they're closed until Wednesday, 28 February. I leave yet another message.

Estrada is on my side. He says he doesn't want me sleeping with the bad hats and sorts me out a space in the guards' canteen where there's a TV and sofa to kip on. I get a slap on the back from him, and we shake on it.

'See you later!' he roars, before dashing off again. He's never still for very long.

Wednesday, 28 February 2001   Meteti

The British embassy went back to work yesterday so, after getting my message, ring here to see how I am. Great, thanks! I have diarrhoea again, but that's no surprise. I also get most of my missing kit back – even my GPS so I know exactly where I am – but I'm not allowed my bootlaces.

The jail is a real cesspit on the edge of an estuary. Hygiene is a real worry, and I'm suffering big time from fleas. If I'm going to catch anything it will be somewhere like this. In the compound there was one hole in the ground used by a hundred men, and no such thing as a toilet roll. For the majority, however, it's little different from what they're used to, as they come from small jungle towns or villages in Panama and Colombia. Rice and beans is certainly the norm.

Later I call the embassy back. They haven't heard anything from immigration and, prompted by my call, try to find out why I am still sat on my arse. At 16:00 I get to speak to an immigration officer, who brings with him a bundle of forms for me to sign . . . yet again. I imagine I've signed ten murder confessions and two attempted presidential assassinations by now. He assures me I will be released tomorrow and will get my visa.

Monday, 5 March 2001   Meteti

Just after 09:00 I spy the fat immigration man hurrying his way across the square.

'It's the fifth of March!' I shout to gently remind him.

'Today,' he answers. 'Today.'

'Yeah, right!' Not that I believe it.

A short while later, he returns and tells me that today he will get permission to put me on a plane for Panama City.

'Plane! . . . Plane! Have you not listened to a word I said.' I am starting to lose my cool a bit here. 'Get it in your head, I won't fly!'

'But . . . but . . . you have to, to get . . .'

'No, I don't!' I storm off to phone Mr Newlands.

'Ah, Karl, good news, the paperwork is through so you can fly today,' says his assistant who answers.

'Listen to me, I will not get on that plane. I repeat, I will not get on that plane! No planes, no buses. When I enter Panama City it will be on foot. I don't care what it takes or what I have to do, I will not get on that plane. I haven't spent two years then risked life and limb to cave in to this bullshit. I just need permission to walk and they shagging well will give me it! If they want to get silly about it, just watch how silly I can get. So you talk to these people and explain just how this is going to happen.'

'But . . . but Mr Bushby,' he pleads.

I'm not going all the way to Panama City, then have to pay a fortune to get back down here. I pace around the square, deep in thought. What if they don't play ball? Would the embassy wash their hands of me?

Meanwhile, some inmates are carrying out repair work to the rest room, replacing wooden support beams. One chap is sawing wood and snaps the saw. The guards give him a hard time as they don't have another and will have to wait.

'Well, just wait a moment,' I say, enjoying the brief diversion. Removing my shirt I open some stitching in the collar and pulled out a wire saw. It has been worth all this hassle – well, almost – just to see the look on the guards' faces, who should have found the saw when they first searched me.

'Well, what else have you got tucked away in there?' they wonder.

I can't help smiling as I unpick some of the stitching in the seams of my clothing and take out my escape kit. There is a small lock-knife, scalpel blades, wire snares, nylon para-cord, a compass, etc., etc. They just look at each other and laugh. At least the wire saw was enough to finish the job.

Then the fat immigration man reappears.

'The phone!' It's the embassy for me; they say they've explained my case to immigration, which, in turn, agrees to let me walk and pick up my visa stamps in Panama City. Yes! Now we're getting somewhere.

I get the 'go' a few hours later. Grabbing my gear, I say goodbye to those I've got to know then get the hell out of here. I follow the immigration man down the main street, and he puts me on a launch on the jetty and tells the boatman to run me to Port Quimba.

'Not a problem, you pay nothing,' is his parting shot.

From Port Quimba, a clapped-out minibus gets me back to Meteti where I head straight round to the police station. Unfortunately, Estrada is in Panama City. When I left here two weeks ago, they'd 'forgotten' to pack my machete, but had assured me they would hold it in the office until I returned. No surprise that they can't find it. I am not happy, not at all. It had been brought back from Borneo as a present many years before by my father and had served me well for two years.

Catching lifts where he can, it takes Karl two days to find his way south again to Boca de Cupe, the place where he was first detained by the police and where he must resume the expedition.

Thursday, 8 March 2001   **Boca de Cupe**

After a good breakfast, an officer signs my notebook as proof that I've been here and I say my goodbyes. Wading back across the river, I immediately take the wrong track. It's easily done. Villages around here are fed by a maze of tracks so while I thought I was heading north, I notice that the river is in fact flowing south. Retracing my steps, I bump into a group of Indians on their way out to the plantations. They put me right. It wasn't an easy track to find and I can see why I'd missed it so easily.

Following the bends in the river, I make Capeti at 09:40. After a quick word with the police, I find the track to Yape, which traces the river, through fields of maize and *plantano* plantations. Virtually all the trees have been cleared from along the river bank but at the end of the cultivation I'm faced with an almost solid wall of vegetation. The track continues through this, more or less in the form of a tunnel and I'm forced to walk bent double, and even on my hands and knees once or twice.

At 11:48 the track drops into a small tributary, and wading across I find I can't pick up the track on the opposite bank. I'm close to Yape, but where? A few minutes later, some locals in a canoe bob past and point me west along the flow. Staying in the knee-deep mud and water, I round the bend and see Yape, and minutes later, walk into Union de Choco.

Stuck here for an hour while the police confirm my details, I press on for about thirty or forty minutes until I reach Vista Alagre. Here, there's a little confusion as to where the track to Pinogana starts. You have to double back then turn west, but first I cross the river, which has almost to be swum now as it is a lot deeper with the onset of the wet season.

It's extremely easy to wander on to another track, and in fact I do twice, but luckily the change in direction sets alarm bells ringing in the back of my mind. You really have got to watch it here. I don't get to Pinogana until about 17:00, where there's another river to negotiate. It's in spate but the police here assure me the height will drop within an hour or so. As it's late, I decide to crash and find a graveyard. 'Excellent!' I camp just behind it in the jungle.

Friday, 9 March 2001   Yaviza

It's 07:30 and I must cross the river. It appears to be the same depth as last night, so what the hell. However, it's not quite that easy without all my flotation aids. Fully prepared, the bags within my rucksack keep it afloat but it's still a struggle to beat the current, which is now flowing strongly. A crowd of locals gather on the bank near the village to watch.

Once across and back in the jungle I find the track. Difficult at first – it's just a small tunnel running through dense vegetation – but it gets easier. It is a wet day, and drizzly, which is good because it keeps the heat down. It takes me about two hours to get to Yaviza.

I cross the suspension bridge into town, and then stop to look back. It is done, I've finished the jungle. Yaviza marks the change back to the road. Sitting dripping wet and stinking in a small shack of a café, I have breakfast then count out my money. Nine dollars! Bugger, not a lot. It won't get me halfway to Panama City. I've been asked by the police a number of times if I wanted to sell my jacket – it's a lot better than the stuff they're using – so I will if I must. We've come a long way together but it's better than starving.

The police don't give me clearance to go until 10:30. I'm now back on an open, dusty, dirt track and the sun has broken through, although there is still a cool breeze that feels good. It's been a long time since I've felt such a breeze, having been surrounded by jungle or walls for so long. Two cops on a motorcycle catch up with me. They want to take a photocopy of my letter from La Palma so one shoots back to Yaviza, while the other waits with me for twenty minutes until his mate returns.

By the end of this long, hot, dusty day, I walk into Canglon, where the police offer me food. I wouldn't mind but I've just spent US$1.50 on a basic meal, 30 cents on a Coke and 10 cents on a small bag of frozen fruit juices called a 'Duro'.

Saturday, 10 March 2001   Meteti

I miss Captain Estrada in Meteti when I pass through at lunch-time but when a pick-up truck stops in front of me on the outskirts, with a load of policemen in the back, he's in the cab. We chat, and I have a few things to add since my 'debriefing'.

I must have covered everything by now. Details of Colombian defensive positions, morale, discipline, location of HQs, communications, troop 'turnaround' and timings, where they were before and where they were going to next, unit sizes, weapons, munitions, rations, equipment, what I'd seen on the commanders' maps in Riosucio and Bajira, plus that of the police HQ in Medellin. What the troops were eating, how and where they were re-supplied. It's amazing what you can get out of troops when you just sit and talk.

I also say what I think about his side. They always carry their weapons with them, which is not the case in Colombia, where slap-dash troops leave them lying around on positions or in the TV room. Discipline here seems much tighter and defensive positions are better prepared. That said, I say I did bumble right on to his force's position in Boca de Cupe without being seen – and that it had been attacked before.

Now I've never asked anyone for money yet, but hey, I don't want to starve and I've served Estrada with my long-range reconnaissance patrol report. He happily hands me US$30. I make sure he realises this is only a loan and that I will reimburse him via the Western Union.

Over the next four days, Karl continues west, and the road turns from dust to tarmac. Running short of money, it is a race to get to the British embassy in the capital before it closes on Friday for the weekend because his re-supply held there has some money in it. To do so, he must step on it and, on Wednesday, 14 March, manages a staggering fifty kilometres to make up the time.

Thursday, 15 March 2001   Panama City

By late afternoon, I'm in the outskirts of the capital. In a matter of moments I go from nothing to a concrete jungle. Busy streets are packed with people shopping, as well as traffic . . . at last! Way off in the distance, the city's skyline of high tower blocks and skyscrapers juts from the hills . . . Panama City. We meet at last. I stand and just stare for a while. The sun is now low and yet the city centre is still more than twenty kilometres away it's so huge. Before darkness falls, I sack it and hide on some wasteland because I don't want to hit the poor housing estates in the dark.

Friday, 16 March 2001   Panama City

Total distance to date: 6671 miles (10,742 km)

I'm awake, packed and on the move by 04:00. It's dark, and will be for a while yet so I ought to miss some of the traffic. The first thing I notice is that this place is far bigger than I'd expected. I somehow imagined that because Panama has such a small population, that its capital city would also be smaller. Instead, it's huge. With the daylight, it explodes into life, but by now I'm well beyond the worst of it and heading for the centre.

At long last, I shake hands with Andy Newlands, 'Deputy Head of Mission, British Embassy'.

'My! Am I glad to see you,' he beams, when I find him in his office in the Swiss Tower. The embassy staff seemed pleased to see me and they're very helpful. Andy has my mail and parcels from the UK and Colombia. All has arrived safely. It's Christmas again. There are cards and gifts from Mother; lots of chocolate, a small Christmas pudding and even a packet of instant powdered custard. Father's parcel contains a new tent, sleeping bag, five pairs of socks, three pairs of trousers, two sweat shirts and two shirts. Indeed a major re-supply. There is a note from Catty with some photographs and, best of all, a card from Adam.

For an instant, I'm alone in the room and sitting by the window staring across the city . . . it's done. I sense I never really appreciated my time in the jungle until now that it is over. It's all so clear to me now, vivid visions of the rainforest, the smells and sounds. I rewind and, fleetingly, relive it over and over again. The faces of the monkeys staring at me from the trees, the fish nibbling my body as I washed in those clear pools of warm water. So much comes back to me.

I feel my eyes wanting to close. Look at the state of me. A tired, ragged soldier and a stark contrast to those in this clean, polished office. I'm so relaxed I can hardly move . . . I don't want to. Aching all over, and very sore, I can't stop smiling.

Saturday, 17 March – Wednesday, 4 April 2001   Panama City

Karl finds Panama City prohibitively expensive. Able to afford only basic accommodation, he had been intending to have another trailer built here but decides against it. Feeling disconsolate, he was intent on moving on quickly when Catty flies over and spends a week with him, which includes his thirty-second birthday. As she has some money, they are able to upgrade to a nicer hotel, which raises his morale. After she's gone, he forwards his excess baggage to the next major destination, sets his alarm for 03:30, then sets off into the darkness for the Bridge of the Americas, which spans the Panama Canal.

Wednesday, 11 April 2001   **Beyond Panama City**

Smooth dual carriageways mean that I'm covering plenty of ground as I make my way into the rolling hills. It's been pretty much jungle or cultivation on either side, but there aren't many places to pick up food or water – and it's so damn hot. What I'd give for some rain. It feels like I haven't seen any rain since I was in Colombia. It's quite the norm to see dark clouds in the far distance to the south-east, and even flashes of lightning, but not here.

But most of all it's the roadkills and the sheer number of snakes I can't get over. I see squashed sloths, pythons, turtles and a splattering of possums, which are all new to me, as well as two alligators, one of which was longer than I was tall. Just imagine hitting an alligator.

'Boof!'

'Dad, Dad . . . hadn't you better go back and see if it's dead?'

'Shut up son.'

When I camp this afternoon just off the road in a wood line, I'm lost in thought in the tent when a metre-long snake homes in on me, or more likely the tent. I saw large black ones in the Darien but this chap was green, with a brown, speckled pattern. I wait until he's up close, about two metres from me, before I move so that he sees me. He stops dead. We stare into each other's eyes. His are large round black ones and totally emotionless. We're still for some time before I make another move to get a reaction. He darts back a few metres then turns to watch me for a little while longer before giving my tent a wide berth and moving off.

Darkness falls and the 'Southern Cross' is back in the sky. I haven't seen it for a long time. In fact I thought maybe I'd seen the last of it. This takes me back to Argentina where it could be seen so brightly above the desert, and I wonder how my old friends from those early days are faring.

SOUTHERN CROSS

A beautiful constellation in the southern hemisphere that people in the northern hemisphere never see. The four brightest stars form a cross, the longer arm of which points to the south celestial pole.

Sunday, 15 April 2001   **David**

Total distance to date: 6966 miles (11,217 km)

As I set off this morning, the land reminds me of the mountains in Colombia or possibly Ecuador. I'm not very high but I'm looking down on to clouds that fill the valleys. To my right, northwards and some way off, there's a long range of small peaks swathed in thick white cloud, a familiar feature I got very used to over a long period. It's comforting in a strange way.

At the end of the day I'm dropping back down to the lower ground and the road is flattening out. It's a long time before I find anywhere to top up with water, and this time it's on a track junction where two shacks serve as a shop. There is very little to buy and once again everything is in small amounts, small tins of this and that, mainly fish. Indigenous people sit around in groups. Women in traditional, colourful long dresses are weaving beside their men who seem hungover or still pissed. Everyone appears to be waiting for buses as they have bags and bundles with them. I don't hang around because the drunks are bothering me and I'm just too hot and tired to deal with them. I knock back two small tins of evaporated milk in an attempt to boost my flagging energy levels. I'm certainly feeling the pinch.

On the move I scan the airwaves with my Walkman and actually get a signal. It must be coming from the city of David as I'm only three days out now. I can tell I'm closing because the traffic is increasing. It's a constant stream of buses and cars coming from the direction of the city, forcing me off the road on to the shagging rocks and stones, which plays hell with my blisters. There's lots of horn-blowing and fist-waving, as well as shouting, from angry drivers who can't understand why this idiot is on the road.

Thursday, 26 April 2001   **Costa Rica border**

I spent a few days recuperating in David, which was just long enough to allow my blisters and sores to dry out. Last night, I stopped just short of the border with Costa Rica. Cleaning up my sore feet, I notice a new potential foot problem – fresh clusters of small pus-filled blisters, which look like spots, but they're not. They seem to be spreading from a central point and you can see them forming beneath the skin. It might be a fungal infection. Anyway, they're sore this morning.

Paso Canoas is the border crossing, but I can't tell where Panama ends and Costa Rica begins in this confused mix of people and vehicles. I find a street-vendor and change dollars for colones. I've just over US$50 which, at C300 to the dollar, gives me C15,000. I find I've walked into Costa Rica without realising so must retrace my steps a short distance to pick up an exit stamp from Panama. It is all very lax and I could have just wandered straight through.

It is then a long haul to a town called Neily. Nothing, despite the border, seems any different although I've crossed a time zone and have lost an hour's daylight. It's the same road, same people and same damn sun.

Saturday, 28 April 2001   Neily

It starts to rain heavily in the late afternoon so I get the tent up smartish and begin throwing my things in. Shamag? Where's the shamag? Bloody hell, no! Not the shamag, for Christ's sake. It's somehow come adrift from the back of the rucksack where I'd stuck it a few hours ago. I sit head in hands . . . tomorrow the sun will eat me alive. Was it at the farm where I stopped for water? I can't remember seeing it. I really need it out here. What to do? Should I go back and leave the rest of my stuff here, or not chance it being nicked? I'll risk it. Out of the wood, I scramble up the embankment on to the road where it's still raining hard. There are a number of houses about, but I don't think I've been seen. I'm in luck . . . a coach appears, heading for Panama so I flag it down.

'Just a few kilometres,' I tell the driver. 'I'm looking for something on the road.'

Off we go with me perched in the open doorway. I don't see the shamag and jump off after about five kilometres. Someone must have picked it up for sure. Now I've got to get back to the wood asap. I'm furious. I get a ride most of the way back and call at the farm where I'd stopped for water. The farmer is actually standing on the road and he smiles when he sees me. Yes! Tell me you've got it, and indeed he has. Thank God! I run the last two kilometres to where my kit is. I'm so relieved to find it's all still here. That was a close one.

Monday, 30 April 2001   Towards San Jose

I reach the coast. I'm taking the more scenic coastal route rather than the Pan American, which promised a 3000-metre climb before descending into San Jose.

Because it's so hot and humid, everything seems to fester. Again, my clothes smell of ammonia and I've got a rash all over my body. I've collected some more sores on my hips and for the last four days have kept getting short bouts of 'prickly heat'. It's not very nice at all, but not too bad as yet. I spend more time on maintenance in the evenings, cleaning feet, sores and other important working parts.

Tonight I pitch tent in the forest, and feel as if I'm back in the Darien. It's just alive in here. It's part of a 'bio reserve', of which there are a number along the coast. A troop of monkeys clamber above me in the trees and I can sit and watch them feed. As long as I don't leave the tent they don't care but if I emerge, they bark alarm calls and scoot. Something else found my tent but before I actually saw what, it growled and ran off when I moved. Whatever it was was large and made me jump as it ran, crashing through the bush. At night it's just so damn noisy, with insects shrilling and frogs croaking. A fascinating place.

Wednesday, 2 May 2001   Towards San Jose

I'm off-road again. Eventually I find the dirt track I'm after, running through a palm oil plantation, which are quite common around here.

Along the way, I step over a termite column, interesting little beggars that I first noticed in the Darien, where they are really prolific. They build tube-like corridors out of what appears to be chewed up wood or mud, which is their own home-made cement. They never seem to stop. Nearly all the trees in the Darien were covered in these networks of tubular constructions. Most mornings there, when I picked up my rucksack, it would have been turned into a termite nest, with once again, a whole network of tube-ways running over it.

In my hotel room in David, I'd noticed a single tube ran down a corner of one wall so made a hole in the tube and timed the termites as to how fast they could repair it. It was generally five to ten minutes per inch. Here on the track, trucks had taken out large sections of the tubes, but the blighters are undeterred. Workers run to and fro moving the materials while construction teams start rebuilding. Other, soldier termites will form a disciplined defence along the lines of the broken tube walls, each one facing out, motionless and evenly spaced. Every one of them knows exactly what they have to do.

Thursday, 3 May 2001   Towards San Jose

I'm still on a vehicle track when a converted military truck passes me, full of eco-tourists, sitting in rows in the back. A little while later I come across them again parked up beside a shack. The gringos are eating at tables. Just the thing for breakfast and a chat, I think to myself. Dropping my kit I walk on to the wooden porch. Everyone just stares at me so I suspect this probably isn't a bar or restaurant at all.

'Morning, is this a private thing, or can anyone join in?' I begin.

Not a murmur. Then the guide speaks.

'Private,' he says.

'Sorry, just thought I could pick up a Coke or something,' I continue.

'There's a place just down the road,' he says.

'Thanks, I'll be on my way then.'

As I am kitting up the guide offers me a drink of juice.

'Hell, thanks, beats paying for one . . . thank you,' I say, dropping my rucksack again.

Then a tourist shouts something I don't quite catch but it was uncomplimentary. I glare at the three tables but no one looks up and they just carry on eating. What a spineless bunch of bastards. I can't believe how unfriendly they are. In response, the girl behind the bar gives me another glass of juice, which causes more muttering. Plainly, I'm not welcome. There are about fifteen of them sitting right next to me as I stand by the wall. There are spare chairs but no one says 'pull up a chair' – they just ignore me. Here we are in the middle of the bloody jungle and they're all upset because I've intruded on their little party.

Friday, 4 May – Friday, 11 May 2001

Passing through San Marcos, Karl picks up some money that his father sent – C36,106.85 (£80) – so is eating well again and taking the hills in his stride. Just two days later, he walks into the capital, San Jose, with 11,537 kilometres behind him. Here, he splashes out on a knife to replace the one he lost in Panama. At C17,000 (US$56), it eats into his reserves but it is a vital piece of equipment. Carried in a sheaf in his combat vest, it makes him look, more than ever, like Rambo, and will, he hopes, act as a deterrent if he runs into trouble.

Saturday, 12 May 2001   Beyond San Jose

Traffic is heavy. Minibuses carry gringos heading for the northern beaches while others drive flash jeeps with surfboards on display. When I pull in for a midday break, the Yanks next to me won't say so much as a 'Hi'. Thinking about it, why should they? Without my trailer, they must think I'm just another backpacker, and one more dishevelled than most.

Not far down the road I find myself standing on the edge of the hills looking out over an incredible view to the west. I can see all the way across the Gulf of Nicoya and beyond. It's one hell of a horizon and I guess I'll be at the Nicaraguan border in five days' time. Tonight, when I stop, I've a cracking spot to camp with a view to kill for, and blow me, not a bloodsucking fly to be found! I'm not surprised Costa Rica is as popular as it is with visitors.

Tuesday, 15 May 2001   Towards La Cruz

Ants. Today I come across a seething mass of ants swarming across the track in front of me. This is the biggest army I've seen. A column three metres wide, which spans the road and even on to the verges, is moving in the same direction as I am. There must be million upon million of these tiny black insects. All move as if under the command of a leader and it's fascinating to watch. The forward edge is a massive group which flows like water over everything, and out to the sides small columns form long probing fingers that never stray too far from the main body. Bringing up the rear, straggler groups file into more columns that eventually drain into the centre like water running from high ground.

Tonight, something comes a'creeping. It's something big and appears a number of times in front of my tent pitched in a dry riverbed. It is on the large side – I know that by the amount of noise it is making – and I catch a glimpse of it once or twice, yet still can't decide what it is. It might be either a very large lizard or a snake, like a python or boa constrictor. Unfortunately, it's very dark and there's no moon. Whatever it is, it's giving me the heebie-jeebies. Up on the banks on either side of me I keep seeing its head pop up now and again, just silhouetted against the night sky like that fuzzy photograph of the Loch Ness monster. It sticks around for quite some time.

Sunday, 20 May 2001   Nicaragua Border

Passing through La Cruz yesterday afternoon – it's the last town in Costa Rica – I'd decided to sack it just five kilometres from the border which is at a place called Pena Blacas. It had been a restless night, far too hot, and I seemed to spend ages scratching and itching. I haven't been able to wash for ten days now and my skin is probably far less than healthy.

Reaching the border, I change my last dollar bill for cordobas (Nicaraguan currency), then spend my remaining coins on a piece of cake and a Coke, before attempting to cross the border. It's then I find I have to pay US$3 to leave Costa Rica. With nothing to lose – I'm now completely broke – I kick up a bit of a stink and the fat man on the desk just snaps.

'Give me your passport!' he yells, clearly exasperated and chops my passport.

But I'm not out of the woods. I'm told I must pay US$7 to enter Nicaragua, but as it's Sunday, it's US$9. What to do? I try pleading.

'You're not entering unless you pay,' says the official.

' But . . .' I stammer.

'We don't care!'

'But . . .'

'We don't care, no money, no entry.'

Only thirty-six kilometres from Rivas and I'm stuck. I have a good think. I could sell my Walkman, but without batteries no one would believe it works. Or perhaps I can call the embassy . . . but it's a Sunday. With nothing to lose, I give it a go and get some answering machine that is barely decipherable as the phone line is so bad. I plonk myself down outside the office . . . now what?

I'm left with just 20 cordobas, which I'll need for the phone. I've kept my cool. Now I just sit outside the building with a hopeless thousand yard stare. Sometimes life sucks.

Then the strangest thing happens. The same staff in the immigration office, who an hour earlier had shut the door in my face – and weren't interested in my newspaper clippings or anything I had to say – call me back into the office.

'We've had a whip-round, each of us giving two dollars, and we're going to pay for your entry,' one announces.

Well, I'll be damned. They don't know me from the next guy and yet they're now paying out of their own pockets for some dippy, penniless backpacker who was dumb enough to get himself into such a mess in the first place . . . how do I do it? I vow to pay them back. I'm on my way by 11:00, soon tracing the shoreline of Lake Nicaragua.

Monday, 21 May 2001   Towards Rivas

Yesterday evening it started raining. The sky crackled with static and flashes of lightning until it turned into a full-blown thunderstorm. It threw it down all night and is still raining this morning so everything is extremely wet. Not that it bothers the spiders.

As I move my rucksack inside my tent entrance, I disturb a very large dark-brown scorpion under the top flap. Digging it out with a stick disturbs a whole host of other creatures, which run amok all over my pile of kit. I don't know why but, ugh, spiders do bother me. I always freak when a large hairy one runs over the back of my hand . . . and right now, I'm freaking big time.

The tent has been invaded in the night. There are spiders of all shapes and sizes and two more scorpions among these unwelcome guests. Mother of God! The scorpions scurry under my rucksack as I jump about in near panic. I've never seen so many creepy critters in one place. They're all over the place, even running up my trousers, both inside and out. Now that does scare me. This is like some shagging horror movie. Bloody hell man, I must get a grip!

I drag out my chest webbing to give this a shake, and find a large scorpion inside its folds, and then another in one of the pouches. I turn out each pouch in turn, and evict yet another scorpion. Pouches that don't contain scorpions are full of spiders and those centipede things. I must be camped right on a huge insect nest – everything is infested with them. I stand stock-still outside the tent in the rain and mud, waiting for anything else to move. Then go through my kit again, slowly. Scorpions are dark brown, almost black, and are hard to find. Finally, and not without some hesitation, I pluck up the courage to put everything on and get moving. Nicaragua is the land of scurrying evil.

Tuesday, 22 May – Monday, 28 May 2001   Rivas

Rivas comes at last – it's a town, not a large city and similar to many places I've passed through recently. For the first time in Nicaragua I get an idea of prices – they're high – and it's quite clear that the cheap days of South America are over. I find a grotty little 'Hospedase' as hotels are called here. Very much your average dollar squalor, except I'm paying US$5, about 50 cordobas – its rooms are more like caves, with a number above each entrance. I get cave number nine.

The town has a Western Union office and even an Internet 'establishment', though little else. I'm forced to wash my clothes by hand in cold water, which just doesn't work. They are still rancid and will need a damn good boil wash – if not two.

It hasn't stopped raining. One morning, it's so torrential that the place I'm staying at floods and I'm left stranded in my room in four inches of water. I leave – more a case of 'abandon ship' than 'check out'.

Right now, I'm feeling very low. At the weekend the town has a large party in the main square, which I attend, but only in body. Every damn thing anybody says, or does, is pissing me off and I sit around for days in this bored, twisted frame of mind. For the past three days, very early in the morning, some lunatic of a holy man has been setting off home-made fireworks outside the church next to where I live. He must have hundreds of the bloody things. Much more and I'm going to stick them where the sun doesn't shine!

It's quite the norm for someone to offer gringos dope from time to time, but this occasion is the first time I'm actually thinking about it! It would be like morphine for a wounded man.

Wednesday, 30 May 2001   Jinotepe

Feeling relatively flush, and I do mean relatively, I hope to stay somewhere just a little upmarket from my usual dives, as it is only for the one night. In fact, I've been dreaming about a night in a clean place with a TV, even Sky or cable . . . wow! But no such luck, there is only one hotel in town that is half-decent and that is US$40, per night . . . obviously a joke. I am left with the one and only alternative, a dog kennel of a squat for US$6.

It's stinking. An old fat woman answers the door, seemingly the same one that I've seen at every other dive I've ever stayed at. She's in the standard uniform of a sweat- and food-stained T-shirt and flip-flops.

'What do you want?' she grunts.

She then spends ten minutes looking for the key and arguing with a huge old fat man who looks as though he's welded to his rocking chair, his feet buried beneath a pile of empty beer cans. We wade knee-deep through a herd of snotty, grubby kids then out into a small courtyard, where we continue through chickens, pigs and three dogs, to cave number fourteen. She forces the ill-fitting door then picks up some rubbish and one sheet from the bed, which has obviously not been touched since the last squatter left or died. All the rooms have double beds, as these places normally double up as a knocking shop if there's a bit of a rush on.

Here I am then, in my square concrete box . . . again. Green-painted walls are peeling and streaked with water stains and rust. A mishmash of corrugated iron sheeting serves as the ceiling and, above me, a single low-watt light bulb dangles from two bare wires taped to a wooden beam. As for the light switch itself, it sparks and crackles when I touch it.

Sunday, 3 June – Thursday, 12 July 2001   León

I must find somewhere to get a new trailer built here. The first place I try is a virtual scrap heap in someone's backyard; the 'engineer', a large fat guy in a filthy and rather ragged T-shirt, doesn't look too promising nor do his two dogs. But the next place appeals; it's a small factory – part of the local Fundacion Politecnico La Salla (Technical College) – and is run by an Austrian. I explain in English what I'm after and spend the next few days drawing up detailed plans.

Having dragged a converted golf trolley over 8000 kilometres I know exactly what I want. Rather than converting a ready-built machine, this time Beast II will be built from scratch, from the ground up. It's a question of lighter aluminium or heavier more robust steel? I decide on aluminium, as steel seems way too heavy.

The city centre feels very colonial with its Spanish churches and a huge cathedral, which is much too large for the town. So the story goes, plans for the cathedral were mixed up on a ship en route for the continent, and this particular building should have been built in Lima. León is a university town. It's full of young people, many of them pretty girls, and there are a fair few gringo travellers, like Nick and Fred.

'Ah! You're not the chap who swam for days down a river in the Darien? My God, you're a legend,' begins Nick.

I like these two. Deciding to hang out with them, I move to their hotel, the Avenida, which is cheaper than mine but just as pleasant.

One afternoon I'm on my way to meet Fred when I pass some gringo backpackers in the overcrowded street market. Among them is a pretty face I automatically focus on. As if this is a scene from a movie, the girl smiles at me then she disappears around a corner. I feel somewhat sad, knowing that I'll never know who she was. Damn it! I think to myself, she was very good looking.

But we *do* meet just a few hours later in a bar. She's Kirsty and, get this, she's from my home town of Hull. Travelling with her friend, Victoria, they've just arrived in town with some Australian bloke they'd run into in Managua.

I am stuck fast, there is no shaking free from Kirsty. Later we stumble into the night and realise that we're both staying at the Avenida. I've not drunk alcohol for a while and so am in a bit of a state, although I'll say in my defence I am holding it together reasonably well. Yes, I vomited twice, in the loo, but cleaned myself up. I swear she wouldn't have known if I hadn't confessed later.

Kirsty is twenty-seven and was born in Hull, but her family moved down south when she was ten. She's very bright – she has an MA in politics – and can argue with anyone, about anything, and win. She oozes with self-confidence, even arrogance, and I can see how some may well find her overpowering. Sadly, she and her friend have to be somewhere else for a few days but she promises to return within a week. León is a quieter, more subdued place without her and I agonise on how, with my deeper feelings for Catty, this girl has literally kicked her way into my life. What's going on?

Kirsty isn't gone long. A few days later, there's a knock on Karl's hotel door and a note is slipped under it. She's back. The next two weeks are some of the best he's had in a long time.

Finally, Beast II rolls out into the daylight for the first time. It's a job well done, certainly for Nicaragua, and has been built to my specifications so I'm happy. Raphael (who built Beast II) and I pose for photos outside the tech college and then I hand over US$400 and walk it back to the hotel. It is not yet complete, however, there is still a lot of work to be done to get the trailer in shape for the road. Small jobs, nothing serious.

The last week is extremely busy. For every item I crossed off my 'things to do' list it seemed I added another two. Kirsty rallies round to help and in fact begins kicking my backside every time I take a breather. She knows I need to get out of here and is determined to keep me busy. However, all that whip-cracking is reserved for the daytime. During the evening we chill-out with other friends at a bar called Payitas. We sit and drink a bottle of rum between us, very cheap, each of us putting a dollar in, yet very effective.

Friday, 13 July 2001   León

The last days always hold an inevitable melancholy when you've got to know people so well, especially someone like Kirsty. But it's lasted longer than any of us could have imagined. Today, we're going our separate ways. After a little time buggering about loading up, I'm 'good to go'. We all breakfast together, then say goodbye. Kirsty spends some time in my arms, neither of us being very good at this sort of stuff, and then I'm away.

Beast II is heavily laden but she moves smoothly. It isn't long before I am out of town and on the main highway for Chinandega, the next town, only forty kilometres north-east. It's a strange feeling to be pulling again, and brings back all my memories of the first Beast. Under a hot sun, I'm soon bathed in sweat.

After fifteen kilometres, I notice a few teething problems. The box – the trailer's container – keeps slipping forward and, as it's only plastic, becomes misshaped. This warping means the lid keeps coming off. Also, the bungees used to strap Beast II to the rucksack are already wearing thin so a halt is in order. I pull in at about 14:00 and park in a dry riverbed under a road bridge. As it takes an age to get sorted out, I realise this is as good a spot as any for pitching a tent, and I cut the day short.

A storm rolls in, and as I sit in my tent eating, the sky explodes with thunder and lightning followed by a torrential downpour. It continues way into the night while I lie in troubled thought, mulling over Catty and Kirsty. They're as different as chalk and cheese, but if I had to choose between them it would have to be Catty. But Kirsty will never know how she'd brought 'home' to me for a month. In that time I felt truly connected to the land I'd left, my England that feels so far away, and is still another nine years in the future.

Saturday, 14 July 2001   Near Cristobal

The heat nearly kills me this afternoon as the temperature must be in the mid-thirties. Waves of heat radiate from the dark tarmac beneath me and I use gauze pads from my medical kit to cover my hands, which are beginning to burn in the intense sun. I'm struggling. I need frequent drink stops but, unfortunately, I'm pretty much pinned to the road by clusters of poor mud-brick huts, filled with the usual gangs of naked children, pigs, chickens and, as always, a plentiful supply of dogs.

To my right for the past two days has been what the locals tell me is the highest volcano in Central America – Cristobal. Recently it's been in the news because of its threatening behaviour. From its crater white steam rises, sometimes heavily and other times just puffs, like a steam engine.

Close to the end of the day, I stumble across a Sandinista celebration. Groups of campesinos have converged on a few roadside bars. Today appears to be yet another 'National Day', an excuse for Sandinistas to party. Rows of trucks and cars, crammed with people, arrive in convoy, headed by girls in hot pants and bikini tops posing on the back of pick-up trucks. Everyone is waving the red and black flag of the FSNL.

I pull over to a small roadside stall, made from wood and straw, just short of the drunken mob, where a group of five local girls are selling snacks . . . but no drinks.

One of the girls – they're all sisters and cousins – invites me to stay the night at their place. It's a madhouse, so much so that I actually set up tent inside the 'boys' room', to which four drunken gimps rock up at about 02:00. What with this bunch, the pigs, dogs and the god-forsaken roosters I'm amazed I get ten minutes' sleep.

SANDINISTA NATIONAL LIBERATION FRONT (FSNL)

A leftist political movement and the main opposition to the Somoza government. In 1979, it emerged victorious from a civil war and – in the face of US opposition, which imposed brutal sanctions – formed a government headed by Daniel Ortega, in office until it lost the vote in 1990.

Karl crosses into Honduras at Guasaule. Issued with a thirty-day visa – long enough to make the relatively short journey to El Salvador – he walks the twenty kilometres to the first town, Choluteca, where he takes a few days off. To better attend to some nasty blisters, he pays a little more for an air-conditioned room with its own shower and lavatory.

Saturday, 28 July 2001   **Beyond Choluteca**

I am stopped twice today by people with guns. On the first occasion a young lad comes from one of the huts alongside the road and walks over to speak to me with a 9mm pistol tucked in his belt. Not a toy, either! Later in the day, two men standing by a pick-up truck on the road pass the time of day with me. One of them also has a 9mm, with a twenty-round magazine stuck in his trouser waistband.

Later in the evening while writing up my notes at a restaurant, where I'm also staying, two men are sitting nearby polishing off their evening meal. Each has a revolver tucked in his waistband. They look like .38s. When they've gone I ask the guy running the place why there are so many guns about in Honduras.

'For respect!' he replies.

In the night, as I'm trying to drop off to sleep, I'm disturbed by a loud bang. It's 01:15, what the hell is happening? For a few moments it's silent again, then there are screams from outside the restaurant compound. I sit up, my heart pounding and realise something is going down. As I'm pulling on my trousers, I pause for a second. The cries are from an extremely distressed man, but even I can make out what he's screaming.

'Please help me.'

What if this is gun play? What if the noise that woke me was a gun? What am I about to get myself into? By now, lights are coming on in the house and the man is banging on the sheet metal gate.

'Please help . . . help me,' he wails.

I scramble from my tent and find the proprietor, a rather large fat guy. I ask what's happening while trying to lace up my boots. There's been a car crash and I peer out over his shoulder. It's dark, but I can see a pick-up truck with a man standing next to it, his arms in the air, babbling in Spanish. Other people are starting to gather from houses around and about. The pick-up has slammed into a large plough and tractor that was parked off to one side of the road. It has rolled at least once before righting itself. I see if there's anything I can do.

Without a moment's thought, I lapse straight back into army first-aid-mode. There's a chap standing in the road with some nasty cuts to his head and he is soaked in blood. Clearly shaken he just keeps repeating his pleas for help as he stumbles from person to person. The man that had woken us in the first place is kneeling over a body.

'My brother, my brother . . . don't die, my brother! Someone help me,' he cries, his breath smelling of beer.

His brother is on his back and covered in blood. He has very obvious head injuries and a rather gruesome shoulder wound. 'Jesus! What a mess,' I say to myself. He's breathing, there is no doubt about that, but he is making a heavy, rasping sound. A thick pool of blood collects beneath his head and, as I feel carefully around the back of his skull, it gives way to a soft pulp . . . oh dear, this isn't good. Thick blood wells from his ears and his eyes are half-open. He's alive but we have to get him out of here.

A large group of people have gathered by this time and are standing about watching.

'Where's the nearest hospital?' I yell.

There's a long pause before someone eventually answers.

'San Lorenzo.'

'Who's got a car, we need to move this guy fast,' I continue. No response.

'Has no one got a car? Does anyone know someone who has a car here?' Again a silent pause before someone speaks.

'There are no cars here.'

At 01:30 in the morning, on a country road close to the border with El Salvador, there's not a lot of hope for a quick move to the hospital. The unconscious casualty is now making gruesome noises when he breathes, and I ease him into a three-quarter prone position so that he doesn't choke on his own blood. His brother isn't helping – he rolls him back over and gives him a shake. I try to get someone to keep hold of this prat, but no one wants to get involved. They just stand and watch, as though it was all happening on TV. No one does a damn thing to help. I dash back to my kit and grab a 'First Field Dressing' from my chest webbing, and another out of my medical kit, along with some gauze pads and crêpe bandages. On my way out of the compound I notice a pick-up truck parked close by.

'It doesn't work,' says the fat boss.

I find the wailing drunk shaking his unconscious brother again. This time, I kick his arse into the road, which gives me a chance to get the work done. I find it hard to get a dressing on the chap's head as I'm trying not to loop the bandage around his neck and obstruct his airway in any way. At the same time I don't want to be putting too much pressure on the back of his head, which now resembles crazy paving. The second dressing goes on to his shoulder wound which has been cut clean and the large flap of flesh has been sliced from the top of the shoulder towards his neck, luckily stopping short of cutting his jugular vein. I can see the bones beneath.

The victim starts to move his body as if making an effort to roll over, yet his eyes and face remain perfectly still. I then strap his left arm with its injured shoulder to his body. It's difficult to see just how bad things are because it's so dark. One of the campesinos has a torch and I go to take it, as mine has no batteries. She jumps back, refusing to hand it over until someone in the crowd takes it from her and passes it to me. Trouble is, the battery is almost flat.

Next thing I know, the pick-up from the compound (the one that doesn't work!) is being driven out on to the road. Yes, this is more like it, I say to myself before, to my horror, it turns off and heads out towards the border. I can't believe these people! Suddenly, there are more headlights in the road so I run out and flag down a passing pick-up, explaining to the two occupants that we need to get this chap to San Lorenzo. They won't help – they pull away leaving me standing on the road in disbelief and a feeling of helplessness comes over me.

More headlights. It's the fat restaurant owner with his son and their wagon. It stops short and they get out.

'No! . . . No! Over here . . . bring the vehicle over here!' I bellow.

They refuse. Christ, now what? They stand with a group, shaking their heads and I go over to them.

'What the hell is wrong now?'

The son states he's been drinking and can't drive. I ask the rest of the group and even volunteer to drive it myself, but the older men just shake their heads and frown at one another. It's as if they're afraid to help.

Another ten to fifteen minutes pass. The unconscious casualty is still bleeding. He moves a little but shows no signs of coming round, not that I expect him to. His head injuries look really bad, but it's hard to know just how serious as the scalp is very vascular and bleeds a lot from the smallest cut. The front of the pick-up itself is extensively damaged; one of its doors has been almost ripped off and bent back on itself and the roof is badly dented. They must have hit the plough at speed as the engine block has been pushed back inside the dashboard. Once again I pick out headlights on the road, and run out to stop yet another pick-up. This time the occupants seem a little more helpful and even the people here give me a hand in explaining what we need. The men in the pick-up agree and reverse the truck closer to the casualty. I get four men to help me lift as I hold his head and neck, slowly easing the victim into the back. He's joined by his brother who seems to have calmed down a little. I grip him and explain he must hold the dressing on to the back of his brother's head.

'Go . . . go on! Get this thing moving!' I bark.

Sunday, 29 July 2001   San Miguel

Yesterday I crossed into El Salvador and now I'm in San Miguel – the second largest city in the country, which is at the base of the 2096-metre volcano of the same name. When I return to my hotel after a spot of shopping, there are some people gathered outside. What's this, I wonder?

They're not waiting for a bus, they're standing around an old boy lying on the ground beside the road. To my horror I see his right foot has been torn from his leg, well virtually anyway, as it's only connected by a few strands of flesh at the soggy ends. His exposed ankle joint and foot are crushed into his shoe, the result of a bus wheel I'm told. Typically, no one is taking control. As I step forward to look at the man, people stop me saying I mustn't touch him until the police get here.

I scatter five dogs that are hanging around, lapping up the blood from the road, then go into a shop next door and grab a plastic bag. I ease the remains of his foot and his injured leg into the bag just to keep the flies and dirt off them. The old boy just lies there as if trying to sleep, probably in shock. There is less blood flowing than one would have expected, so I decide not to try and tourniquet it. There's nothing further I can do, so leave it to them and head back for a shower.

Karl heads on, beyond San Miguel to Usuluatan and the surfing capital of Las Libertad. It is a journey punctuated by two equal irritants: mosquitoes and constant police checks.

Thursday, 9 August 2001   **Towards La Hachadura**

During the afternoon I pull into a mishmash of wooden stores on the roadside. It's all very busy with campesinos getting on with their lives. I re-supply with pasta, plus this time some fresh green tomatoes, onions, toilet paper, candles, milk powder and a new set of batteries. While here I also take the opportunity to fill up with three litres of water to last me through the evening. But just as the woman is refilling my bottles, there's the screech of tyres from the road.

As I turn I hear the terrible thud of an impact and see a bicycle folding beneath the wheels of a car, its rider sent rolling across the tarmac like a rag doll. I'm getting good at this now. I run over to the scene just as the car reverses off the bent and twisted bike, steers to the right of the body and drives off at speed. Hmm. The victim is face down, blood running from his mouth and I can see bits of teeth. He's breathing, unconscious, but breathing. A large crowd quickly gathers and an old man attempts to pull me away saying, 'No, no, it's OK, he's alive. Best leave him.'

After a very quick look at him, I can see no other obvious injuries and the bleeding from the mouth appears to come from a facial injury. People are now pulling at his arms and legs and drag him off the road to the shade of a tree.

'Do you know what you're doing?' I yell.

'Yes!' is the reply.

A group of men sit the unconscious casualty upright, holding him by his arms while three of them begin fanning him with their straw hats. I try to explain they'd be better off laying him in a coma position, but no one seems to be listening. I decide that time would be best spent looking for transport.

'Who's got a car here?' I ask.

This is met by the same blank expressions as my previous experiences, so once again I attempt to stop traffic on the road. I eventually halt a red pick-up and begin to explain that we have an accident victim that needs to get to hospital. Others from the crowd then switch on to this and help me to convince the driver, who rolls his eyes as if to say 'Christ, why me!'

The crowd is still fanning the poor victim and even slapping him on the back.

'Let's go! . . . get him over here!' I plead.

The group of men hoist him, none too gently, off the ground and carry him over to the pick-up . . . which is now full of other people!

'Everyone off the back of the pick-up please!' I request.

'But it's our taxi!'

'Not now it's not, it's an ambulance!'

Once the back of the pick-up is clear I turn around to find the men stuffing the poor blighter into the front passenger seat, and I mean stuffing, there is blood running everywhere. Cursing loudly, I lift the chap out while trying to explain how this is just not the way it is done. 'Help me!' I shout as I carry him around to the back and slide him in.

The locals argue that he'll fry in the sun.

'Don't worry about that, lie him on his side, and keep him on his side,' I insist, the heat being the least of his worries.

'He needs to stay like this! Look, he's got blood in his mouth . . . keep him laid on his side!' I repeat. More confused stares from those tending the victim.

'Just you worry about his breathing!' I sigh, as the truck pulls off and, at the same time, the helpers roll our friend on to his back. It's a good drive to the nearest hospital or even the nearest town. This place is incredible. Is this is a bad month for accidents or is it the norm? If I'm hit and left unconscious in the road, I don't much fancy my chances.

Karl crosses into Guatemala on Friday, 10 August at the small fron-tier post at La Hachadura. It is hot and humid and rains heavily, and a new tent has several design faults and doesn't keep the water out. The way through fields of maize, sugar cane and grazing cattle is hilly and punctuated by a series of volcanoes, one of which belches plumes of smoke and steam and creates a fog that hangs in the air. After four days, he walks into the city of Escuintla, where he is look-ing forward to seeing Catty again.

Tuesday, 14 August – Friday, 24 August 2001   Escuintla

Total distance to date: 8044 miles (12,953 km)

A 'coming in day' is always a pleasure. I look forward to the chance to wash, let sores and blisters heal, sleep well and eat like a madman for a few days while I recuperate. I remember some great ones – Perito Moreno, Esquel, Santiago, La Serena, Antofagasta, Arequipa, Loja, Quito, Medellin and Panama City. I even get a puncture this morning but it doesn't faze me – no messing, simply strip out and stick in a spare inner tube and I'm on my way. It's that easy with these quick-release wheels, not the pain in the arse it used to be. I've noted that my tyres are still in good nick. They don't seem to be showing the same amount of wear as they did with the previous trailer. This may well be due to the fact that I'm using two towing shafts now as opposed to a single main shaft.

I call Catty. She's heard nothing about her visa application. Half the problem is that I've arrived earlier than anticipated which hasn't left her much time to get sorted. She's no idea if she will make it and I can't afford to hang around as I'm paying US$5 a night for a room and can hardly afford it.

In the meantime, I conduct a chaotic phone interview with the BBC. Five minutes into the call and everything's going well, when the old woman that runs the place with the phone gives me grief for spending too much time on it. I'm now being interviewed while attempting to keep this woman quiet and at arm's length. She's giving me a hard time now, insisting I hang up, then threatening to cut me off. I want to sound sure, sophisticated and succinct, but I'm sure I'm stuttering and stammering, caught between trying to answer the questions and placate this old trout.

Her husband arrives, all stone-faced, insisting I hang up. I've no choice – I apologise and hang up. The old woman storms off leaving her other half to explain that, here in Guatemala, you also have to pay to receive a call.

'It's the phone company,' he says. 'They're corrupt, the lot of them.'

On the twenty-first, Catty calls to say she can be here in four days' time but, in the end, she doesn't get the visa – it's been refused. The problem is that she's Colombian and the countries around here get nervous at the mere mention of the place. I hope that she can make it to Mexico, although the further north I go the more expensive air travel will get. I've nothing to keep me here now – I'm leaving directly.

Saturday, 25 August 2001   Beyond Escuintla

I'm into more hill reps (a rep is army slang for a 'repetition', as in fifty press-ups). At the top of one lump, I'm gasping for breath, literally melting on the newly laid tarmac and trying not to breathe the stifling air rising from it. The legs are really working hard after a week off and, consequently, I'm plagued with cramps when I stop for the night. My calves and thighs ripple and twitch as though something large is living inside my legs. I sit in my tent and watch them – they seem to have a life of their own and, squatting in the bush, trying to go to the loo, I leap about with sharp cramps and fall over with my trousers around my ankles.

It'll be six days to the Mexican border. According to the map, the hills don't stop until then so it's going to be a hell of slog.

Sunday, 26 August 2001   Towards Tecun Uman

Police patrols cruise past then slow down and I'm warned several times this is 'a bad road'. They don't just mean the traffic – they also mean the thieves. They offer me a lift in their pick-up, which is nice of them.

Later, I come across an old man on the roadside. He looks like a hobo and his sack seems to contain just rubbish. Clearly he's having problems as I saw him trying to wrap a rag around his foot. I pass by, but in the end just can't leave him there. I can almost feel his pain, having been there so many times myself. This will only take a minute so I double back and offer help, telling him I have stuff that can improve things for him. At first he's a little unsure as to my intent, but when I show him some of my medical kit he is over the moon. His wellies have opened a small sore on his ankle and although his Spanish is terribly hard to understand I work out he has been walking, or had to walk, two days to get to his goal. I simply clean up his wound and shove a dressing over it.

The old chap's soon as happy as a campesino with a basket full of tacos. I give him a bottle of water and head off.

Wednesday, 29 August 2001   **Towards Tecun Uman**

I meet some old German guy heading east this morning. He's in flip-flops and looks distinctly well-worn. He asks where we are and how far it is until he can find a place to cash traveller's cheques. Apparently, he's been robbed at the border and they've taken his money, watch and shoes. This had happened on Sunday when everything was closed, so he'd set off on foot (never a smart move), and has now been at it for three days. Needless to say, he is suffering somewhat. He obviously hasn't thought this one through.

I break at a Texaco station. This is where I often take a few moments to observe people passing through. Here you see the extreme differences between city folk passing through and the local campesinos. Mr City Slicker, with his five-year gym membership body, cowboy boots, tight jeans, silk shirt and greased-back hair sports a 9mm pistol (chrome-finished so that it goes with his jewellery) in his belt holster. He is merely popping in for cigarettes, while his drop-dead gorgeous girlfriend waits in his shiny Range Rover.

Parked next to him will be a pick-up full of tatty campesinos, those in the back soaking wet from a shower. They have dark sullen faces and gaze at me with fixed stares. They don't even blink.

It's now thirty-five kilometres to the border at Tecun Uman, which I intend to hit tomorrow. The thought of reaching Mexico has a bit of a buzz to it. It's been one of those distant goals that it's difficult to imagine I'll ever reach.

Chapter Seven

MEXICO

Thursday, 30 August 2001   **The Mexican Border**

Tecun Uman is the grottiest frontier town and not somewhere to hang around in. I end up trailing my way through shady backstreets until I find a shabby-looking office, where I pick up my exit stamp. An obviously destitute young girl then helps me by explaining in clear English what I need to do and where to go, not that I need this information now. She's very efficient; she tells me at which point I'll no longer need Guatemalan quetzals, and that it'll be pesos from there on. Dutifully, I give her my remaining loose change.

I eventually find the first checkpoint across a bridge on the Mexican side. It's all very seedy, and an anticlimax. I'd been hoping for the chance of a classic photograph, but can't see a 'Welcome to Mexico'-type sign that would have made a backdrop. It's all rather subdued here, but with thirty-seven kilometres to the next town, Tapachula, for now I'm looking for a place to sleep on the edge of town. I eventually come across a large truck park that is surrounded by a high wall and has armed guards on the gate. I give it a moment's thought, but then opt for a field nearby.

Friday, 31 August – Monday, 3 September 2001   **Tapachula**

Tapachula is a pleasant surprise – it's clean and more modern than I'm used to. But as a consequence, lodgings are expensive and the cheapest I find is 85 pesos (US$10) a night.

"The Beast—Its set up.

1 ltr water bottle (×2)

'LANDS END' water proofs

main kit + sleeping bag within rain cover

odd bits bag

tools, spare parts

bungy

washing kit

tent

'Kitchen':- pans, brew kit etc

food + water

tent

sleeping bag

roll mat

food + water

water bottles

water proofs

Kitchen

Kit Store

December 1998,
Argentina.

tent

sleeping bag

roll mat

Positioning of the kit/equipment on the Beast.

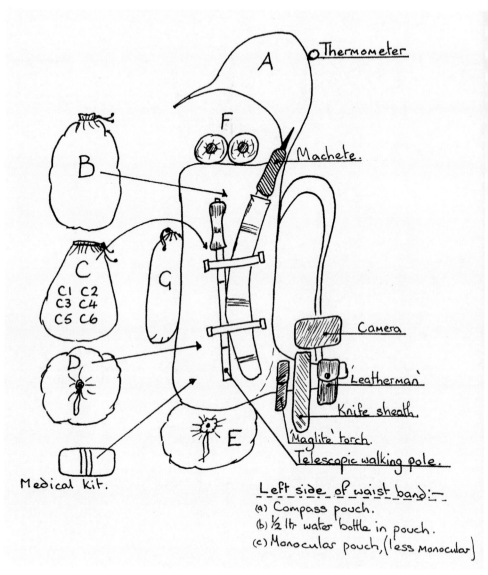

A · Thermometer

F

B

Machete.

C
C1 C2
C3 C4
C5 C6

G

Camera

D

'Leatherman'

Knife sheath.

E

'Maglite' torch.
Telescopic walking pole.

Medical kit.

Left side of waist band:—
(a) Compass pouch.
(b) ½ ltr water bottle in pouch.
(c) Monocular pouch, (less Monocular)

The equipment I carried after leaving the Beast, donkey and horse behind to climb over the Andes into Ecuador, September 2000.

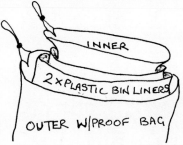

This was then placed inside the bergen and four 2 litre plastic bottles were slipped down the sides of the bergen and one at either end.

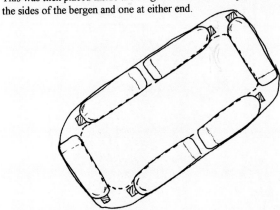

Riosucio. Drawings showing how I turned my rucksack into a flotation aid for the swim down the river, 31 January 2001.

I also used two 2 litre bottles under my 'Op's waistcoat' as flotation for myself, as well as four smaller bottles in the pouches.

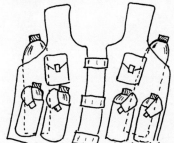

The end result worked perfectly, keeping my head and the top of my shoulders just out of the water.

Swimming down the River Atrato using floating debris to camouflage the rucksack and myself,
2 February 2001

Drawing of the very thickest part of the jungle, 9 February 2001.

THE ROAD PHASE.

HAIR DYED BLACK,
SKIN DARKENED.

CLOTHES RENDERED DOWN TO
LOOK LIKE THE REAL THING.
DYED WITH DYE, COFFEE,
BOOT POLISH & DIRT.

THERE IS ALSO A SURVIVAL
KIT & ESCAPE MAP SEWN
INTO THIS CLOTHING.

SMALL BAG TO KEEP
'DAY TO DAY' THINGS
HANDY.

RUCKSACK HIDDEN
BENEATH A 'RIG' OF
SACKS.

CONTAINS:-
JUNGLE KIT.
FOOD.
NEW BOOTS.

THE OLD PAIR OF
'ZAMBERLAN' BOOTS
CUT DOWN, BRUSHED BLACK,
FULL OF HOLES & LOOSE STITCHING.

The mode of dress I adopted when leaving Medellin to walk northwards up the road towards the Darien Gap, disguising myself (as best I could) as an itinerant. This was all discarded when I entered the jungle.

The equipment I carried through the jungle of the Darien Gap.

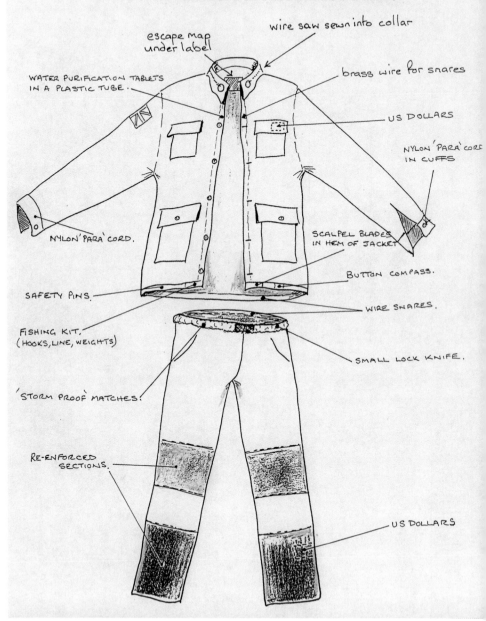

HIDDEN ESCAPE/SURVIVAL KIT
ITEMS SEWN INTO CLOTHING

escape map under label

wire saw sewn into collar

WATER PURIFICATION TABLETS IN A PLASTIC TUBE.

brass wire for snares

US DOLLARS

NYLON 'PARA' CORD IN CUFFS

NYLON 'PARA' CORD.

SCALPEL BLADES IN HEM OF JACKET

BUTTON COMPASS.

SAFETY PINS.

WIRE SNARES.

FISHING KIT. (HOOKS, LINE, WEIGHTS)

SMALL LOCK KNIFE.

'STORM PROOF' MATCHES.

RE-ENFORCED SECTIONS.

US DOLLARS

The emergency equipment sewn into my 'jungle uniform', which would give me a fighting chance of escape, and survival, if captured.

I sense I'm going to struggle in Mexico with money. On my first night in town I eat pizza and ice cream, which I immediately regret. I then find a place selling tamales, which are basically pasties made from maize with a scrap of meat or fruit in them. This is more like it. They're as cheap as it gets and I like them. From now on, I intend living on them.

I sit gloomily in the café, and what makes it worse is that it's the weekend. Long-legged Latin-looking beauties stroll past in high heels and short, tight skirts, blowing me kisses as they go on their way for a night out. It takes overwhelming self-control to sit it out. The walls of the café begin to close in around me and isolation starts to bite. I really do want to go out on a bit of a bender but just can't.

In two days, I've spent US$100. I just can't figure out how. I know I spent too long on the Internet, which is one of my favourite escapes. I also had some film developed as I couldn't wait to see the photographs – this has to stop. I replaced most of my consumables; the batteries, film, food, alcohol, soap, note pads and pen, and then paid to give my clothes a really good wash. That's all.

Once out in the countryside, the population thins out and Karl is able to find places to sleep without being stumbled upon by people all night. He also crosses a time zone and gains an hour, which means first light it is 06:30 and last light at about 19:30.

Roads running parallel with the Pacific coast are narrow and dangerous and he is sharing them with fast-moving heavy goods vehicles, coaches and minibuses. Once a coach comes whipping past, seemingly only millimetres from his sleeve. The small flap that covers the petrol cap has been left open, sticking out from the side at ninety degrees, and it catches Beast II with a terrific bang. This gives him a scare, as do the graphic close-up photographs of mutilated road accident victims that appear in all the newspapers on a daily basis. It rains a lot and his tent is leaking like a sieve.

Friday, 7 September 2001   Towards Tonala

I'm invited to stay by some people working at a quarry. One of these chaps is your stereotypical bandito from a spaghetti western. He's a big burly man with a huge drooping moustache and sounds like

Speedy Gonzales in the cartoons. Westerners assume all Mexicans sound like this but, in fact, it's only those who come from the north. I love listening to it, and sit there suppressing a chuckle.

The nightwatchman readies his fire for the evening and I'm surprised to see that he is only using three thick pieces of wood. As I watch he places the three large logs together end first. He then simply cuts slivers of the dry inner wood and fills in the gap between them. Putting a light to these wood chippings until they glow, he then leaves them to smoulder in the breeze, and before you know it they burst into flame. Every now and then he adds a few chippings and the whole lot burns steadily all night, as a thick layer of ash, surrounded by the glowing ends of the three logs, keeps it going, allowing him to heat a pot of coffee whenever he likes. It's an impressive lesson. Normally, getting a fire going in this weather is an arduous task.

Tuesday, 11 September 2001   Tonala

At about twenty-five kilometres, and after a long day, I finally reach Tonala. I need to take a good break here and get myself cleaned up. The roads are long and flat at present and you can watch cars disappear towards the horizon until they become dots that fade out in the heat haze. When I finally arrive in town, sometime in the mid-afternoon, my first move is to collapse in a small restaurant. The town itself is quite a small place and is basically a clone of most other Latin towns in Central America.

Once my eyes are back in focus I notice that the TV is showing a burning skyscraper in a large US city . . . Christ! That's New York. I strip off my equipment and just as I'm about to sit down, still watching the TV, a passenger airliner slams into a second tower, next to one that's already burning!! What the hell is going on? I stand stunned by this picture of a world gone mad. The TV news crew rabbits on in excited Spanish and I've not got a cat in hell's chance of figuring what's going on from them. I'm desperate to get more information, but it's hard to get the true picture at this end. I end up glued to the Internet.

Tuesday, 25 September 2001   **Towards Tangolunda**

I bump into three bike-borne Canadians – Rob, Trent and Debbie – heading for Chile. Four months into a year-long trip, they sit on the roadside with me for a couple of hours. They tell me of their days up in the Californian desert in July and August, where the temperature nudged the high forties, forcing them to cycle at night. It turns into a warm one here, but it appears things might get even hotter, as weather forecasts put the daily temperature at 39–40° C further north.

Towards the end of the day I come upon a stretch of road that takes me straight back to a time just north of Santiago, Chile. Exactly the same, with those low trees, cactus, rocks, a hint of sand and dead, yellowing grass. I feel my stomach twist with a sense of longing for a place I wish I could see again, but just for a while I feel as though I am back there and it gives me a rather strange buzz. It gets better as well because as I climb on to the high ground I've a breathtaking view. Both behind and to my front I can see the road disappearing off to the horizons laid out like one long ribbon. To my left, the land falls away into a vast expanse before reaching a lagoon and finally the sea. To my right, distant mountains fade into deepblue mist and the shadow of clouds. The view to my front is like looking at a postcard from northern Peru. It's almost creepy to see it again, like stepping back in time.

Wednesday, 26 September 2001   **Towards Tangolunda**

Off to my right, I see what appears to be a cloud of smoke, yet it's moving in a strange fashion. I stand still and watch this for a short while before it dawns on me that this isn't smoke – it's a huge swarm of bees. It is rolling across the desert towards me, but luckily, at the last moment, it sweeps past, its outside edge some six to nine metres to my front. Had I carried on walking instead of gawping at it I would have been consumed by the sinister cloud.

Sunday, 30 September 2001   **Towards Tangolunda**

I find a strange dead thing on the road today. I'm used to snakes, bats, crocodiles, dogs, sloths, skunks, foxes, huge lizards, turtles, possums and rats, but this one is a revelation, bringing back memories of a past life . . . it's a rabbit.

Back up on the high ground I have this marvellous view of the beaches and once again they scream temptation, however there's a swamp between me and paradise. Out to my right there are hills and what appear to be massive areas of wild bush. There is still a tropical feel to things. The place is crawling with huge bugs, flies, lizards of all sizes, frogs, monster car-eating spiders, plus snakes and scorpions.

Hmm . . . scorpions. Yesterday, I stopped for a Coke and was chatting to a group of rather loud taxi-drivers when one of them screamed and pointed at my rucksack. I glanced around and caught a glimpse of a scorpion's claws as it appeared on top of my sack . . . and it wasn't a small one! One chap brushed it off with his hand. It hit the ground and ran back towards my feet, where I stamped on it with my boot. It might have been living in my rucksack for several days.

Looking for somewhere to sleep I come across a track junction with a signpost indicating there's a restaurant down by the sea, a kilometre away. This is as close as I'll get, so what the hell. I rumble down the track of sand and stone, around the shoreline of a lagoon and then out and on to the coast. Here I locate the abandoned wreck of the restaurant. Nearby, I find a chap in his hammock amid a clutter of nets, fishing boats, six dogs, some crates and a mound of assorted rubbish. He is good enough to give me a bottle of pop from his shack. I decide to sleep up top, by the old restaurant. The fisherman disappears and leaves me to myself. So here I am with my own villa and a sandy beach. I strip off and go for a swim then lie for a while at the water's edge, watching the vultures overhead and the pelicans as they skim across the waves. Large frigate birds, their red throats inflated, soar above me, almost stationary in the air as they are held in the strong onshore breeze. It reminds me greatly of Chile.

Wednesday, 3 October 2001   Tangolunda

For about a week, I've noticed that the climate is changing. The first indication was an increase in cactus trees, due to the drier air. The webbing straps on my equipment also feel different, having turned oddly dry and stiff. They creak as if I'm on an old wooden ship. The salt stains have returned and my clothes are not always soaked through – now it's just around my waist and the top half of my body. When exertion causes me to breathe heavily, my open mouth is dry and I'm gagging for water.

Mexico is not as I had thought it would be. From the maps, I'd been expecting the coastal roads to run along the shoreline, like the roads in Chile, but they are set much further back. I also imagined there would be more desert, but I'm told this is confined to the very northern end of Mexico and, even then, there isn't much.

There's no habitation on the road at all now and my water runs out not long after midday. This is a nightmare as the temperature has just reached its peak. I'm in big trouble. With the sun feeling as if it's just six inches from my head, the heat is outrageous and is also reflected from the road, so I'm inhaling hot air.

At my twenty-kilometre point I come across a road junction with a sign indicating that the town of Tangolunda is four kilometres off the main road. The area around the road junction is an extremely well trimmed plot of land and at first I expect to find a café or something. There is grass, neatly clipped trees and hedgerows, but nothing else other than a large statue of the Virgin Mary.

I calm down and take a good look around. Clean new road signs, neatly trimmed, extremely green grass, flowerbeds and even a little island in the middle of the junction that has been landscaped with cactus plants and a pool of water . . . a pool of water. Where from? There has to be a standpipe. I drop my kit and search for it. Yes, found it – I help myself.

Sunday, 7 October 2001   Puerto Escondido

After only eight kilometres, I crest a hill and see Puerto Escondido arrayed before me on the coast. On the way down, through the palm trees and over the thatched roofs, I glimpse white surf and sandy beaches, complete with early-morning surfers. A Canadian stops me – he lives here and is running a few restaurants so I accept his invitation to have breakfast on the house.

I can see the attraction of this place and why it's full of gringos. It's also chock-a-block with some good-looking girls as well. Surfboards are parked everywhere and groups of gringos are just hanging out having a good time. But I'm merely an observer. I'm struck by an extreme feeling of loneliness and sense how far from all of this I really am. It may be an amazing beach and the biggest tourist attraction around, but I just feel like an outsider. I must leave it alone. I let it pass me by.

I decide to move out. That is until I feel sharp pains in my stomach indicating I'd better find a loo . . . fast. The nearest place turns out to be a restaurant just outside of the town. It seems as if my insides are in turmoil yet again, so I waste no time and take antibiotics straight away. It transpires this place is also a hotel. With that knowledge I'm in another battle with myself, one half reasoning that it would be a good idea if I just crash here for the night and by tomorrow the drugs will probably have got the infection under control and life will be a damn sight easier. After all, why suffer? To this the other half states the simple fact that I can't afford it.

I cave in. I've wasted half the day so, if I do leave now, I'll only get twenty kilometres. I may as well sit tight. The trouble is, the town below leaves me troubled, distant, bored, and lonely. I've no TV and the room is disturbingly silent. I become increasingly frustrated about everything and nothing. All I have going for me at the moment is the flame that gives me the impetus to keep walking and to survive. Some of the time it annoys the crap out of me. It's all happening nearby; fun, life in general and yet it may as well be a million miles away.

Friday, 12 October 2001   Towards Pinotepa Nacional

I'm on the road for 07:40 and moving well. I'm feeling happier as I've loosened the purse strings slightly, which means I'm able to keep my energy levels up. It costs but the world is a far better place and the distances seem to whizz by.

At the end of the day, I'm in the company of campesinos again in a small village. I'm invited to sit and drink with them but decline, just settling for water. The house has a backwoods feel – it's made of wood and mud bricks. Pigs, chickens and turkeys busy about us while the dogs declare war on the gringo. I sit with a rather large elderly lady, her big fat son and his friend, plus a cluster of kids aged five to eighteen. The son sports a large thick 'Mexican' moustache and has a pot belly that hangs over his shorts. His friend, who turns out to be a cousin, has a rusty old 9mm tucked into his belt. Apparently, he belongs to a group of vigilantes that protects the village.

An old man joins us. From what I can understand he employs a group of people who work in the fields and they are now standing crammed into the back of his pick-up, waiting patiently to be driven home. The old man stops for a drink, although it's quite apparent he's had a lot already. He wants to know why I'm here, having fun, when my country is at war. (Britain is backing the US in its ongoing invasion of Afghanistan.) I'm also asked how I expect to cross the US with the war going on? I have the feeling the locals seem to think this is World War Three, and I get questions to that effect.

Sunday, 14 October 2001   Pinotepa Nacional

My cousin, Jason Metcalfe, is due to arrive in Acapulco on the eighteenth on a cruise ship – he's the gift shop manager. Unfortunately, I must be at least a week away, as it's more than 200 kilometres from here. Jason rings my hotel on the Thursday and tells me he's only got eight hours ashore so there's no way we'll be able to meet up (it's four and a half hours on a bus from Acapulco). That's a damn shame, but he tells me he's going to leave some money for me with someone he knows in the town. I explain that it was my intention to pass around Acapulco as it's obviously well out of my price range, however he insists I have to see it and so will leave me some money to help. What a guy!

I expect a blazing email from Father wanting to know why I'm spending so much. At the moment I'm eating well and consequently moving well and life is not filled with pain, suffering and misery . . . but somebody, somewhere has to pay. I've already been here longer than I planned and have spent more than I should have, leaving myself short for the trip to Acapulco . . . well short. I'm as depressed as hell again, and not looking forward to setting out tomorrow, which isn't normal for me. I begin to feel that there isn't a lot to look forward to any more, just the same old hot road.

As I lie here on the bed, watching the squeaking ceiling fan slowly rotate, I start to dream. I might end up somewhere back along the road in the deserts or in the jungle. I yearn for the clear pools of water in the dry riverbeds in the middle of the Darien. Or sometimes it's the villages of Paya or Pucuro, a couple of the most tranquil places I've ever known. Right now these memories are the only thing that seem to save me from complete despair.

Monday, 22 October 2001   **Towards Cruz Grande**

Yesterday I crossed the state border from Oaxaca to Guerrero. It was marked by a military checkpoint, where they shuffled through my passport and kit before allowing me to continue. The roads smell of death, with rotting corpses everywhere. Not only dogs but horses, cows and donkeys, which are all allowed to wander quite freely.

I'm back down from the hills so find myself returned to a green tunnel of high vegetation that encroaches on the road on both sides. This makes for some pretty scary moments on blind bends. Mexican drivers have two speeds . . . fast and faster. There are many pick-up trucks loaded with people literally hanging from the edge, with gritted teeth and wide white eyes. I can see the look of terror on drivers' faces as they come whipping around a corner and notice me.

This explains all the carrion. Around here a decaying large animal will simply melt into a pool of black goo, and the smell is totally overpowering. I always seem to find a nasty one when I'm gasping uphill. A few good lungfuls and it's a real fight not to vomit.

At midday, I find water at the base of a steep cliff face. Looking upwards, I stare straight into the eyes of a coyote, all reddish-brown with patches of silver-grey and a long, slender jawline. I've seen a good number of them in this area, but a lot more just recently. I guess they live off the roadkills.

Wednesday, 24 October 2001   **Cruz Grande**

I must reach Cruz Grande, where I'm told there's a cash dispenser. It's a long day – thirty-eight kilometres so I get a wriggle on. It's difficult to see many similarities but since September 11, people keep calling me 'Bin Laden'. I guess they're a bit short of information from the outside world and I suppose I do look a bit odd. I've long hair, a strange coat, chest webbing and a face full of hair. I get it everywhere I go and the locals think it's oh so funny. Campesinos don't ask me where I'm going because it's obvious – I'm a gringo so I must be heading for Acapulco.

A favourite enquiry is 'Why is he dressed like Bin Laden?' This is usually followed by 'Why is he selling ice cream . . .?' 'If it's not ice cream then what is he selling . . .?' and 'Why else would he be pulling a cool-box if he isn't selling ice cream . . .?'

It's kind of odd, but you associate 'Aaahhh, gringo!' with Mexicans, however from the first day I arrived here in Mexico I've been referred to mostly as 'Quado', meaning 'Whitey'.

Cruz Grande is a grotty little town of 12,000 souls. Having found the cash machine, I decide to clean up and crash in a hotel. I'm charged 100 pesos for the night, then as I'm still standing at the desk, the next people to come along – some Mexicans – are charged 60 pesos for the room next to mine. I go to war. I kick up one hell of a fuss and I'm given 20 pesos back, which is the best I can do. Gringos are obviously considered rich pickings; they will blatantly overcharge you. I bet I've been turned over a few times before already. It's endemic here.

Sunday, 28 October 2001   Acapulco

Total distance to date: 8830 miles (14,219 km)
I gasp my way up and up until I eventually stand atop the hills gazing down upon a city of high-rise hotels and palm trees, and Acapulco bay's blue waters with two cruise ships at anchor. Now it's down, down to the seafront to begin my hunt for as cheap a place as possible. I get shunted all over but have little luck and become quite tired. I also pick up a lot of strange looks from people, who just don't know how to take me. As far as everyone is concerned I'm a tourist, having just arrived by the plane or boat. What's with the ice cream-Bin Laden thing, man?

By late afternoon I come across a place in the back streets that charges 120 pesos (US$12). I'm sure I could find somewhere cheaper, but I've had enough for one day. I'm forced to strip Beast II down in order to get it in. It's not bad though, and well placed with an

Internet café in the next street, and only two blocks from the seafront and a huge shopping mall and most of the supermarkets.

Waiting for me at the Internet café is a message from Jason.

'Sorry, but could not leave any money as no one would take responsibility for it.'

Bollocks! Oh well, I'll stay for a day or two. I'll keep myself to myself and stay away from the shops, beach and a world of miniskirts, high heels and legs, as well as a collection of some of the best-looking girls you're likely to see. I take a look at the beach, with its jet skis, cruise boats and parascending, but don't go back.

The cleaning woman hands me my washed laundry.

'Why, thank you very mu—' My jaw drops . . . I'm about to go loco down in Acapulco.

My 'pilgrim's' coat (my extended walking shirt), is now a most delightful two-tone combination – white on the top half while the lower half is now bright pink!! A vision flashes through my head of me setting about her with the garden furniture outside my door. Instead, I duly pay her.

Tomorrow, I'll soak my shirt in an attempt to bleach out some of the colour. I can't see Bin Laden wearing pink.

ACAPULCO

On Mexico's Pacific Riviera, it is the ultimate beach resort and a magnet to the rich and famous, many of whom have holiday homes here. Its curved bay and harbour are among the most beautiful in the world. It's an expensive city. The glitzy parts are a different world from the squalid streets, dirty hotels and crowded shops and buses, which are only two minutes' walk away.

Friday, 9 November 2001   **Beyond Petatlan**

Beyond the coastal town of Petatlan, I'm mobbed by a pack of barking dogs. Taking a swing at one, I catch the toe of my boot on the tarmac and tear the sole from the upper. Now this is a bit of a disaster. The sole has come off from halfway but is still held on by the heel. I push on regardless to the next small village, my sole slapping about like a crocodile's jaws. I've still got a long way to go before I get my next pair in the re-supply at Manzanillo so I must do a running repair with an all-purpose glue.

Back on the move and the boots are fine and by the end of play I reach a string of villages. Having been laughed at in Petatlan and having had a plastic Coke bottle bounce off me from a passing bus, I'm not in the most diplomatic of moods when two more dickheads think they'll have a laugh at my expense.

'Where's the war gringo? Ha ha ha,' one calls out.

'C'mon, let's go fight a war, ha ha ha,' shouts his chum.

I assume their remarks are prompted by the way I'm dressed. Dropping Beast II, I start walking back towards them. Make no mistake, I'm itching for a fight. The two suddenly grasp that things aren't quite so funny any more, as I swiftly start and finish my own minor war on the roadside. On reflection, I overreacted and these poor blokes weren't to blame. I leave the scene feeling I haven't helped myself. It is not a smart move to make enemies in these parts and these two will probably run me over in a truck in a day or two. I must exercise a little more self-control.

Sunday, 11 November 2001   Beyond Petatlan

On the road, two men come sprinting out of the bush towards me armed with sticks. I have very little time and almost in panic pull my machete . . . only to find that the two young blokes are pissing about chasing one another. Christ Almighty! The adrenalin still pumping, I replace my machete with trembling hands. I then begin to think about what would happen should I swing for someone on a dark night and do some real harm, or even kill them. I'd no doubt end up going down for manslaughter, be it in self-defence or not. I think I'll give consideration to getting a baseball bat. Giving somebody a good whack with that or splitting them in half with a machete may make all the difference in the eyes of the jury.

Tuesday, 13 November 2001   Lazardo Cardenas

Lazardo Cardenas is just your average run-of-the-mill Latin town. I get myself a room for 80 pesos (US$10) – it's not bad, with a toilet and shower – and enjoy a shave and clean-up, before getting something to eat. I invest US$10 in a lightweight, portable personal defence system (baseball bat). It may just be worth it one day.

There's black news from Mother. It appears her job is in jeopardy as the workers at the factory where she works have been given notice that it will be closing. A good number of the workers have been making small weekly donations to the expedition and this has obviously been a vital source of income. Bad news for Mum, and the rest of the workers of course, but with a knock-on effect that my only permanent source of money is about to dry up . . . now what?

I lie awake barely able to sleep. What's going to happen? How bad could it get? This loose arrangement with my mother's workmates – they chip in a little each week to keep me going – has been going on for more than two years now. It's been a lifesaver but I suppose I've been waiting for it to break down for whatever reason. Now that the factory is closing, putting my mother and her friends out of work, I wonder how they must be feeling? This is just bad news all round.

Wednesday, 21 November 2001　　　　Beyond Lazardo Cardenas

Still tracing the ocean, by the end of the day I climb a cliff top where there's a shack of a restaurant. I crash-land, panting like a dog. Once I've calmed down I order fried fish as it's only 25 pesos, which is as cheap as it gets. It's one hell of a view from up here. I'm looking southwards out to sea.

The fish duly arrives and I tuck in, quite enjoying it. That is until I get about halfway through – I'm suddenly wracked with pain. A damn fish bone lodges itself in my throat . . . bloody hell! It won't budge! Every time I attempt to swallow it's as though someone's cutting my throat. Oh, Christ! Now I try not to draw attention to myself but that's quite hard as, believe me, it's extremely painful. In desperation, I fill my mouth with food then swallow . . . bloody hell! My eyes are full of tears and whatever it is, it's still stuck fast . . . shit! There's nothing else for it.

'Er, excuse me, can I have some salt, please?' I rasp.

I take the small plastic bowl of salt to the balcony that hangs over the edge of the cliff. Now drooling with saliva because I can't swallow, I'm attracting some attention. Other diners watch, obviously bemused because I'm forcing salt into my mouth. It has the desired effect and my face turns inside out . . . yet I don't vomit. Bugger this – more salt perhaps? I gulp a second larger helping. Yep, here it comes.

There's a slight pause, followed by a wonderful display of projectile barfing off the balcony and out to sea, which, thankfully, takes the obstruction with it. I'm consumed by a wave of relief, which is spoilt somewhat by the fact that the barfing continues for another couple of goes. Apologising, I have to explain to the baffled chef, with my extremely sore throat, that it's not his cooking.

Thursday, 22 November 2001   Beyond Lazardo Cardenas

I'm back in the hills again. It's late in the day before I find a place that sells drinks. I ran out of water earlier and have been suffering somewhat, so I put two Cokes away before being forced to buy some bottled water because the place won't give me any from the tap. I ask how far it is to the next village and almost choke when he says it's sixty kilometres. I check out the map . . . worse still, it's all uphill and I feel my heart sink.

I continue along these roller-coaster roads. Reaching the foot of one of the climbs, I rest with head in hands. I just don't feel as though I can make this bitch of a climb right now. I've nothing in me, I'm all burnt out. It's been one helluva day and I've got no option but to get on with it. It takes a good while, well over an hour in fact, to make the six-kilometre climb.

Once over the crest, I lie out in the road and gaze skyward like a dead ant. I can't even have a good slurp, as I need what little I have for tonight. I just want to sleep.

Then a passing car stops, clearly concerned that a gringo is lying face-up in the road.

'You all right?' asks the driver.

Without sitting up, I incline my head to see white people with blonde hair. At first I assume they're foreign tourists but in fact it turns out that they're a cosmopolitan Mexican couple, obviously quite well-to-do as they're in a shiny four-wheel drive. They speak a little English.

'Do you have any water?' I croak, still barely moving from the horizontal.

They hand me a litre of bottled water. Result! This is what I need to do from now on – just play dead in the road. I gaze at them through red, watery eyes and give them a pained smile.

'Keep it, drink it all,' they offer.

This is good news. At least now I don't have to kill them for it.

Saturday, 24 November 2001   Towards Manzanillo

In the late afternoon, can I buggery find anywhere to camp? It's a well-populated stretch with evenly spaced farmhouses and roadside shacks and full of one-eyed campesinos with three-legged dogs. Everywhere I look I'm being watched, and a motorcycle cruises slowly past me a couple of times looking me over. This place is definitely giving me the creeps.

In a bit of dead ground, I cut off into some scrub. It's thick with thorns and a real pain in the arse, but it offers good cover. I can't think anyone will notice I'm here if they haven't seen me coming in. No such luck. A family group of about twenty people pass by with their bundles and, of course, it is the children in the party who spot me.

After a little while, two older kids arrive on bikes, locate me and then disappear, which is, I guess, a reconnaissance mission. For whom, I wonder? I soon find out. At last light a pick-up pulls in sharply from the road and men in black are leaping into the bush. I hear weapons being cocked as they converge on my position. It's the police. Of course, they have to come when I'm halfway through my pan of pasta, so I sit and wait to see what they do.

'Out . . . where we can see you . . . all of you!' is the command.

As I leave the tent, five M16s are trained on me from all about. I can't help but smile, my mouth half full of pasta.

'Who else?' someone barks.

'No one, just little old me,' I respond.

One of the more expendable of these heroes is commanded to go forward and scan the tent. He does so, M16 first. Another goes with him as they creep forward and slowly one of them reaches forward with his left hand, tentatively fingering the camouflaged sheet over Beast II. His comrade stands close by, M16 in the shoulder. It's getting fairly dark now and quite hard to see, yet no one has thought to bring a torch along. I just stand, spooning pasta into my mouth.

On balance, I certainly would not have come storming in here as they did. They could have taken me by surprise rather than coming in accompanied by screeching brakes and cocking rifles. Those should have been 'made ready' (cocked) well before they got here. There is then a series of routine questions and a lecture about how unsafe it is to camp near the roads around here. I'm advised to use the hotels on the beaches. Yeah, right, as if. They tell me this is a dangerous place and if I stay here it will not be their responsibility if anything happens to me. They decide to leave me, but not before one fool decides to unload there and then, and ejects a 5.56mm round on to the ground . . . where it's too dark to find it.

Now that this is over I'm left feeling very insecure. Every nutter for miles around will soon know I'm here. But rather than move I decide to upgrade the defences. There are four ways into my area, three of them through the wood. Two of these approaches are quite open and anyone could move along them almost silently. I therefore rig up bent-over thorn bushes across the tracks, which if 'released' will spring back noisily. Seeking out everything that is dead or dry, I throw armfuls of twigs and branches on likely approach routes. If anyone attempts to get near me now I'll know. Next to me, between the tent and the field, is a wire fence. I cut the bottom strand of this and remove it so that I can come straight out of my tent, under the fence and into the field. As far as anyone coming from the field is concerned, you have to scale the fence first and I've arranged a good number of nasty thorn trees on top of this.

Thursday, 29 November 2001   Manzanillo

Total distance to date: 9306 miles (14,985 km)

I expect problems with my visa as it runs out tomorrow. I bet I can't get it sorted here and consequently they will send me to Mexico City – that's a twenty-six-hour round bus trip. It has to be said, I have a pessimistic head on at the moment, but that's the way life here has made me. I arrive at about 10:30 and I check my email. A distraught Catty informs me that they turned down her visa application yet again. This is the last thing on earth I need to hear right now.

Immigration is on the second floor of a large government building. Inside, naval officers stroll to and fro in crisp white uniforms, carrying black briefcases and with ID tags roped around their necks. I hand over my passport to a girl behind the desk and ask about extending my visa. I'm delighted to find out that I can, thank God! A group of three girls then busy themselves going through my passport, and also get a look at my infamous newspaper cuttings.

I get an audience with Blanca Leticia Escoto Gonxalex, who is in charge. A cheery middle-aged woman, she sits on her throne with a baby in her arms who belongs to a second woman – a Canadian – who's sat in front of the desk.

'Come in, come in,' says the queen bee. 'Tell us about your walk, young man.'

I do and she seems very impressed.

'Look!' she beams, 'a new baby born here in Mexico.'

The baby's mother now lives here and as we chat her husband and family arrive. The family have lived in Britain for a large part of their lives, in fact they've only recently moved here and have opened a restaurant in a beach town not far north.

By now I've attained celebrity status with the staff.

'Get this man a new visa!' orders the boss, and before I know it we're all posing for photographs, someone has rung a local radio station and I'm giving an interview over the phone, live, in Spanish.

Realising that my visa extension lasts only three months, and it will take me at least four months to reach the US, Blanca has a letter drawn up requesting authorities to help me out if there's a problem or when I next need a visa. Yes! The Canadians extend an invitation to stop over at their restaurant, Romeo's, in Melaque (only sixty-one kilometres north), for a good meal and a bit of a rest. Wow! It's all working out just fine, then.

Discovering that I intend to cross the US border at Nogales, Blanca's eyes light up again.

'My son lives there!' she announces. She gets straight on her mobile to her son, Basich Escoto, a civil engineer living on the American side of town but who is working on the Mexican side. She passes the telephone over to me and I speak to him for a short while, and again I'm invited to stay when I reach the border. He even extends the invitation to my family if they wish to meet me there.

Despite all this good fortune I still find myself back at the hotel sitting in deep depression, staring at my feet, still with the weight of the world on each shoulder. I just can't get Catty out of my head. There remains only one option . . . that I fly down to see her in Colombia.

Back in Guatemala she'd offered to pay for my ticket. I was prepared then to give it a go, and as far as I was concerned it doesn't compromise the spirit of my journey although I'm not sure what others might think. But the way I'm feeling right now, I don't give a big rat's arse about what other people might think. Red tape and increasing air fares mean that I will soon be out of range so I must act now.

She's been the focus of so much for so long. Every night I spend alone, every testing moment, Catalina has been my escape route and offers hope. I'm not prepared to let her slip into history so easily. Logistically, I can leave my kit with my new-found Canadian friends in Melaque, which is a few days' north of here, so this is indeed a rare opportunity. Yes, I'm uneasy with the idea of back-tracking but there's little doubt in my own mind that an escape for a little while is what I need.

With plans to visit Catty beginning to come together, Karl leaves Manzanillo on 5 December. Beast II looks impressive with new The North Face and Zamberlan company logos and his home-made Union flags. A day later he arrives in Melaque, where he finds Romeo's restaurant and his Canadian friends, Luke and Anna, who feed him and give him a room with a view in their three-storey house. Here he locks away Beast II and his kit, takes the bus back to Manzanillo and catches another for Mexico City and an onward flight to Medellin via Panama City. He stays with Catty until mid-January, before returning to Melaque.

Tuesday, 15 January 2002   Melaque

Melaque is teeming with Canadian tourists, nearly all from a place called Salt Springs, an island off British Columbia. Despite all these English-speaking voices I feel subdued and cannot converse with anyone. Many times I'm asked what's wrong as I spend most of my time staring into space. But that's just me. Catty occupies my thoughts and the fact that I'm about to embark on 'Year Four' also plays on my mind.

It is worth noting that last year, fifteen days after I'd passed through Mutata on the Medellin to Turbo road (which I used on my way to the Darien Gap), all the towns along the stretch were attacked in a large FARC offensive. This year I left Catty and Medellin on the same date as the previous year, and on that day a three-year peace deal between the FARC and the government broke down. Government troops have moved in to take over an area the size of Switzerland that had been ceded to the FARC as a concession for them attending peace talks. The FARC have now withdrawn into the hills and Colombia is bracing itself for the inevitable response.

Karl hits the road on 17 January. After a month in the cool climate of Medellin, he struggles to re-acclimatise to the extreme heat, high humidity and no rain. Although the roads have fairly decent surfaces, the route takes him into hilly country and the climbs are steep and demanding. The traffic is light, mainly consisting of holidaymakers on their return leg to Canada and the US. He's gone 'soft'. For the first few days, he endures sore feet and bad blisters and must kick-start the healing process. When he camps on the nail-hard ground, he doesn't get much sleep and the nights are cold.

On Friday, 25 January, he drops into the Bay of Banderas and the town of Puerto Vallarta – a haven for rich tourists with its palm-fringed drives, expensive hotels and private condos.

Saturday, 26 January 2002   Puerto Vallarta

I'm stopped by a man who, at first, I take for a rich tourist. Jose Luna is a well-spoken, middle-aged Mexican and drives an amazing Audi Sports TT, a most beautiful car. Very interested in what I'm doing – he says he's a keen traveller – he invites me to stay at his place, which just so happens to be right where I'm due to end the day anyway.

Jose's house absolutely blows me away. Set in wonderful gardens, with palm trees and flowers, it boasts a swimming pool and jacuzzi. There are also workshops and a tennis court, as well as three other cars in the driveway. I am given a room in an annex and have my own shower and loo, as well as an amazing view out across the bay. What can one say?

Next day, we hit the beach. There's Jose's wife, his two sons and two friends of theirs, Canadians from the Yukon they'd met travelling. The family squeeze me into a spare wetsuit for a spot of sub-aqua. I remember I'd been down to thirty-five metres when I did a bit of diving way back in my Northern Ireland days . . . although the water was a tad colder than the Pacific Ocean. Out among the reefs it's an amazing world, full of coloured tropical fish. Stingray, pufferfish and angelfish, in fact, you name it, it's down here. We spend hours in the water and someone bags a lobster and some fish for supper.

Before I turn in, Jose gives me 2000 pesos (US$200), the most anyone has ever given to me on the road. What can I say? He has also printed twenty Goliath Expedition T-shirts for me in his silkscreen printing room, where they make T-shirts advertising his restaurants. Blow me, I only go and leave them behind.

Wednesday, 30 January 2002   **Towards San Blas**

For a moment, I think I've gatecrashed a Saga holiday. Around noon, I pull into a small village café to find it's full of elderly Canadian women, more than thirty of them, along with some others from the US. They've gathered together in their motor homes from various trailer parks to form a ladies' convoy that is heading north. It seems to be the done thing as a number of convoys have passed me today, almost all of them bearing Canadian window-stickers. The noise these old girls are making is deafening. Their voices are far louder and higher pitched than those of Latin people. It's like sitting among roosting seabirds . . . a nest site of gibbering gannets . . . and everyone is wearing name-tags.

They're very nice to me. In the end I'm almost dragged to my feet and made to address the group, explaining my trip to whoops and applause. This is followed by a whip-round and they take a lot of photos. I am presented with a bread basket full of money – notes and coins – which comes to just over US$50. Good God! I'm loaded, and have never had so much money in my pockets. I even have to tighten my belt to ensure that my trousers will hold up under the weight of the coins. I'm now carrying US$300. What a cracking start to the New Year.

Thursday, 31 January 2002   **Towards San Blas**

Where the road divides, I take the more minor-looking option. It traces the coast but it means that I will avoid some extremely steep climbs that the major route has in store. This will take me to San Blas, a place renowned for its midges and an old Spanish fortress.

My new road looks minor but at least it's tarmacked and I'm pleased to say there's little traffic, mostly just stuff from the local farms. Just beyond some dotted houses, I notice an open quarry that is nearly hidden from view above the road. I decide to pull in for the night at this rather dusty site.

With their built-in radar, some children soon find me. It's been a while now since I've had much trouble from the rustics; I don't get the stares and constant annoying presence because there are a good number of gringos about and I'm not a novelty. But now, away from the popular places, I'm the best thing these kids have ever found. The cry goes out . . . gringooooo!! . . . and kids begin to flock into the area and, ten deep, place me under surveillance.

Soon they start to dare one another to run closer and shout. This starts to get a bit wearing. Then, suddenly a rock hits the tent, thrown from down on the road. Right, that's it, I decide and I undo the tent fly net to put on my boots. Just as I stick my napper out . . . smack! It takes a few moments before I come to and gather my senses. I put my hands to my face then find them covered in blood. The rock struck me just left of my nose above my lip and it's streaming with blood.

'Little bastards!' I yell.

I am never going to know which one of them threw the stone, so decide to take my revenge on the whole hamlet. Quickly throwing on my boots I'm off, baseball bat in hand, screaming down the track and across the road where I surprise two women standing next to a pick-up truck.

'Where are they? Where are all the little bastards? I'm going to eat every one of them,' I bellow.

Now it has to be said that the appearance, apparently from nowhere, of a wide-eyed screaming foreign devil, covered in blood and waving a baseball bat, is fairly alarming to say the least. Sure enough, it terrifies these two. They freeze in horror and then simultaneously burst into tears. I spare them, and move on down a second track to where I find a man with a heavy sack on his shoulders.

'Where are those kids? You'd better find them, and you'd better tell them good!' I bluster, now waving my bat in his face. The terrified man stumbles backwards.

'If I see them again I'll beat them to pulp! If anyone bothers me again tonight I'll kill 'em!' I continue.

Raving away in a mix of Spanish punctuated by the appropriate English swear words I make my point by slamming my bat into the racks on the back of his truck.

'Do you understand me? . . . NO MORE STONES! In fact, not one squeak! . . . Go on, tell them.'

'Yes . . . yes!' he says, lowering his sack and making his way down the track without it.

I start to make my way back to the tent, blood dripping from my face. I pass my two original victims who stoop in a huddle, still bawling their eyes out. Christ! I'm hopping mad, that stone really hurt. After my completely over-the-top performance I know there will be little chance of any more problems. A couple of minutes later I see the pick-up pull off with a number of children sobbing away in the back.

The rock has put two holes in my face, but it isn't as bad as it had looked once I've cleaned it up. It's at that point I discover I've split my bat right down the middle . . . Aaarrrgh!

Friday, 1 February 2002   Los Cocos

Before the end of play, two guys stop me. One of them has a thick white beard and deep, piercing eyes and looks just like Gandalf. I soon sense that I'm dealing with God-fearing hillbillies. They're from Washington State and staying down at a place sixteen kilometres from here on the coast, at the beautiful Los Cocos beach. I get an invitation to stay overnight and this suits me as I'm about right at the end of my day anyway.

The place they're staying at is a run-down hotel, the Dolphin. Gandalf (I forget his real name) is living here with his wife until they can get a place of their own.

'Just wanna place for ma chickens 'n critters,' he drawls. His critters are, I gather, a horse and donkey.

His wife is a rather large lady with white hair, pale skin and super-bright red lipstick who speaks even more slowly. They tell me they have moved to Mexico because the US has lost the Lord. Here, I'm told, they can spread the 'good word' because the people have open hearts and will listen. I refrain from arguing or letting on I'm not persuaded and just continue to listen.

'Ya know how ya got this far, don't ya? . . .only with the Lord's blessing!' he pronounces.

A blank look from me.

'So who ya gonna give the credit to when ya done?' he asks.

'Er?'

'Who ya gonna give the credit to?' he repeats, in a deep, booming voice, while staring into my eyes. I imagine some might find him intimidating, but his fire and brimstone act is falling on stony ground.

'I'll think about it,' I reply.

I'm kipping in a concrete compound in an abandoned building next to the hotel, which is fine by me as it's nice and secure, plus Gandalf is kindly paying for my supper.

Others are holed up at the Dolphin. This evening, once I'm established in my compound, I'm invited up to Gandalf's room for a chat. When his wife lets me in I'm almost brought to my knees by an overpowering cloud of dope as six others inside puff away on reefers and pipes; a 'boho' couple, two lads who work for or help Gandalf, his hillbilly mate and his wife. Tonight's topics range far and wide, from local issues – planting, chickens, crops and irrigation – to world politics. Everything good of course somehow boils down to the grace and will of our Lord, to which everyone repeats 'Hallelujah, Hallelujah, yes sir indeed, Hallelujah.' I'm offered a smoke but decline. I sleep well.

Monday, 4 February 2002   **Towards Mazatlan**

Rejoining the main highway 15, I now have 70mph, long-distance heavy freight trucks and coaches to concern me again as I walk facing the oncoming traffic. The last few hours of the day seem worst. Unlike the winding hilly stretches, which meant traffic had to slow, now there's nothing to prevent these convoys from passing me at top speed. Worse still, I've no room to get out of the way.

When a convoy passes, it's the second, third or fourth vehicle that worries me most as they drive right up each other's arses. Sure, the guy in the front vehicle sees me and swings wide but the guy in the second truck has no idea nor have those behind him, giving them a fraction of a second to react. I'm sometimes forced to jump or I'll certainly get hit. I've got weeks on these roads. I'm a gibbering wreck.

Wednesday, 6 February 2002   Towards Mazatlan

I have a closer than usual shave, but this time with a group of cars. The first vehicle moves out to go around me, but leaves it until the last second, consequently number two, who is virtually clinging to the first vehicle's bumper, gets a shock and has to swerve sharply. This means number three hits his brakes and swerves, while number four careers off the road on to the rough . . . and straight towards me. In my mind's eye, I have this image of frozen faces twisted and distorted in terror as the driver fights for control. Veering towards me, the car then swerves violently back on to the road in a cloud of dust, screeching tyres and scattered gravel. How did it miss me?

Wednesday, 13 February 2002   Towards Mazatlan

This is easily the worst day on record. Time and time again I'm almost scraped by convoys of heavy traffic, with one group coming head on and another from behind. There is a steep drop of over a metre next to the road so it's a poor escape route.

Before midday, a two-trailer, twenty-four-wheeler (or more, I really wasn't counting), packing some real weight, is approaching and, again, the driver doesn't see me. At the last moment, its wheels lock and it starts to skew sideways towards me like a block of flats, billowing smoke and scarring thick black lines of rubber along the road's surface. I hear squealing brakes from the cars, trucks and coaches behind it as everything judders to a halt.

It's mayhem but no one has been hit. Head down and shaking, I keep walking, weaving my way around the lorry and the other vehicles parked at crazy angles behind it. Two children, scared senseless, are sobbing in the back of one car and are comforted by their mother.

Almost on top of them, is a large, long-distance coach . . . people are going mad and I'm taking a lot of flak. I wonder how I've survived this far. It only takes just one of these drivers to have been on the road for too many hours, to be nodding off at the wheel . . . I'd be a goner.

This evening, I sit just inside the tent, chopping away at my vegetables and mulling over my near misses. I pause and find I'm looking into the eyes of a large grey hawk that is sitting on top of Beast II. Hunched, with its head pulled back into its body, it glares in at me with bright, sharp eyes. It remains like this for about twenty seconds as if waiting for me to move. Then, using the breeze, it stretches out its wings and lifts effortlessly into the air and over my tent.

Thursday, 14 February 2002   Towards Mazatlan

I'm ten kilometres from Mazatlan when I wave to a cyclist on the other side of the road, who is heading in the same direction as me but with the flow of traffic. He is clad in a helmet and Lycra shorts, riding a flash super-lightweight racing cycle. He gives me the thumbs up then clenched fist as he passes. He obviously views this road in a similar way to me.

Just three hundred metres or so later, I crest a hill and there he is again. Only now he's on his side, off the road, surrounded by a group of concerned bystanders. His bicycle is twisted and smashed beyond recognition. Nearby is the coach that I presume is responsible for taking him out.

The people, some of them from the coach, place a jacket under his head. The police arrive, don't seem in a rush to do much, and just stand about scratching their heads. I go over and take a look at my friend. As it turns out he's in reasonable nick, conscious and well aware of his state. He tells me it's just his left arm and shoulder, and there appears to be little else wrong. The police decide that as they are so close to town they will call an ambulance rather than attempt to lift him into the pick-up . . . a good move at last.

Karl arrives in the swirling city of Mazatlan, overlooking Olas Atlas Bay, on 15 February. It's expensive here. Not intending to stay very long, his fortunes improve when he meets Jose Roberto, the sports section editor of Noroeste. *Very interested in his story, the editor even finds him a place to stay. As a consequence, two full-page pieces appear while he is here – one in* Noroeste *and another in* El Sol. *When he leaves on 21 February, he camps for the night, as near as damn it, on the Tropic of Cancer, reminding him of when he crossed the Capricorn line in Antofagasta, Chile. He begins to notice that the air feels drier and the humidity lower and his clothes have a strange 'plastic' feel to them as they begin to stiffen up.*

Saturday, 23 February 2002   Beyond Mazatlan

It's a hot one today. So much so that all the black plastic buckles on my kit are starting to soften up and Beast II's aluminium frame is too hot to touch. This road is quite quiet, just a steady trickle of traffic, so I'm not dicing with death. There's little shade to be had as there are no trees near the road, however I do find I can rest out of the sun beneath small flyovers built for local campesino traffic. It's nice just to be able to lie out in the cool shade and gaze skyward into the deep-blue vastness, with only the odd vulture, swift or even frigate bird crossing my field of view. I didn't realise just how large frigate birds are until I'd watched them buzzing the small fishing boats down south. Giant flying machines, they cut a menacing figure in the air.

Being relatively close to the sea, I get the benefit of a cool breeze most of the time. I've had a slow puncture for a while now and it has never really bothered me as I just used to pump up the tyre every morning. Unfortunately today it's going down somewhat faster so I've had to cut the day short to fix it. Anyway, I find a nice spot to camp, from where I can just see the sea.

Tonight I'm happy – there's not a biting bug to the found. I'm out of my tent and sitting in the darkness where I stargaze in the cool air. It's a three-quarter moon, which means a bright night, but the stars still shine like you never did see, with tall cactus silhouetted against them. Now and again the shadow of an owl will glide silently past against this starry backdrop. On the seaward horizon, I can see small pinpricks of light from ships and along the road north I can watch the tail-lights of trucks passing down the valley before climbing the hill and disappearing. This is what I've been missing.

Thursday, 28 February 2002 **Culiacan**

Total distance to date: **9835 miles (15,837 km)**

Culiacan is the capital of Sinaloa State. It's a large city, so large that I was thinking seriously about missing it, as I have to detour to get there. All the same, money and food, as well as email, are waiting for me and I think I ought to make a big effort with the regional press.

Outside the editorial offices of *El Debate*, I get talking to a man who has also been in there. He's Carlos, and seems like a pleasant chap as, after a while, he offers me a place to stay. He lives in the suburbs, in a humble home with his extremely pregnant second wife, who is due to go into hospital on the following Tuesday. It's a Caesarean job, so a case of coming ready or not. I get to sleep in the concrete shell of a spare house that Carlos is also renting at present. It's rough but I soon square it up.

Carlos is a working-class Mexican with little money to spare, but seems happy with life. He does PR for local would-be politicians and arranges press conferences, and he's keen to set something up for me. I take it with a pinch of salt, although by the following day, he has a list of twenty local journalists from the national TV, press and radio to call. He's the real thing. He intends to invite them to a spot in the city centre outside the cathedral where press conferences are held.

On Saturday I meet Carlos's eldest son from his first marriage, Carlo, and Carlo's friend, both of whom are pilots in the Mexican air force, flying counter-drugs surveillance ops. Mexico has very little in the way of an air force; like the rest of Mexico's armed forces, it has no real offensive capability, acting more as an internal security force for combating drug traffickers. The Mexicans call it a war, and the very epicentre of that conflict is here in Sinaloa. It is the second largest area of drug production in the Americas, topped only by Colombia. The whole of the Central American drug business is run by two cartels, both of whom are based here, where the godfathers also live. Sinaloa is so rooted in the drugs business it's become part of its culture. Most of the local music here is in the form of folk songs about drug smugglers. When you wind up shot you get a song written about you, as a rule. Just across the road from the State Government Headquarters in the city is a church whose saint is also the patron saint of drug smugglers. I forget his name but I'm not making any of this up.

CULIACAN

Home to Mexico's infamous narcotics industry, the capital of Sinaloa State nestles between the Pacific Ocean and the Sierra Madre mountains in the country's north west. For decades, its fertile fields have produced not only soybeans and sesame seeds but vast amounts of marijuana and heroin destined for the US market. Sinaloa's poor campesinos have made it big growing and selling drugs and networking their way from the foothills of the Sierra Madre to the US border, which is just two days' drive away. So engrained is the trade in the city's culture that there is even a patron saint of drug smuggling – the legendary bandito, Jesus Malverde – whose image is seen dangling from the chain necklaces of many young Culiacan men.

Carlos's press conference, meanwhile, gathers pace. I smile a lot, but I'm still not convinced he'll pull it off. As the week progresses, his wife goes in to give birth but the anaesthetist is not working so there's a couple of days' delay. Carlos is running about like a madman, to and from the hospital while still arranging things for me. During this period his car goes offline and ends up in a garage. I can see veins throbbing in his neck and temple, which makes me wonder why he's putting himself out for some penniless backpacker he's just met.

Saturday is the press conference and all my kit is moved lock, stock and barrel down to the city centre where I set everything up. Within just a couple of minutes cameras start appearing from nowhere and suddenly I find myself surrounded by the press, microphones thrust in my face and cameras running. There are reporters from the national TV, radio and newspapers as well as a couple of local chaps, about nine groups in all. Not a bad turnout and our biggest press bash to date. Crowds of passers-by stop to watch and this all adds to the atmosphere. I'm in my element and find I have no problem giving a presentation. I think it went very well and everyone seems to agree. Just to put the icing on the cake, an elderly woman comes forth from the crowd, puts her arms around me and tearfully claims I'm a very important message for the world. She gives me

God's blessing and marks me with the sign of the cross, wishing me all the best while wiping away her tears.

As Carlos prints logos and posters for local festivals and performances, I also get introduced to a good few people in the art world. I start getting invited to festivals in town and further north on my route. I meet the director of the forthcoming Poets' Festival and he invites me to appear as a guest to give a talk to a group of interested poets ... poets? With a flourish, he produces some poems for me to read, watching eagerly for my reaction.

'Yes ... they're great, I really do like them,' I say, struggling through a few. I can't pretend ... I'm a complete philistine. I just can't connect with these people at all, but I try. Maybe I can learn something or broaden my horizons.

I'm introduced to a man we shall call 'Bob', a choreographer of contemporary dance, and a charming man, who makes Julian Clary look like Arnold Schwarzenegger. Bob takes a liking to me straight away, but I'm glad to say he set me up with one of the three female students in his contemporary dance class, a girl called Lupita. Bob is also a festival director and is well-liked.

Bob invites me to lunch in town and brings along Lupita. She's fun, clever and unusually tall for a Mexican girl, being not much shorter than me. In her early twenties, she moves like a princess and has the features of a high-born Spaniard. Over lunch, Bob goes on and on about the importance of contemporary dance and its history. I must have shown some enthusiasm as I find myself being taken to watch the group perform in Cosala, a place a few hours' drive away.

With the audience, most of them old campesinos, I watch these city girls lurch about the stage to their New Age music. I can't say I am much wiser afterwards and nor are the natives but the girls and Bob are keen to know what I thought.

'Yeah! That was excellent, went down really well,' I enthuse.

We grab a pizza then leave. The girls are in high spirits. They sing all the way home and, get this, Lupita plays 'feely feely' with me, while her friend sitting behind runs her hands through my hair. This is two-and-a-half hours of unexpected heaven.

The following evening is my last here. My newfound boho friends want to give me a send-off but the evening has a violent conclusion. Outside a disco that wants to charge us an extortionate amount to get in, I catch sight of a strange movement in the shadows down a dark side road, about a hundred metres away. I slip away and find a pitiful sight. A dog, obviously hit by a car, has a broken back and is trying to drag its paralysed rear end slowly across the dirt. The poor thing is trembling, no doubt with pain. It doesn't know what to do next – it's horrible to watch.

It gives my palm a faint sniff. I place my hand upon the animal's head and it sticks to its blood-matted fur. It lies down. It isn't going anywhere. Here in Mexico it will be left to die slowly and painfully but I can't leave it. I unearth a large rock, at which point Lupita joins me.

'What's up, let's go, we're off!' she urges.

'Er, just give me a second will you. You go back to the car and I'll be there in a moment,' I reply.

I stand over the creature. She seems to know just what to do and lies her head down against the road. I lift the rock above my head and bring it down squarely on target. The dog turns to rubber immediately, its skull crushed. She hadn't felt a thing. I'd done the right thing. I return from the shadows to where the group is standing below the streetlight, their faces contorted in horror. Looking down at my shirt I now realise I'm splattered with blood from head to foot. The girls stand wide-eyed, hands over their mouths. I even have blood splattered on my face.

'The dog . . .' squeaks Lupita.

I have some explaining to do. (A pointer for all you chaps out there: beating dogs to death with rocks is not the best way to impress girls on a night out.) Luckily the decision as to where to go next has come down on the side of taking a whole heap of drinks back to the lads' pad so off we go, me sitting in the back with the girls. Suddenly I find I've a lot more room than I had earlier.

Saturday, 16 March 2002   Beyond Sinaloa

Back on the road and tabbing along, minding my own business, a rather flashy 4 × 4 goes past and pulls in on the other side of the road to my front. Out jumps a woman, who comes trotting towards me. She just wants to say 'hello' and asks if I need anything. As it happens she appears to have no idea as to who I am or what I'm up to, but seems quite keen to natter. The story is that she's a thirty-year-old divorcee from Tijuana on her way back north after a short break. She is casually yet well dressed and gives the impression that she's a professional of some description . . . so the way things turn out comes as something of a surprise.

I'm chatting away when the conversation suddenly takes a bizarre turn.

'Aren't you ever scared of women raping you on the road?' she says, laughing.

'I should be so lucky, but I promise to put up only a token resistance if you try,' I reply, equally risibly.

'Are you serious?' she says.

'Yep! Drag me into the back of your motor . . .' I confirm, still, having a laugh. That'll teach her to go down that road, I thought. She laughs nervously then really surprises me.

'Do you have a condom?' she brazens.

The next thing I know she's making space in the rear of her 4 × 4 . . . Later, we go our separate ways and I carry on to my thirty-kilometre point, reaching it with time to spare. *Who* was that woman?

Friday, 22 March 2002   San Miguel Zapatitlan

Making a drinks stop in a village called San Miguel Zapatitlan, I chat to some chap. I ask him where I can get powdered milk but he doesn't think I'll find anywhere for a bit on this road. But I don't worry. I know I'll be fine as I have enough for today.

On the way out of town he reappears, this time in his car and gives me two tins of milk powder, four dollars' worth . . . good lad. I offer to pay but he refuses. He then comes straight in with an odd question.

'How do you get by with relationships, do you have any?' he begins.

'Er . . . well, it's a bit difficult,' I reply, rather disarmed by his seismic switch from powdered milk.

'What about sex and that?' he continues.

'Sex and that . . . well . . .' I'm lost for words.

'You see, I was wondering if you and I could have a sexual relationship,' he asks.

I think it's time to run for the hills.

'No,' I say firmly. 'I don't think that's going to be possible . . . but thanks again for the milk.'

Sunday, 24 March 2002   Sonora State Line

As I approach the state line with Sonora I pass a vehicle inspection point and also a 'Pest Control Road Checkpoint'. I find I get treated just like any other truck.

'Is your load all right and clean?' asks an official.

'Yep, sure is,' I assure him.

'No need for me to check?'

'Nope!'

'Come on then, push on through.'

After this detailed inspection the trucks move on to be sprayed with a cloud of pesticide. Hmm. I might as well. I wander over and stand by the trucks, close my eyes tightly, hold my breath and wait to be enveloped in the paralysing mist.

'Yes, that's it . . . get some of this ya little bastards,' I growl, as I re-emerge, probably poisoned.

My cloud of flies rapidly diminishes as I cross into Sonora, my last state in Mexico and Latin America. For once, I'm virtually pest-free.

Tuesday, 26 March 2002   Navajoa

I know I'm close to a town when the smell of dead and rotting dogs reaches its peak. I'm stepping over corpse after corpse, most flat and dried, but some still wet and sticky as I walk into Navajoa in the afternoon.

It's a small place but I'm still directed to all four corners, looking for somewhere to stay. Three hours later, I get lucky. That said, it's a cesspit. Those running it are totally astounded – they never have a gringo staying – and they can't believe what I'm up to. It's the map on top of Beast II that really catches their attention and consequently I get a room for free in what, by night, doubles as a rock-bottom whorehouse. It's not as if I'd look a gift-horse in the mouth, but con-sidering the state of the room it's hard to believe anyone would pay for it anyway.

I spend the next day in my room sitting in silence. I think about Catty. I'm also thinking about my son, Adam. I have missed so much of his early years – would he know me? He means so much to me but what can I do? I just have too much time alone, too much time sitting stewing over things.

Monday, 1 April 2002   **Beyond Navajoa**

Emerging from a heat haze, I spy a long-distance biker up front. I haven't seen any of these for quite some time now. This guy is heading south and I'm surprised to find he's an Argentine; he set off from home for Alaska but ran into visa and money trouble in the US and, consequently, must return to Mexico City to sort out the paperwork, before continuing his trip. He has to manage on US$4 a day, and if he's not sleeping in the bush he uses Red Cross stations or fire stations, mostly the latter. I might have been able to use these two locations if I'd had a bit more mobility. On these roads he puts away 100 kilometres per day . . . Christ! Think of it – 100 kilometres a day! We stand and talk for quite a while about all sorts of things.

'Look,' he says, 'rubbish everywhere . . . and this traffic . . . whoosh . . . whoosh, all the time!'

'Tell me about it.'

'Everywhere you sleep there's human waste and toilet paper!' he bemoans.

'Tell me about it.'

'. . . the place stinks.'

I nod in complete agreement.

Tuesday, 2 April 2002   **Towards Guaymas**

From my tent this morning I watch a flock of quail, with an odd quill on their heads, running amok through the bush around my tent.

In these parts, it has been a doddle to find a place to sleep because the local population is thinly spread. This afternoon, however, I'd pitched the tent when I see a group of cowboys moving cattle through the bush. Luckily they are just far enough away not to see me but then, as if by magic, men appear and set about working on a large electricity pylon ten metres from where I'm camped. Their hammering draws the attention of the cowboys and they canter over for a look. I just sit, shaking my head. There are hundreds of pylons out here, in a vast open expanse, and everyone for miles around is here . . . working on the one closest to me.

One of the cowboys comes along the fence line. Seeing my tent, he just stays and watches me from the other side of the stock fence, about three metres away. Somehow I know this is not the end of it and sure enough thirty minutes later two horsemen approach through the bush, this time on my side of the fence. One stops short but the other comes forward and as he rides into view, complete with large hat and boots, I'm alarmed to see he's wearing his neckerchief over the lower half of his face like a bank robber. In fact, both are.

They weren't when I saw them earlier, moving the cattle. Both are now just short of my tent and, merely by their eyes, I can tell that they are local Indians.

'Anything I can do for you?' I ask.

Without dismounting, one reaches into his shirt's breast pocket and asks if I want a cigarette. I thank him but decline, however he still takes a cigarette from the packet. He's obviously not thought this one through. I watch intently. Unless he pulls his mask down, he'll struggle with this cigarette but he and his accomplice just turn their horses around and leave.

I really didn't need to be barefoot now. As soon as they go, I pull on my boots and follow, but being on horseback they are soon well gone. I rush back to the tent. Being recced by, I think, Yaqui Indians in masks is unnerving and now they know I'm alone. It is time to get out of here. I throw everything into Beast II and move out across the road, over a railway line and into the bush until I find another spot to hole up. I don't need to go too far as they will have assumed, as everyone does, that I'm on a bike and therefore will be long gone.

Karl spends a week in the port of Guaymas, set in a lovely bay backed by purple desert mountains on the Gulf of California. Having traced the same coastline for three years and five months, this is the last time that he will smell the ocean or walk along its shores until he reaches the Bering Strait in Alaska. He sets off again on 12 April, turning inland and taking the road for Hermosillo, capital of Sonora

State. This is where Catty had applied for a position as a civil engi-neer – sadly for them both, she didn't get the job.

Along the way, a car is heading his way when its rear tyre disinte-grates; there is a lot of banging and smoke and then the whole wheel breaks away from the hub and comes flying towards him. Luckily it passes over his head with bits of rubber flying everywhere as the car speeds past. It doesn't even slow down, it just carries on. This hap-pens often. No one changes worn tyres in this part of the world.

He is wearing warm clothes in his sleeping bag again, and prefers the cooler evenings to all those sticky, hot and humid nights in Central America.

Sunday, 21 April 2002   Towards Santa Ana

Because there is secure fence running all the way along this road, finding places to sleep is a real problem and any lay-by doubles as a vast toilet. If I do find an unfenced spot with sufficient cover from view it's obvious that a lot of other road users have spotted it too, when looking for a quick toilet-stop. Hence the last few nights I've been sleeping in virtual cesspits, having to shift aside tons of used toilet paper so that I can erect my tent. I sleep with the smell from countless piles of human waste when on either side of me there are thousands of square kilometres of open bush and sand . . . all behind the flaming fence.

This afternoon, close to yet another lay-by, I cut myself a space behind some bushes so that I can't be seen from the lay-by and get the tent up. Not much later, a pick-up pulls in loaded with a family of campesinos. The vehicle is also packed with chairs, tables and plants in plant pots, all crammed on to the back of the rusting pick-up. Granny campesino starts forcing her way into the bush with a hand-ful of toilet paper, looking for a spot well out of view, and heads – you've guessed – straight for me. It's only a matter of time . . .

'Oh, My God,' croaks the old dear, reeling back and stumbling towards the lay-by.

Next it's the turn of the kids.

'Look . . . look . . . there's a gringo living in the bush,' they scream.

The pick-up empties as the entire family now stands peering at me through the bush, only a few metres away.

'Look . . . look. There's a gringo,' they chorus, like a flock of demented squawking parrots. Good grief.

Monday, 22 April 2002   Towards Santa Ana

I'm in a wayside restaurant. As I collapse in a chair a rather large woman waddles over cradling a screaming child in her arms. On approaching my table she lifts up her T-shirt producing one party-sized breast, which she promptly stuffs into the baby's mouth. That shuts it up.

'Yeah, what you want . . . food?' she charms.

I'm about five days from the US border. It's kind of strange but no matter how I try I can't imagine that all this will disappear . . . no more Latin America. I just can't believe it. You know, I'll miss it. For all the whining I do, I bet I'll miss it.

Tuesday, 23 April 2002   Santa Ana

In the small town of Santa Ana, I email my father. I tell him I expect to be in Nogales – the border – in about four days. This Internet café is run by an American, or should I say, a North American, as local people get quite upset if you refer to Yanks as Americans. They look down on North Americans, considering them to be recent, colonial arrivals. On the other hand, this chap doesn't have too many good things to say about the locals as he finds them impossible to do business with, stating that all they want to do is sleep. That said, his girlfriend is a Yaque – a pure Indian – and he reckons her people are the most racist you'll find. They have little or no tolerance of the mixed races that populate this country.

'My girlfriend is a Yaque and would not spare a penny for the starving members of any other peoples,' says the café owner. 'Conversely, those of mainly Spanish descent – the Latin people – wouldn't piss on an Indian if they were on fire.'

Friday, 26 April 2002   Towards Nogales

I find it's time for a toilet-stop. I have to hide away in a very tight spot between a large cactus and some thorn bushes. Squatting in an unseemly position with my trousers around my ankles I end up with my long hair being caught in the thorns . . . Aaarrgh! Then a thorn pierces the top of my ear . . . Ouch! I can't move . . . Aaarrrgh! Gritting my teeth I make an effort to struggle free, but only end up backing my bare bum into the cactus . . . AAARRRGH!! The four-to-five-centimetre needle-sharp spines are tipped with tiny barbs. Just the merest touch and they stick like superglue and pierce the skin so easily.

I'm in a real state. My pants are around my ankles and I'm stuck fast to thorn bush and cactus. The pain is almost indescribable, and certainly no joke as I'm now bleeding from all over the place. I try to disengage myself but it only makes things worse. Hell's teeth, how my eyes water and it takes me an absolute age to escape. I've a multitude of tiny puncture wounds. Thank God no one has stopped while I'm stuck there. The good thing about these cactus (if there are any good things), is that unlike the thorn bushes the cactus spines don't snap off, leaving you with more problems.

On the road, someone gives me a large watermelon – it's my evening meal as I've run out of everything else for this final night's camp in Mexico. When night falls the temperature drops rapidly. As soon as it is dark I walk up a hill from where I can look down on Nogales, lit up below. I spend some time there, not quite able to fully appreciate the moment. Tomorrow is the 'coming in day' of 'coming in days'! Nogales, this is it! The end of Latin America! The end . . . it just doesn't seem real.

Saturday, 27 April 2002   Nogales

Total distance to date: 10,333 miles (16,639 km)
This morning, I push into the town centre and find a rat hole of a hotel, yet still have to pay US$15. Going through my usual routine I turn on the shower and get a cold trickle of water. Things don't change. I grumble and gasp under the ice-cold dribble . . . fifteen dollars! Anyway, there's no time to waste as I have to go out and get things sorted. The first thing is a haircut (not looking forward to that at all) and I must give my kit a real good scrubbing. It's now midday so I have to get myself in gear.

Dad's latest email says there's going to be media waiting for me on the border and I am under orders to get myself looking presentable. I lose 60 per cent of my hair, reverting to a pre-expedition appearance, looking like something from 'N Sync'. I'm not too keen on this new well-scrubbed image.

Later I go down and recce the border crossing point, trying to anticipate any problems and checking that I can get Beast II through the pedestrian gateway. It looks a tight squeeze but it's possible, and a far better option than pulling it through the traffic entry point, as this will be packed solid with little room for the likes of me. I decide to check things will be OK with the US Customs people, but they just look at me as if I'm a retard.

'If you're a pedestrian, sir, then you cross through the pedestrian entry point . . . don't you?' says a patronising official in his booth.

'Yes, but I'll be pulling a large trailer and . . .'

'Well, sir, then you would have to drive through with all the other trailer homes at the appropriate entrance point,' continues this counter cretin.

'No, it's a box on wheels and . . .' I get that look . . . 'Oh, it doesn't matter.'

I look around. I see that my interest in the crossing point has caught the attention of the US police.

'Hey, Frank, think we might have a nutter here,' I overhear an officer say.

NOGALES AND ILLEGAL IMMIGRATION

Karl crosses from Sonora, Mexico, to Arizona, USA, in Nogales, the bustling city that straddles the border. It is here that he heard about the fateful journey in May 2001 of a group of Mexicans trying to cross illegally into Arizona, which cost the lives of fourteen. The group of twenty-five Mexicans were seeking a new life of better jobs and higher wages but half never made it after their guides – known as coyotes – abandoned them in temperatures of 46 °C. Every year hundreds of thousands of Mexicans brave the desert heat and cross into the US where they earn tax-free dollars that sustain their families back home.

Sunday, 28 April 2002   **Nogales**

I've just today to kill. Before I check out of this dreadful hotel, I stand and stare at myself in an old, faded and cracked mirror for a while. I look so different now that I've had my hair cut. It has been long for the best part of three and a half years and I now hate it so short.

Everything seems oddly surreal as I stroll down the main street. Is this really it? Is this the last time I'll enter a Latin town and look around the streets that now seem so familiar to me? Closer to the border itself, Nogales changes dramatically into a huge tourist hot spot. The streets are full of shops and restaurants to accommodate throngs of US day-trippers. I sit with a coffee in a packed café, surrounded by Yanks, just listening to the babble of 'English'. I hang out all day, sitting and thinking over all that has been and gone. I look back over some old maps and trace my route. Cities and towns that for so long had been nothing more than simple black ink dots on my map are now faces, places, times and emotions. There are street scenes, landscapes and volumes of memories. The maps come alive. Catty now seems so far away, in a different world, and it doesn't feel good. All day I sit and observe people going about their business.

Tomorrow I will not wake and see the women sweeping their doorways and shop stalls clear of dust. Gone will be the squeaking wheels and cogs of the ageing tortilla machines, as will the crowing roosters and barking dogs. Today is a time for reflection, as tomorrow will indeed be a new dawn.

I'm not going to bother with a shitty hotel tonight. Instead, I get in with the Mexican soldiers up on the border post and sure enough wangle myself a spot on the floor to kip on . . . just six metres from the USA. I sit and joke until late into the night with these lads of Mexico's 24th Infantry Battalion. I crack jokes in Spanish. I realise just how good my Spanish has become.

Chapter Eight

THE UNITED STATES

I'm about to cross into the United States when two chaps – one in a photographer's jacket with a camera hanging around his neck and the other with a note pad in hand – approach me.

'You must be Karl,' begins Mitch Tobin, a reporter from the *Arizona Daily Star*, who interviews me while the snapper snaps away. They follow me as I make my way along the covered walkway to a large terminal and the pedestrian port. Inside are four turnstiles and a gate for large luggage and shopping trolleys. I slot into one of the two queues and file forward to have my ID checked by the officials. It's not as strict a going over as I'd imagined. US citizens can get through with only a driving licence and local Mexicans seem to be using some form of a pass. It's finally my turn and I have to slide BII through the gateway to be looked over by the police. It grabs a fair amount of attention and raises some eyebrows but doesn't cause any problems with the US Customs. Minutes later, I fill in my 'green card' then pay $6 for a ninety-day visa – I'm in Arizona.

Blinking back in the sunlight, I'm greeted by a small posse. There's Daniel Corbett and his cameraman from KGUN 9, a TV station from Tucson. Daniel is a former BBC weatherman . . . now there's a thing. There is a female reporter from the local newspaper, the *Nogales International* – she's Genevieve H. Gutierrez, or 'Gigi', and another guy that I don't immediately recognise because of his short hair – it's Sammy. He is an old pal that I got to know after we met in Cuenca, Ecuador. He lives in Las Vegas.

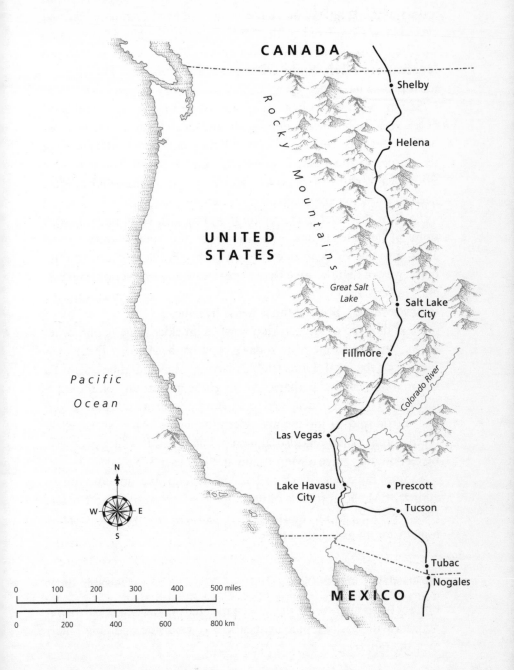

This side of town is a completely different environment; everything is open-plan and well spaced out, on the sidewalks there is plenty of room, plus they have ramps at regular intervals, so no more slamming up and down the kerbs, and I can even use dedicated cycle lanes. Compared to the Mexican side, Nogales USA is quite small so I don't have much of a choice of hotels nor is there an Internet café – apparently, I'll be pushed to find them anywhere as most people have their own PCs.

Sammy, who works in a bar, generously stumps up for a real good hotel, very flash. I have a good wash and clean up and then we cross back to the Mexican side where I will find an Internet café. Crossing the border at this point is so easy it's just not true. You just walk through a turnstile, with no ID check at all. And coming back, I just need to show my green card.

Back in the hotel that evening the press girl, Gigi, joins us with some of her friends and, after drinks by the hotel pool, we cross again into the Mexican side of town as the US side has little to offer in the way of nightlife. We have a great time and everyone gets pleasantly merry. Back at the swimming pool, we take a quick dip – in fact, very quick, because the water is freezing.

Next day, I'm in the hotel lobby when an elderly chap approaches having recognised me from today's copy of the *Arizona Daily Star*. Next door the local 'Lions Club' is having a lunch and he asks if I'd like to join them and perhaps give his group a short talk on the expedition. Of course, I'm delighted to so Sammy and I are taken next door and introduced to the mainly elderly members. After an excellent lunch during which Gigi also shows up, I do my stuff, which goes well. Better still, they have a whip-round and I trouser $75.

Sammy must head back to Las Vegas. Gigi fixes me up with an address – Mexican friends of hers – where I can stay tonight before I start walking in the morning. She also has me over to her place tonight for an excellent supper.

Wednesday, 1 May 2002   Towards Tubac

I'm about to step on to the Interstate Highway when a patrol car appears with flashing blue lights and a voice inside booming loudly over the tannoy.

'Get off the highway,' it orders and the car pulls in front of me.

'You can't use this road to walk on, boy, it's against state law,' informs the patrolman. 'I can ticket ya, you'll need to be using the "frontage road" instead.' (The frontage road is a single-lane road running parallel to the Interstate.)

This is not a problem, however I seem to get it wrong again. Without realising, I end up back on the Interstate once more because, altogether, five roads are running parallel with each other so it's easy to be confused. I'd followed a sign for the frontage road yet ended up on the right-hand two lanes of the Interstate. I'm well impressed with these frontage roads though, because they even have a bike lane and there's bags of room. I walk twenty-nine kilometres.

INTERSTATE HIGHWAYS

The equivalent of the UK's motorways, France's autoroutes and Germany's autobahns, they are double-carriageways with a central reservation and hard shoulders, and have controlled access on and off a slip road. It is illegal to walk along these highways so, as the police did not class Karl's trailer as a vehicle, he is often ordered, where possible, to use the frontage roads. These are the relatively minor roads running alongside main highways, often on both sides, for the use of local traffic. In rural areas, they usually give access to farms and fields, and in towns, to motels, shops and gas stations.

Thursday, 2 May 2002   **Tubac**

Last night, George McQueen and his family had me to stay – they're friends of Gigi. I promise them that I will call in at a local school just three miles into my route to have a word with the children. Feeling the effects of a barnstormer of a breakfast, I see the banners that read 'Welcome Karl' before I hear children's voices chanting 'Karl, Karl, Karl'. This appears to be a real treat for the kids, ranging from six to sixteen, who attend this small country school in the village of Tubac. It's kind of strange having to talk to such a wide age-range. Would the younger ones understand anything I was talking about? I attempt a watered-down version and both the teachers and kids alike seem happy. I answer a million questions.

This afternoon I'm sitting beside the road in the shade of a small bush, when another cop car cruises past before it stops and reverses until it is in front of me. Out steps a dashing young chap in gleaming white T-shirt and khaki police shorts. His must be the most casual of police uniforms I've ever seen. He seems more concerned with whether or not I'm fine, saying he'd seen me sitting here and just wanted to be sure I was not in trouble, as people sometimes are in this heat. Had I been asked to leave the road before, he wonders? Well, yes, I explain, but say there is some confusion because frontage roads stop and disappear from time to time. The cop is decent.

'I'm not going to say you can't use the highway as this isn't my jurisdiction, me being part of the Sheriff's Department and not Highway Patrol, but you could find you end up in trouble,' he says.

I assure him that I'll do my 'absolute best' to stay out of trouble.

I pull in at the next roadside restaurant. I'm not intending to eat, just to have a drink, but some old folks recognise me from the news-papers and I'm treated to a free meal. I'm asked to sign a menu as they have a special wall plastered with menus signed by the famous or crazy. Have you noticed how you can never think of anything appropriate when someone puts a card under your nose? This isn't easy for me and I'm under pressure. Off the top of my head I come up with the following, which I'm quite pleased with:

'Don't you get lonely?' they ask.
'Look behind me, do you see them?' I reply. 'Behind me are the dreams of a million men. We're an army, a powerful thing that won't be stopped. These dreams are always with me – and, together, we're heading north and we're feeling strong.'

Bloody marvellous. I sign it Karl Bushby, World Walker. The café owner loves it.
'Wow, man, that's so true . . . yeah man, it's, like, so deep!'
More cash donations!

At the end of the day I reach the outskirts of Green Valley. Gone are the days of reaching a major road junction to find one grotty little pit, with the choice of warm or hot Coke. Now it's a whole set of burger joints. McDonald's, Burger King, plus pizza palaces and gas stations. And even at the gas station you can have a choice of six different flavoured coffees, all of which taste great. I sit in the McDonald's, reading newspapers, until darkness falls. I then pick up one more coffee before I wander off to find a bush by the main road to hide behind.

Next morning, Karl is ordered off the highway again by another patrolman, when a BBC news team descends. Over the weekend, they aim to make three separate short news-bites for BBC Breakfast Time, Midday News and the Evening News, each of them a little different. The BBC book Karl into the Western La Paloma, in Tucson, which, at $300 a night, is the most lavish hotel he has ever stayed in. Next day, they hire a helicopter and film him in the Saguaro National Park, which goes swimmingly well until National Park Police take exception to the helicopter.

Filmed and interviewed walking into Tucson, the BBC return him to the park where he pitches his tent framed by the setting sun and spends the night. Next morning, they catch him crawling from his sleeping bag and putting on his boots. Rushing him into town, he is featured at an equipment store being fitted with new Superfeet footbeds – special inners for his boots. The shoot is over. The crew have a whip-round – they give him $100 out of their own pockets – before returning him and Beast II to where they found him three days ago.

Monday, 6 May 2002   Tucson

Dropped off by the crew yesterday, I used the backstreets into Tucson. I crashed at a motel, which set me back only $25, then caught myself on Channel 13. As I was watching, the phone rang. It was the Indian family that ran the place, phoning from the front desk.

'You're on TV! You're on TV! Oh, wow, it's so cool . . . and you're here in our motel,' shrilled the voice. I'm a celebrity.

This morning, I find a solitary Internet café. I'm now able to start contacting those people that had left email invitations for me to stay at their homes, which is a huge help. It's a little cold-blooded, though, contacting people in this way. I have things to do, lots of things. I need to contact any interested local radio and TV and also get some form of permission permit that allows me to walk on the Interstate Highways. If I can't manage this, progress will become a lot harder and slower. I also collect a re-supply parcel from the central post office.

I've decided to lodge with someone called Steve List and he meets me in town with his pick-up. He lives with his girlfriend, Jenny, twenty minutes south-west of Tucson, and I intend to stay until at least Friday. He lets me use his phone and the Internet, so I can keep pace with all the ensuing madness. It's like being catapulted to another planet. I have to sit still from time to time trying to get my head around it all. Everything is moving so quickly. I have more than $200 in my pocket, all donations. And within forty-eight hours of the BBC news item being shown in the UK, Father has been inundated with emails and phone calls, plus there are nearly five thousand hits on the website.

Jenny lets me have a spare laptop from her office for $100, which is an absolute bargain. I've dreamed of a laptop for quite some time but until a month ago it had been far from a reality. I get the green light from the lads at home to pay for it but when I do, Jenny, in turn, hands me an envelope from her boss containing $100. How generous.

I get to see the Permits Office people in Tucson. As I anticipated, this is a tricky one. It was the police that put me on to these people and now this lot are trying to throw me back to them. Both are concerned for my safety because of the 'volume' of traffic that flows between Phoenix and Tucson. They needn't be. Compared with where I've been recently, they're empty. I couldn't die on these roads if I tried. The good news is that the Interstate has a 'frontage road' running all the way to Phoenix so there's no real problem if I stick to it.

Saturday, 11 May 2002   Beyond Tucson

I get pulled over by a copper who is responding to a call from a member of the public requesting he check out 'a madman in a cowboy hat and some kind of Boy Scouts uniform, pulling a cart in the middle of the road'. I explain that, in fact, this makes a change as I used to be Osama Bin Laden pulling an ice-cream cart. This amuses him.

It doesn't take me long to assess that the US believes it's under imminent attack. When I enter burger bars mothers that have missed me on the news gather their children and keep them well away from the potential 'school shooter' or suicide bomber. I soon sense that 'security' people in shops and cafés are watching very carefully. Another thing I notice is that there's no one on the streets. Other than the odd person, no one walks. I've seen no girls younger than forty and then only at a distance, whizzing by in a car or on a bike. Having said that, I was surprised to come across a whole pack of girls, a netball team or something similar, that were all jumping up and down across the street from me outside a pizza parlour, shouting Karl! Karl! I'm beginning to think I'm some sort of a pop star.

This afternoon, I pitch my tent near a railway line. The ground shakes all night long as I'm close to an automatic level crossing. I'm deafened by the trains giving it maximum with their horns.

Monday, 13 May 2002   Eloy

This heat is sapping: it's touching 40 °C. It's a record-breaking temperature for this early in the month. My kit is almost too hot to touch and I flinch when I brush against Beast II's aluminium. At the end of my tether and red-hot, I decide to crash in some redneck bar. I try in vain to pull the trailer into the entrance way rather than leave it outside where I can't see it, as there are no windows in this dark dingy bar. The staff freak, thinking their time has come at the hands of some suicide bomber. There is a bit of a stand-off. I've little or no energy left for diplomacy or even good manners but the locals are still good to me, despite my pathetic performance.

Beyond the bar I push on for only a mile or so until I reach the edge of a small town called Eloy. Tiredness is beginning to show through. I can't wait to call a halt. I seem to get my head together and best rest when I'm alone in my tent. It is my home and there's nothing quite like it really. It's often far better than the bed in a strange house.

The next leg – the 360 miles (580 kilometres) to Las Vegas – will take about twenty-one days. In these temperatures, Karl is aware how serious an undertaking walking in the desert will be. This might be the US, but he knows that it will be no walk in the park. He will need to carry water and lots of it.

Tuesday, 21 May 2002   Beyond Eloy

Still in the Tucson suburbs, I stop for a bite at a fast-food joint. I get the evil eye as soon as I walk in – I guess these city people just don't like the way I must look. I ask the girl at the counter for some food and she turns into a startled rabbit and tries to catch the eye of her boss. Why, for Christ's sake, I'm human.

'Why are you looking at him?' I ask her.

No effect and so I ask again, only a little louder. This time, I get served. I'm now on the offensive. It doesn't take much to send me off the deep end . . . and this is worrying. I seem to swing from one extreme to the other. Not far up the road I pull into a gas station, as I need some fuel for my stove. I've tried this on the way up from Tucson but it was explained to me that I can't fill my fuel container from the pumps and, consequently, I couldn't get any fuel. I try again here. After a lot of huffing, puffing and whining, I pay $5 for a plastic gas can and then try to fill it up. I have not been very pleasant to the woman on the desk. Now, it's self-service here, unlike Latin America. I struggle with this relatively hi-tech pump, following the instructions, yet can't get anywhere. What the hell is wrong with this thing? After ten minutes, I'm feeling stupid now and do not want to have to ask but I'm left with no choice. I go back inside the shop, where the woman is now grinning.

'Yes,' she says. 'You have to pay me first, then I activate the pump.'

'And you thought you'd just sit and watch me, didn't you?' I reply.

She just smirks, with a look that says 'That's right, prick'. I almost have to use deep-breathing exercises to calm down. She gets her money, as I throw coins on to the counter and storm back out to the pump. I don't want this plastic can, but it's the only way I'm allowed to take petrol. And even then the minimum amount is far too much for me. I take what I need from the can but I'm left with it and its remaining contents. I can't leave it by the pump so walk back to the shop with it. As I enter the woman goes mad.

'Get it out! You can't bring flammable liquids in here,' she wails.

I give the can to some guy who's just driven in, then storm away. Later, when I've cooled down, I realise that none of this would have happened if I had been a little more civil in the first place. I don't even know I'm doing it half the time. I'm convinced half of Phoenix would line up to piss on my grave if I get run over. I'm becoming too self-indulgent. I've no patience and I'm expecting too much of complete strangers. What's wrong with me?

Wednesday, 22 May 2002   Beyond Eloy

Just before midday I meet a group of deaf cyclists. It turns out that they are cycling across the US from the west to the east coast on a fund-raiser for the 'Deafway Students Scholarship Fund'. I get 'talking' to one guy, or rather doing my best to communicate by pointing and gesticulating before he reads the plaque on Beast II. Suddenly, I'm a hero again. I sign T-shirts, hats and all sorts of things, accompanied by a lot of photos. It's strange being among a crowd of people who are obviously quite excited and yet are making no sounds – there's just a lot of hand-signalling. They give me a T-shirt with their logo on that everyone signs and $50, which at first I'm dead against, given what they're doing. They insist I take it. Taking money from them doesn't seem right at all, and in fact I'm never totally happy accepting donations from anyone.

Thursday, 23 May 2002   Prescott

Not far down the road a white pick-up pulls over in front of me and a middle-aged couple – Anne and Walter Horn – climb out. The softly spoken Anne explains that they've been looking for me for over two days. They hired this wagon in the hope that I would accept an invitation to rest at their place.

Their daughter, Tracy, runs her own PR business and thinks that she can help me with publicity in the US. She is in Prescott, a long way off to the north. I agree to the plan overall as long as they can return me to this point at the '81 mile' marker, which won't be difficult to find again. We load up Beast II and are on our way.

Prescott is a one-hour drive to the north, out of the low-lying desert and up into the hills and pine forests, including a huge scorched area where only a week ago a massive forest fire had flared to within a couple of miles of the town centre. The town basically stands in the midst of the forest and it's such a shame to see all this damage. We drive straight around to Tracy's. Sure enough, she heads her own PR company, and with her five colleagues works from an office at her home. In truth, they normally only work within Arizona and there's no guarantee of publicity nationwide, however I'm welcome to chill out while they try. Why not? It's very nice here.

Tracy and her friend and co-worker, Patti, are my age, single and obviously having fun. Patti is slim, very attractive and dresses to kill. We get on from the word go – in no time at all the sparks between us are almost visible. Trouble is, with Catty weighing on my mind, it's appalling timing. I've quietly decided that I will ask her to marry me if that is what it takes to be with her – I've no idea if she'd accept.

I wonder if there is some way that we can write her into the plan, perhaps in a support role? I have to know how she feels. After all, I would be asking her to chuck everything. I put all this to her in an email – it's no surprise when she says that she can't commit. I don't doubt that she loves me, but joining me would be such a big change in lifestyle – giving up all of her home comforts, job, family and good living is a step too far.

Within a very short space of time, I've moved in with Patti at her very smart house in the desert, a way south of town. It doesn't feel right and I don't feel good about it, but I'm not going to whinge or make more excuses. I do what I do to get me through the day and maybe the next one. Right now I need to be with someone. I think Patti understands. It's a beautiful home in a beautiful setting, and I'm living in luxury with her and her twelve-year-old son and four-year-old daughter. She is a brilliant cook and I eat like a king. I had originally only intended to spend a couple of days in Prescott, but soon realise that there is actually a lot of potential to get some US national coverage. We're making good progress on the sponsorship front, with a number of companies supplying either equipment or money, and although this takes the pressure off, we still need a lucky break that will find a donor prepared to help with the estimated £40,000 I need to cross the frozen Bering Strait.

A day or two before I leave, Patti read some of the diaries. Maybe she hadn't realised, or didn't want to, just how much I do feel for Catty and she is definitely hurt. All day, I knew something was very wrong, but it isn't until the evening that she finally confronts me. She'd 'given me her heart, home and bank account . . . and all the time I'd been thinking of someone else. Had I not really cared about her at all?' Of course, I do care very much and I'm extremely grateful for all she's done for me, but, hey, we're both grown up and we know what's going on here. We knew from the start. Yes, I am cut up about Catty, but she's not here and might never be . . . life goes on. And I think Patti needed me in the same way I needed her.

I decide to stay an extra day, as tomorrow, Saturday, is Anne's birthday, so of course I hang around for that. We have a great time. Walter, Anne's husband, is a really excellent guy and very funny. I even buy Anne a present; it's the first time in three years I've bought anything for anyone. It felt good. Next day, Patti hires a truck and, after a few tears, leaves me where Anne and Walter found me.

Under a clear blue sky, the temperature is 39.8 °C when Karl sets off northwards towards a land where it hasn't rained for four years. The road is quiet with little or no traffic and he spends the first night under a bridge. With sun up at 05:00 and nightfall at 20:00, given the heat, there is too much daylight and the nights are too short. By midday, he is forced to find shade in a ditch close to the road, as the temperature on the thermometer in his rucksack is touching 50 °C.

From now on, he sets off before 05:30 because, by 10:00, temperatures hit the forties, and he has to rest up in the heat of the day, before continuing into the night, wearing a fluorescent vest. On these roads, walking at night – particularly when there is no moon – is hazardous because this is the main trucking route and there is now no 'frontage road' or even a hard shoulder to walk.

SPONSORS

Just two corporate backers, Zamberlan – Karl's walking boot supplier - and Superfeet – they make insoles for his boots – have been onboard since the outset. After eighteen months, they were joined by The North Face, which supplies his equipment and clothing, and in 2002, Softcom (Mail2Web), a Canadian web-hosting company, was the latest to become involved, sponsoring him and his website.

Thursday, 13 June 2002   **Parker**

It's in the high forties again in an arid land that now has no trees at all. With little or no wind it's a kick-arse day and by the time I pull over to camp and hide from this firestorm, life is pretty unbearable. I remember how, yesterday, I emptied the 'hot' water out of my bottle to replace it with cold outside a café in the village of Bouse. As it hit the tarmac, it turned into a cloud of sizzling steam. I've never see anything like it. Right now, the water in my bottles is so hot that it scalds if I spill any on my skin. Earlier, while walking, I'd splash some over me – it hurts at first but you feel cooler after a couple of seconds as it evaporates. It's just a fleeting pleasure – within a couple of seconds my skin is dry and any breeze that there might be feels like a blowtorch.

Everything emits a heat haze. I can almost hear the stony sand crackle like hot coals on a fire. I can't sleep, nor can I stay still in any one position. If I remain for too long on my side or back the heat from the ground begins to burn me. Christ! I'm drinking as much water as I can but hot water is unpleasant, and as for eating . . . forget it. I've completely lost my appetite.

If I sploosh myself from time to time to stop the burning, I just waste precious water. Sunblock turns to liquid and containers leak everywhere so my kit is a real mess. Black masking tape melts, comes undone and literally falls off my kit. I keep getting nosebleeds. It has to be the dry air playing havoc with the lining of my nose. All in all, this is not much fun. I planned to lay up here until 17:30, but come 16:00 I just can't take any more. On top of that my water is running very low, so I break camp and get on the move.

After only a short while, I come across Parker, a small town on the Colorado River. It's dry and dusty, but an oasis none the less. Iced water has been the only thing on my mind since I left Bouse and I crash into a small café, virtually wiped out, so damn tired. I down four large glasses of orange juice with ice. To be in this cool air-conditioned café is such an intense relief I decide I'm going to rest in town tomorrow – and maybe Saturday – and clean up a little. Besides a new inner tube, I need some different food for the road. I can't cook in this . . . no way! You could put a gun to my head but you'd never get me to even think about putting hot food near my mouth.

It's clearly quite a fun place. SUVs (sports utility vehicles) and cars pulling speedboats, jet boats and jet skis are parked everywhere and Mexicans in flash sports cars come and go with scantily clad girls. The motel is $45 and I pay almost $10 for my orange juices. I took out $100 from a cash machine when I arrived . . . and it's almost gone. Jesus, I can't keep this up. If the lads back home had not found me some sponsors life could turn incredibly grim.

Saturday, 15 June 2002   Towards Lake Havasu City

I change tactics. Following the Colorado, the road from Parker to Lake Havasu City – my next main target – has a hard shoulder and this should take two days. Rather than being microwaved in the desert during the daylight, I'm going to walk through the night and should be able to reach a river where I can then lie up through the next day and possibly get some sleep. The following night should get me to Lake Havasu City.

I move at 19:00. It's still red-hot and in the forties, but the sun is dipping so it will cool a little. The road begins to undulate, though not too steeply thankfully and, as it's dark, this is definitely a new experience. The route is framed by canyons, hills, sharp peaks and jutting rock formations on either side of the road. I can smell the river so I must be close to it for much of the time. By midnight, it's 20 °C and I find the going very easy, making good time under the bright starry sky. My target is a camping ground twenty-four miles (thirty-eight kilometres) from Parker. Here I am sure I can hide out and at least I'll have access to water.

At 04:00, almost on the dot, I arrive at Cattle Cove Sports Park, a camping site and marina. I creep past the office, find myself a spot to hide and get the tent up. I just want to sleep. As it's still dark I try to grab a few hours before sun-up but only manage about an hour before the sun hits the tent and does its worst. It's impossible to sleep so I sneak out into the park in search of a waterfront café. I can't stand it in that tent – I need to get out of the heat.

At sun-down, I move. There's some huffing and puffing as I climb back up to the highway and lope off into the darkness on a slight yet continuous incline. Later into the night, I spot a car parked up on the right. Initially, I can see its lights but as I approach the lights go out and I lose sight of it. The next time I see it is as I pass by. An electric window purrs and a female voice asks if I'm thirsty.

'I'm always thirsty,' I reply.

'Karl, it's Patti! Heyyyy!'

She'd been looking for me all day, not knowing I'm now only walking at night so I'm pleased she persevered. With her is a huge cool-box chock-a-block with ice, drinks and food. We sit and talk for a while and she decides not to drive home tonight but to get us a room in Lake Havasu City. Off she goes to find one while I push on. The total distance tonight is only fourteen miles, which means I can sleep, as I will get there at about midnight or 01:00. Not too long afterwards, Patti reappears and gives me the details of the motel before disappearing back into town to wait for me.

Just 500 metres from the motel, spokes start popping out from one of the wheels and puncture the inner tube. Luckily Patti has left me with her cell phone so I call her and she rescues the Beast II . . . what luck it was her being here now.

Monday, 17 June 2002   Lake Havasu City

I say goodbye again to Patti in the early evening, when she drops me where she rescued me yesterday. It's about twenty miles (thirty-two kilometres) from here to the junction with Interstate Highway 40, which is my goal. It is a steady climb for most of the night, a long, slow drag and I'm extremely tired. Walking nights and sleeping days sounds simple, but it's not really working too well yet. It's hard to reprogramme to this new routine.

By 01:00 the moon has set and it's very dark. I can't make out much and I'm constantly losing my night vision, blinded by car lights. For hours, my mind has nothing to focus on, no details except the stars. There's just nothing to see. I get very sleepy and feel as if I'm walking in a trance. By the end of the night, I'm completely whacked, and just south of the highway junction I call it a night hoping maybe to get a little sleep while it is still dark.

Tuesday, 18 June 2002   Towards Needles

I'm slower than I want to be. I arrive at the Colorado River at about 01:30 and begin looking for a place to sleep. I'm having no luck here and end up getting very pissed off and exhausted, losing the dark hours and precious sleep time. There's just no place to hide away. All around the river area are buildings, sub-stations and pumping stations with fences and 'No Trespassing' signs. I wind up having to go back out into the desert and finally find a place to sleep at 03:30, not good. At 05:00, it's light and I'm wide awake.

The temperature soars. It's a gruelling day and suffocatingly hot. My water is so hot that if you hold the bottle for too long it starts to burn your hand. All I can say is that it will be hard, if not impossible, for you to imagine just how hot it gets out here unless you have experienced it . . . it's literally incredible! My very best friend and secret weapon is the plant-spray. With enough water I can keep myself wet and not have to pour hot water from the bottle, losing a lot of it in the process. I use it all the time. The day drags slowly on and on occasions I think I might fall asleep, but just as I drift off I suddenly snap to. 'Oh, come on, sleep for crying out loud,' I plead. Of course, the more you try to sleep, the more you can't.

Tuesday, 25 June 2002   Towards Las Vegas

Walking at night isn't the way ahead. To get me to Las Vegas, I decide to walk whenever I get up in the morning and do the first ten miles (sixteen kilometres). I'll then rest up and set off walking again between 19:00 and 20:00, getting some sleep later in the night.

This morning, off to one side of a road junction, down by the river, I locate the first of three water caches that Sammy – my Vegas friend – had agreed to leave for me. I had been told that there was nothing much in this area, but find, to my delight, a gas station that I can hide behind and some cold water.

By 19:00 I'm on the move again, on a long straight road through a very bleak landscape consisting of sand, stones and the very occasional patch of dead scrub. In the darkness off to my left is a bright glow in the sky above the McCulloch mountain range. From this general glow a piercing finger of light points skyward as though it is solid. This is one of the brightest lights in the world, fired out of the top of a huge pyramid . . . the 'Hotel Luxor' in Las Vegas.

Sammy meets Karl in Henderson, a small town on the outskirts of the metropolis, where he will be able to resume his walk without having to enter the city itself. He has just moved into a new house he bought only days before. It's his first home, so things are a little topsy-turvy – there's no furniture – but not that it bothers his house-guest, whom he takes on a week-long party circuit. Patti also comes to stay – their relationship is still on.

In a few days' time, Karl is to meet the journalist Jonny Beardsall who is coming to interview him for the Telegraph Magazine. *Jonny will be spending two days walking with him in the desert. Does Jonny know what he is in for? And just how fit is he?*

Friday, 5 July – Monday, 8 July 2002   Las Vegas

Total distance to date: 10,863 miles (17,521 km)

The writer arrives on a direct flight from Gatwick. It feels really strange waiting by the exit gate listening to British accents. There are Brummies, Scousers, you name 'em they're here . . . most of them young males and looking for a crazy time. I hold a sheet of card with Jonny's name on it, but he knows what I look like, having seen photos of me. Looking like I do, I guess I'm hard to miss.

There he is. He wears a Panama, short-sleeved shirt, purple cotton trousers and a pair of brown brogues . . . without socks. No luggage either . . . just a small day-sack. He's very laid-back and has a well-forged Sandhurst accent. With no plans as far as accommodation goes – this is cool – he can crash on the floor at Sammy's.

Tonight, the jet-lagged journo has to be dragged out on the town when he could have done with some sleep. But, hey, this is Vegas. As I found out, you don't get away with it that easily even if, like this poor bugger, you're dead on your feet.

Daylight arrives and we're off. Sammy drops us in Henderson. It's a good few miles before we're clear of civilisation and finally find ourselves at a desolate desert checkpoint. This is the entrance to a state park and for first time ever I have to pay to walk on the roads. It's only a few bucks and the *Telegraph* coughs up. To my concern – and not a little surprise – Jonny is walking in a short-sleeved shirt, shorts and his brown brogues (still no socks), plus the same Panama hat, of course. He assures me he will be fine and says he wasn't going to shell out for a fancy pair of walking shoes just for the sake of two days. I'd have thought a pair of trainers would be ideal, but Jonny tells me he doesn't have any of those either. He explains that he's done a fair amount of running, both marathons and fell running, so I think he'll probably be a damn sight fitter than me. He explains he only ever wears spiked fell-running shoes or those old army-issue 'pumps' as we used to call them, a kind of white gym shoe. Christ, I think, this guy must be hard as nails.

But it's hot, and getting hotter as the temperatures race into the forties. Very quickly Jonny begins to feel it. The guy has just got off the plane from London, so I guess this is to be expected. A few more miles and he really does need shade and rest and I become a little concerned. Needless to say, we're in a bad-arse desert with not a hint of shade or anything to hide under, so I have to put my tent up and get him inside out of this killer sun for a bit. The temperature nears 50 °C – the world is on fire. There's no real escape from the heat but at least in the tent he is out of the midday sun.

Spotting the tent, two park rangers pull up. From them I learn that I'm not allowed to pitch a tent out here or sleep outside a designated campsite. But in this case they are not that concerned as we're only taking a rest stop. The rangers get on to their paramedics and ask them to come out with some water for us, not that we really need it as we're carrying more than enough. However, a rather flash paramedic unit does turn up with ice-cold drinks so I'm not complaining.

A little later we push on, albeit at a slower pace. This is only fair – Jonny isn't acclimatised so I can't expect him to move like I can. Come the afternoon and the temperature is as high as it's going to get and, Christ, it is hot. The scenery roundabout here is impressive. A few miles to the east you can make out the bright blue green of Lake Mead. In our immediate vicinity, though, it's just the harsh desert, devoid of anything green. We don't go on for too far as I find a culvert beneath the road, which without doubt is the best and most enjoyable place you're likely to find out here. It's just big enough to stand up in.

Jonny realises just how good it is to crawl under the road and escape from the killer sun, but you will never escape the heat, the burning air and that intense bright glare reflecting from the desert sands and rocks. Settled into our underground home, the interview continues with Jonny using a dictaphone. There are lulls of tired silence before we start chatting again.

But this culvert won't do for the night so we are left with the problem of finding somewhere to hide where we won't be clocked by the authorities. Up a bank and off the road, I manage to find some dead ground and we kick a patch of sand clear in a dry streambed, which is hidden in a small gully. We eat tinned food that Jonny bought in Vegas – fish and fruit, which is a luxurious change from the dry stuff that I would normally be eating.

Progress the following day is painfully slow, way too slow for me. Poor Jonny's feet are having a hard time of it. He's picked up a lot of blisters very quickly. You might get away with wearing leather shoes without socks in England, but not in these conditions. After short breaks, which we take frequently, he suffers until his feet warm up again. I sympathise fully with his plight, having been there many times.

Yesterday and today, photographer Michael Kelly and his assistant have been ambushing us along the way. They've driven from Los Angeles and are working for the *Telegraph*. They spend hours and shoot rolls and rolls. Standing around for these long periods is a drag out on the road, but the end-product should be good, and probably the best shots to date.

Come the third day and I notice a marked improvement as Jonny starts to get into the environment. Having applied yards of tape to his feet, we're moving a little faster now but I think his spirit of adventure is wearing a bit thin. I can hear the disappointment in his voice when we reach the bottom of a steep valley and cannot find a culvert, or see his face illuminate when we do. I know exactly how he feels – the least little thing can mean so much out here.

Later this morning we wait by the roadside. After a while, a pick-up appears, like a mirage in the heat haze. It's Sammy. It's back to Vegas for a brief chill-out and clean-up. It's now Sunday and later today Jonny must catch his flight home.

With twenty-seven days left before Karl's ninety-day US visa 'waiver' expires, immigration in Las Vegas tell him that to apply for a visa for a longer period, he has to leave the country. (The waiver enables British citizens to enter and remain in the US for ninety days without a visa.) With nothing else for it, Karl takes the bus to the nearest border – a twenty-four-hour journey via Los Angeles to Tequener, Mexico – where officials on the Mexican side ask for $24 to let him enter. Injudiciously, he bluffs his way through without paying, confident that this will be as straightforward as it was in Nogales and that he will have no problem getting back into the States with a fresh visa waiver. This is not the case.

As his current waiver still has nearly a month to run, Karl learns that he can't be issued another and must apply for a visa. To get around this, he removes the waiver slip from his passport and pretends that he is entering for the first time. US immigration smells a rat. Electronically swiping his passport, they discover the existing document. Warned not to try anything like this again, he is allowed back into the US on his current waiver.

Because he knows that he will have to leave when the ninety days is up, he wonders if he might fly to Colombia, get a bona fide visa, and also see Catty again. This is a bitter blow to Patti; their relationship falls apart and, much to his regret, he loses a good friend.

While Karl considers this, he is also aware that the sponsor, Superfeet, is expecting him on 8 August at the huge Outdoor Retailer Show (ORS) in Salt Lake City, where he and Beast II have been given their own exhibition space. There is a good chance for some extra publicity as well as making valuable contacts. He doesn't wish to miss it.

I return to Las Vegas. On that long, long bus trip, I am deep in thought. Maybe all this could have been avoided if I'd paid a little more attention to the visa rules in the US, but I really hadn't been warned that there could be these unforeseen pitfalls. I also think long and hard about my relationship with Catty. It is a fact that we, or at least I, feel we are slowly drifting apart. Despite trying to convince myself time and time again to let her go, I could not. I'm in a confused mess, added to which is the relationship I had with Patti. But now the fact that I must leave the US to get my visa means that, perhaps, I can see Catty and try and hold our relationship together. This would be a dream come true, but I can't risk missing the ORS. Or could I do both? Perhaps I can pull this off.

As the remaining days on my visa rapidly tick away, it seems as though everyone I know in the US, and those involved with the expedition back in Britain, are all working hard contacting embassies, appealing to governments and the US Immigration Service. Time and time again all our leads would turn up in dead ends. If I've a hope of making the ORS, I think I must really leave for Colombia asap. Others, meanwhile, urge me to sit tight in case there is a last-minute reprieve from somewhere. But, as time goes on, it becomes clear that a stay of execution is unlikely – I must leave the US if I want to come back again.

In truth, it's just as well I have Catty in Colombia because I am running out of options. Luckily, Superfeet put $2000 in the expedition kitty a couple of months ago, so I have funds, and book flights straight away and fly to Medellin. I have a hunch my best chance of a new visa is the US embassy in Bogotá. Straight away I approach the embassy. I find I need an appointment for which I have to pay $65, and this is just to get me a date for an interview. I eventually get a letter confirming the date of my appointment . . . 1 August 2003. Not quite what I'm looking for.

I am in a long queue – Catty is in it, too – because many Colombians want to go to the US. Her interview is not until October. The decision by the US immigration people as to whether or not she can travel could be make or break for us. If she doesn't get it all hope is probably gone. For now, there's still a chance. I talk to her about the possibility of becoming part of my ground crew but despite her strong feelings for me, the expedition is 'my dream, not hers'. This admission seems to seal our fate. She also tells me that if she doesn't get a US visa, it could mean the end for us.

But at least with my unexpected trip we have a fresh chance to talk it through. I have always felt that I'm asking too much of Catty. To leave her family, home, work, and all the security she has. She had never been outside of Colombia until the trip up to Panama, so how can I ask her to give up her life and come with me into the unknown, without any real idea of how we could make it work?

The rigmarole over Karl's US visa goes on, with continual emails and faxes flashing between Colombia, England and the US. But although he manages to bring his interview with immigration forward, it's still weeks away. Then, in late July, he gets an email from Gigi, his reporter friend in Nogales, who has spoken to the US consul in the town on his behalf. As directed, Karl faxes his passport details to Nogales and hears that he can be issued with a new visa.

It is now 2 August and the ORS starts in six days' time. With no time to lose, Catty trawls the Internet and finds him flights that will get him there on time. It's time to say goodbye again. She tells him that 'she would be with him to the ends of the earth'.

The first leg of the journey is to Panama. Sitting in the aircraft, he looks down on the jungles of Central America, remembering those days when he was down there looking up at night at aircraft heading north, trying to imagine just what it would be like to sit in all that comfort.

He can see the whole of Costa Rica from top to bottom, coast to coast, and can trace his route all the way. From Mexico City he flies on to Hermosillo where his bus arrives in Nogales in the early hours, and he gets a few hours' sleep in a cheap fleapit right on the border.

Within a very short time he has a new six-month visa. Meeting Gigi, she drives him straight up to Tucson to catch his flight to Salt Lake City. With clear skies over the deserts and the Grand Canyon, he arrives in Salt Lake City on the evening of 7 August, just in time for the show.

Evan Wert, Marketing Director for Superfeet, meets Karl at the airport. Both he and his crew are overjoyed to see him as they've put a lot of effort in and knew that it was touch and go that he would make it. Karl is booked into a first-class hotel, and Beast II has been picked up from Sammy's in Las Vegas and transported here. Everything is in place and good to go. All he needs is some sleep.

Thursday, 8 August 2002   **Salt Lake City**

Total distance to date: 11,277 miles (18,159 km)

I get a phone call to my room at about 07:00. It's Evan from Superfeet, asking where I am? Bloody hell. I hadn't altered my watch and I'm an hour behind. A bit of panic dressing and I rush over to find five guys in the car park waiting for me.

To get the maximum publicity, I am to walk into the Outdoor Retailer Show, which in fact is only a block or so from the hotels. I set up Beast II and change my clothes. In doing so, one of the guys recognises the Parachute Regiment tattoo on my right shoulder.

'Ha! That's what Dennis has on his hat,' he exclaims.

It turns out that Dennis – the boss, and creator, of Superfeet – is a former Regimental Quartermaster of 2 Para! Well, I'll be damned.

I'm overawed when I see the massive conference centre, and then the press group waiting for me. Here I meet with Shannon, the company's PR girl who set the whole media circus up. Before I even reach the building they start with a roadside interview taken by the local TV news crew. They then follow me indoors, dragging Beast II and all behind me. Once again I'm taken aback by the size of this place and the vast numbers of people within. It is indeed a big deal.

If you're an outdoor freak, you're in heaven here. For Superfeet it's a perfect piece of product promotion. Here are the insoles that outlasted seven pairs of boots . . . and here's the man himself to tell you about it . . . Karl Bushby. Throughout the morning, I'm interviewed by TV and newspaper reporters. There is also a news crew following a TV personality around – someone from one of those 'reality TV' shows, 'The Survivor', or something similar. It has to be said she's currently TV's top totty, a drop-dead gorgeous girl who had come second on the show, and is herself a presenter. I get to chat with her on-camera.

After the show Karl manages to get a lift back to Las Vegas so that he can carry on from his 'walking stop'.

Monday, 19 August 2002   **Mesquite**

It's a straight climb and a good hard slog up on to the Masa (Table) of Mesquite, a high flat plateau. Once up there, there's a stiff wind, which takes the bite out of the heat. For some reason there is also a haze in the sky that also keeps the sun off a little until midday when it really heats up. There's no cover, nothing, nothing at all.

Eventually I find a small culvert under the road. It's pretty tight to get into but once in I find there is just enough room to sit up. I tidy the place a bit, making some room for myself, dragging out rubbish and tumbleweeds, while checking it for snakes and scorpions. Once finished I've just about had it, knackered and very tired. I have to leave Beast II outside, next to the road.

I inspect a whole bunch of new blisters. Rather than wait for them to burst while I'm walking, I open them now, clean and cover them again. Once this is done I sit in a daze, surveying my limited world as through a porthole. I just can't keep my eyes open, but if I lay down neither can I sleep. God! This is just so frustrating. I raise my head to take a look at Beast II only to come face to face with a snake. I flinch, as does the snake, but it's still no more than an arm's length away.

Short of a weapon, I reach for the McDonald's water spray. Very slowly I pick it up and twist the nozzle setting to 'fine jet'. Armed with this handy deterrent, I give him a quick burst in the face, making him retreat a couple of metres. Two more bursts and he slithers away. He's probably never seen this much water before. He's not a 'rattler', but is light-brown in colour with reddish-brown bars down his back.

I can't sleep. The temperature is 45 °C in the shade, probably because there's no wind under here. Thank God for my water spray! Again I hear a car pulling in above me, but this time it's accompanied by the sound of a police radio. Oh, Christ! It's time to face the music. I scramble into a better position where I peer out to find a concerned but jolly-faced police officer. He'd been sent to investigate a 'sick man' lying ill in a culvert . . . or at least that's the report. Well, at least I get some more water.

Thursday, 22 August 2002 Virgin Gorge

For once, it was a cooler night so I slept well under the stars just in my sleeping bag. I eat some sandwiches for breakfast and I'm on the move by 06:40. After several miles, I'm at the mouth of the Virgin

Gorge, which winds through the Virgin mountain range. Visually, it's a break from the normal barren landscape. The entrance to the gorge is a welcome sight with its huge rock canyon walls that provide me with much-needed shade. Unfortunately, the respite is short-lived – once around the next bend, I'm in the direct sun all day.

The road is narrow so I decide against walking in the dark. This commits me to the full twenty miles (thirty-two kilometres) in daylight. I reason I may be able to manage it today as temperatures are a little less than their normal 'killer' state, around 38 °C. Having said that the day is still very hard going, being mainly uphill, as I begin the climb for Salt Lake City.

Growing low on energy, the day begins to drag out and my mind tends to focus on ice-cold drinks and little else. Those last few mile markers do their usual trick and somehow find a way of walking away from me, but eventually I climb out of the gorge and back into the desert. Finally, I come to rest under a road junction flyover and here I sit out the last of the sun's rays.

I make a new friend. A small brown flycatcher lands next to me and, as I sit still, hops closer. I'm amazed to find that it will sit on me, trying to pick off the odd fly that buzzes around. I take the cap from one of my water bottles, pour a little water in and place it on the ground next to me. The bird jumps down and drinks from it. I soon realise that even if I move the bird does not seem to mind. I tap the little chap on the head with my finger and he will just jab at me with his beak.

Saturday, 31 August 2002   Towards Fillmore

I hurt. I'm on a constant hobble, limping most of the time. I had to give myself a paratrooper-style pep talk earlier this morning – I must get a grip and stop whining about sore feet and just get over it. It's only twenty-three miles, less than forty kilometres, to the next exit from the highway and that has a gas station, which is a very convenient target.

I eat a hearty breakfast in last night's gas station and move well, but by midday the little toe on my left foot is driving me nuts. I have to do something to try and relieve the pain, so I cut a chunk out of my footbeds to give it some more room. Once again both my little toes are just large blisters – deep blisters that are very sore to the touch, even where the nails used to be. They don't seem to want to heal and just get deeper. But still they don't, and won't, slow me down.

This is real cowboy country. Yesterday, I was passed by an authentic wagon train, even driving a herd of horses with them. They had a small girl with them who could not have been more than five years old, nipping about on horseback as though she was born on it. She looked so small on such a huge animal.

Sunday, 1 September 2002   Fillmore

Now I know why my feet have been so bad. I cast my mind back to Salt Lake at the Outdoor Retailer Show. Just before I was due to leave one of the Superfeet team was fitting me with new footbeds, and trying to explain better ways to get my boots to fit and stop any blisters. What, I wondered had they done with the extra pair of insoles? I know they gave me a spare set, but I can't for the life of me recall where they are.

I stop, take off the boots, and have another look under the footbeds. Obviously I've done this before, but what looks like the bottom of my boot . . . is not! Using my knife blade I dig out a snug-fitting extra insole. For the love of God! These must have reduced the size of my boots by half a size or more. That's why I've been crippled. The sensible thing will be to let these blisters heal for a while now that I've found the cause.

Karl finds a room at a group of gas stations that cluster around Exit 163, just a short distance from the town of Fillmore. He intends to rest for three days to allow his feet to heal. Finding a chance to connect his laptop to the Internet, he learns that Superfeet has donated $10,000 to the expedition. Not only that but Hi-Tech, makers of the Magnum boots, whose representatives he spoke to in Salt Lake, are talking about a deal which could realise a further $15,000 per year. This boosts his own enthusiasm for having a mobile support team in Alaska, a team that might include his friend with a Land Rover, Dean, whom Karl met in Mexico, Sammy from Las Vegas and, depending on her getting the visa, Catty. He doesn't feel this would compromise the aims of the expedition.

After four years, and the worst drought for seventy years, it starts to rain. The scenery is beginning to change. Now less than a week away from Salt Lake City, he gradually leaves behind the desert belt of the northern hemisphere and starts to see trees and vegetation again.

Wednesday, 11 September 2002   Fillmore

An email from my father rips my cosy world apart. His simply deals with facts, things that don't sit well in my world of dreams. He can't know this but sometimes it's only the dreams that hold it all together for me. This life of mine is pretty fragile and can be shattered like glass. He explains how none of my dreaming or ranting will overcome the problems we have at present. But all I can see is the fact that someone is telling me I'm about to lose my girl!

I'm seeing red, as well as feeling nauseous deep down. Anger swells up as I sit with my eyes closed, attempting to bring my rage under control. It appears that the chaps back home believe that having a support party is not the direction that the expedition should be taking. They believe we are unable to fund such an undertaking and that on top of that a support team would detract from the overall credibility of the expedition. That it would take away what makes the expedition 'saleable', that it would take away some of its 'mystique'. There's no bloody mystique about sitting in a dark, empty tent every night! It sucks! Well, bugger me . . . people won't be entertained if I lose my mystique? At last I know why I am here then, it all makes sense now.

Anger gives way to a deep sadness. Catalina . . . it's all about Catalina. I don't move, I can't muster my thoughts. My mind is panicking, scrambling . . . will I lose her? Could I let her go?

In mid-September, Karl arrives at a hillside apartment an hour's drive from Salt Lake City, Utah. Re-equipping himself with cold-weather gear is his immediate preoccupation and Sammy, his friend from Las Vegas, comes up to drive him around the city collecting it all. He also needs a new container built for Beast II to carry it all in. Using two plastic utility boxes, he has these converted to his own specifications into a single, much larger box. Having seen Karl on TV, the engineer at a plastics workshop doesn't charge for the work.

While he is here, he meets two Germans who are also walking the Americas, this time from north to south. Pulling a steel trailer – it weighs about 112 kilograms – and sharing the workload, they are averaging the same distances as Karl. They exchange much useful information; rather than go through the Rocky Mountains, they went east and down through Edmonton then Calgary, a route that appeals to Karl. Although they had nineteen encounters with bears, they tell him that moose are more of a concern, particularly if you surprise them. In turn, Karl warns them that using the rivers of the Darien is not the answer for them as they flow in the wrong direction for those moving south.

On 3 October, Karl leaves Salt Lake – a city founded by Mormons and still the centre of their world – and resumes his journey north-wards on the 89 North, a route that parallels the I-15. Mormon hospitality knows no bounds and he stays with more Internet-diary followers, Lee and Dale Huff in Centreville on his first night out, and with their son, Derek, in Ogden, a day later.

Over the next few weeks the temperature drops; leaves on the trees turn a golden brown and when it rains in town, there is a covering of snow in the surrounding mountain tops. Winter is on the way.

Tuesday, 8 October 2002   **Logan**

An even colder night and a thicker layer of ice on my tent. Without too much hanging about, I get up, pack up and move around to the front of the gas station, where I have my breakfast in Burger King. I stand for a moment while the first rays of the sun warm me up. Strange, but it only feels like five minutes ago that I was in the desert.

I walk ten miles to Logan. A few days ago, I caught up with Laura Lee, a journalist I first met at the ORS. I'd called the other day to let her know I'd be passing through Logan, where she lives, in the next day or two, so we put together a quick interview for a local newspaper that evening. She says I can stay.

Yesterday was a big day for Catty, as she was going to the US embassy in Bogotá to attempt to prise a visa from their grasp. I was feeling fairly confident, but she was less so. Her applications for

Guatemala and Mexico were both refused which shows how hard it is for a single girl. The US Immigration Service finds that none of the girls from Latin America who get visas ever go home again.

In town, there's no email or word from Catty. This is not a good sign and I feel a deep despair setting in. Sure enough, she emails to say that they have refused her a visa. I feel nauseous and can hardly believe I'm reading it. Then the sadness turns to anger. It appears they wouldn't even look at the papers or letter that she had with her. This is indeed as dark a day as I can ever remember.

Although a big blow, it's not that much of a surprise to Catty. She's losing hope and thinks she will never see me again. For two years she has been at the forefront of my dreams and at moments like this she's the one thing that holds me together. It's just too painful but I'm not prepared to accept it at all. I must be able to do something.

In my desperation I had suggested that if all else fails, we should marry, in Colombia. Plainly, I was running out of ideas. But as she's a sensible girl, she doesn't think it's great idea because it still might not work – yes, we'd be married but we could still end up living apart if she isn't allowed into the US. I'm pinning my last hope on the State Senate in Idaho, the next state on my route.

Wednesday, 16 October 2002   Preston

Temperatures at night fall to around –5 °C. Although my sleeping bag is rated down to –7 °C, if it's anywhere near zero I'm frozen and find it difficult to sleep even with spare kit on. I should have found a more substantial bag in Salt Lake City so this is a bit of a cock-up. Climbing out of my bag and into a stinking – and literally frozen – set of clothes is nothing short of horrible. I so hate the mornings.

As I walk, Catty is on my mind. How, I wonder, can I get in touch with the Senate or the Governor's office when I'm out here? As I mull it over, a car pulls over and a large elderly woman wearing a Burger King uniform of all things squeezes out. She's a member of the press. I go through the ritual of explaining what I'm up to when she lets on that the State Governor is actually in Preston today. It's a long shot but, getting all excited, I ask her if she can fix up a meeting with him. She agrees to the mission and shoots off for town.

I switch up a gear. I actually break into a run, the first time ever I have run with the trailer, and soon eat up the few miles to Preston. To get his opinion, I phone a chum, another Dean, in Pocatello – a place on the route a few days' further north – for his thoughts. He gives the impression that he has some sway in the political scheme of things but tells me that, in truth, the Governor is not, in fact, the right guy – I need to be speaking to the State Senate.

Putting on the brakes, I look skyward. I'm soaked in sweat. Sod's Law, I think to myself, but that's the way it goes. Just at that moment a car pulls up. Out steps Larry Bradford, who just happens to be a State Representative. He asks if I'm the guy who wants to speak to the Governor. Unfortunately, the Governor has already left.

Friday, 18 October 2002   McCallon

I'm back on the I-15 Interstate, which is bordered by flat farmland. Tonight in a small town called McCallon, I crash in the Moose Hollow Café. This place is a real classy log cabin. The walls are crowded with taxidermy. But the deer heads and antlers are dwarfed by a massive moose head which must have been shot by a tank. Apparently, all this stuff has been shot locally so this place is a real hunter's bar.

The natives seem very friendly. I get talking to two men, both the size of Grizzly Adams with long beards. Real mountain men. They tell me stories of how they survived in extreme conditions in these mountains, and how, one winter, they were cut off by snow and had to shelter in a cave for two months. They've run to fat, but I'm assured they were a lot leaner once. It's quite funny really. As we are talking, a family turns up and as the youngsters catch sight of these two, they scurry back out again and won't come in.

Neither of these big guys has a full set of teeth, and what they do have stick up like gravestones. I sit talking until it gets late and then push on down the road for a little while until I find a gas station with a truck park to hide up in. It's already cold and the temperature drops to –7 °C during the night.

Tuesday, 29 October 2002   St Anthony

The world is looking very grey all of a sudden and the trees have shed all of their leaves. It's still very dry, however, although there is some cloud about at present. It is definitely colder though, with day-time temperatures hardly picking up at all and I see a huge truck coming down from the north with great chunks of ice and snow falling off the rear.

On leaving the town of Wexburg I stop at a gas station and top up with some breakfast. When I re-emerge, it's snowing! It's quite heavy, in fact. This is the first snow I've seen this year, and I guess it's the start of a very cold six months. Brrr.

Although it's settling fast, this is wet snow . . . and it sucks. As soon as it lands on me it begins to melt, making things pretty miser-able. It is soon quite deep. Snowploughs create banks of slush at the sides of the road and it's all too apparent that I haven't got the right boots to deal with these conditions. Unfortunately, the Gore-Tex waterproof trousers that I have 'ride up' and snow and slush finds its way into the top of my boots. I need some snow gaiters and goggles because the snow is being driven into my face and sunglasses.

I end the day in the little town of St Anthony. Here I run into a chap who is a supervisor with the forestry commission. He's read about me in the newspapers and also seen me on the road. We get chatting away. He has a little pad up here where he stays if he can't make it home for the weekend so I'm in luck tonight. Because he covers vast areas and can be out for days on end, his outdoor kit is second to none and he offers me a lightweight sleeping bag and some snow goggles. He also finds me a 'Thermarest' (a self-inflating air sleeping mat to insulate against the cold ground). This is good news as I wanted to buy one of these, however thought they were too expensive. With this comes a cracking little inflatable pillow.

Forestry workers also get issued with US army ration-packs when 'in the field', and he gives me some of these. I'm looking to stock up on food anyway as the chances of re-supplying myself on a regular basis dwindle as the distance between the small towns increases. Unfortunately I can only manage to get four of these ration-packs into Beast II, so this will have to do. The rations are terrific – you just add water to a thin piece of sulphur compound material, which cre-ates a chemical reaction, heating the meal almost instantly.

Karl crosses from Idaho to Montana and into the Rocky Mountains. Climbing over Reynolds Pass at a height of 2050 metres, he also crosses the 'Continental Divide'. At this point all the water that falls to the west runs off into the Pacific Ocean and all to the east finds its way into the Mississippi River and the Atlantic. The fishing season is over, as is the best part of the hunting season so every business has closed down for the winter and it feels just like a scene from The Shining.

Monday, 4 November 2002   **Towards Ennis**

Outside my cosy hideaway it's blowing hard, but the snow is starting to melt and looking thinner on the ground. Prominent snow-covered mountains are within view; the Madison Range, with its highest peak of 3385 metres, runs northwards on my right and the Gravelly Range is to my left.

I'm following the Madison River up a dark black valley when I chance upon a small fishing and hunting store . . . and lo and behold it's open. I push my luck by going in to see if there's anything this log cabin can offer in the way of food. A large glass-fronted fridge stands empty but for two small pots of yoghurt . . . yes! I take these two pots of gold to the checkout where a happy-faced, chubby man with a large, thick moustache grins at me. He picks up the pots, squints at them, then drops them in the bin.

'Sorry, these are out of date,' he says.

'Bollocks,' I hiss. I stand and stare longingly at the bin. 'I don't suppose you have anything else, anything at all. Er, coffee perhaps?'

'Sure,' he continues breezily. 'Ya want coffee . . . ya hungry?'

He leads through to the back, up some stairs and into a lavish kitchen. Log cabins just aren't what they used to be. He makes me a cup of coffee that almost tears my head off, but it's hot and wet. Result.

Thursday, 7 November 2002   **Towards Ennis**

I pitch the tent in a large culvert under the road that looks more like an underground aircraft hangar. It's out of sight as well as out of the wind and the receding patches of snow. Just at present, life in my little green home is pretty good. I have some extras, like my new lightweight sleeping bag, plus I still have the fleece bag liners – they're excellent. I'm so warm that I can keep my damp socks and clothing on and come the morning, it's dry. My only problem now is it's all so comfortable I don't want to get up in the morning.

But in the early hours, in pitch darkness, I wake suddenly, on instant alert. Something else is in the tunnel. Suddenly it makes a rush for the tent! Within a split second the tent wall bulges as something tears at the material. Jesus Christ! I've not had time to even get out of my bag! What the hell is it . . . a bear, a mountain lion . . . or what? Phew. It's tumbleweed. Two very large tumbleweeds had been blown into the culvert and had come bouncing through before getting caught up in the lines of my tent. Their coarse, spiky, dry branches made an almost deafening noise as the wind tried to tear them loose. I sit wide-eyed and panting, heart pounding, pumped full of adrenalin.

Karl stays in Helena for almost a month, awaiting news from the US embassy. When it comes it's the worst that it could be: officials refuse Catty a second interview and their initial decision stands. This, he thinks, could mean the end of their long-distance love affair. With no reason to sit tight any longer, he sets off again on the I-15 heading north for Great Falls on 14 December.

Monday, 16 December 2002   Somewhere Near Wolf Creek

It's a little chilly and there's a stiff breeze, but still no signs of snow. I have a problem with a wheel coming loose. The bearing housing is unscrewing – this will eventually damage the bearings, a disaster as I have no spares. I have no second spanner or pliers to tighten it, only my Leatherman, which on its own cannot do the job. Bugger! It doesn't look or sound very healthy.

I'm now in a very remote area. Holding my breath, I carry on, wobbly wheel and all until I find the next settlement, which is a detour well off the highway. I find seven houses among a number of farm buildings. After knocking on every door and a search I realise that there's not a soul to be found. Christ, all I need is one spanner but I'm forced to wait until 15:30 when someone arrives and I'm able to get the job done. But it's 16:00 before I'm back on the highway, and time to find a hole to hide in. I've lost half a day – a real bummer – and now it's almost dark.

Half an hour later, I do the dumbest thing imaginable. Recently, I switched from ordinary gasoline to Colemans' fuel to use with my stove. This is clear and I've been keeping it in one of my plastic bottles. In growing gloom I fill one of my pans from this plastic bottle, thinking that it is water . . . then put it on my stove to boil. At this point I'm in my tent, which is all closed up nicely as the wind is now blowing a gale outside.

Preparing my food, I notice that the pan is boiling already. Then the fumes ignite. Within a fraction of a second the temperature in my tent climbs from −7 °C to something akin to the surface of the sun! A bright fireball rises and dramatically fills the inner chamber of the tent. This, however, isn't the time for panic. With due haste, though as calmly as I can, I reach for the pan handle through the now blue flames and, unzipping the tent, ease the pan into the night. Once in the wind, it becomes an inferno and roars away like a blazing oil-well fire.

This has only taken a few seconds . . . my mind is still wondering why my water burst into flames? Talk about confused. Miraculously, I'm unharmed. Hair is missing from my hands and face but that's it. Had I knocked over the pan, I would have been doomed, as the tent would have been flooded with burning fuel. Clambering outside I suffocate the flames and then, still not quite with it, pick the pan up by the handle. Sssssss. I'm branded.

Further north, the Rocky Mountains begin to give way to the flat expanses of the Great Northern Prairies as Karl moves through the sleepy towns in the top part of Montana. The fields are a buff sand colour, with all the crops cut down to stubble, and it is unusually mild for December.

Wednesday, 25 December – Friday, 27 December 2002   Conrad

I arrive at sunset with a sore back and feet, and find myself eating at a gas station café called the 'Town Pump'. I've not been here long before two very good-looking girls with a camcorder turn up. Judging by their excitement you don't get a lot of 'celebrities' in town. They end up inviting me back to one of their parents' house where they are having a bit of a bash with friends and family. Very posh house it is too, obviously reasonably well-off.

I'm not even sure what they think I am, but even though I've just pulled fifty-four kilograms for twenty-one miles it probably never occurred to them that I might not be in my best party head-banging mood. Lots of people and noise but I don't know anyone here. They're all a decade younger than me, college freshmen, or some still at high school, and I've got the feeling that I'm a disappointment. But I am grateful to be here. It's Christmas and I could be sat alone in some gas station. As I sit here, a glass of wine in hand, I can't help but dwell on where I was this time last year . . . with Catty. I've tried as best I can not to go there but can't help it.

We move location now but it's just the same; a house full of kids, beer, dope and very loud music. I'm drunk and getting drunker, sitting on the sofa with a dog sleeping on my lap . . . just like some granddad. Some eighteen-year-old girl is pissed off with me and calls me dull and moody. I smile and explain: 'No . . . I'm just older.' Eventually, everyone leaves for yet another house, but I remain behind and kip on the sofa.

The following morning I'm hungover with a hellish headache after a night of wine and tequila. I think I'll move on tomorrow but on the way to the café, I notice bad pains in my right knee. I panic a little but I'm convinced it will pass if I rest up for the remainder of today.

I continue to meet up with lots of folks in Conrad. As news spreads, people come down to the Town Pump just to meet me. I'm sitting at my table signing autographs as if I'm at some kind of a book signing. At one point I have seven college girls fussing over me. It's all very flattering.

The pains in Karl's knee persist but he decides to make a move and sets out from Conrad. Although it is mild at first, the weather changes and it starts to snow and turns to rain. It is cold at night – around –6 °C – and he decides to rest for two days in Shelby, the last main town in the US, where friends from Helena pay him a surprise visit and book him a room in a motel.

Next day – New Year's Eve – just nineteen miles (thirty kilometres) from the Canadian border, he pulls into the 4 Corners Bar at Exit 379. He has barely seen a soul on the road all day and inside, just two elderly men are sitting at the bar. But it isn't long before

*others start to turn up, most of them oil-field workers from
Oilmount (population: ten) and from Kevin (population: thirty-two).*

*Those at the bar are friendly enough and ask him to sit and have
a drink with them when they see him working alone at his laptop. He
has a few drinks, but as he's sleeping out tonight, doesn't drink too
much and stays just long enough to see in 2003. Just around from
the exterior door and under the window is Beast II. Like most nights
when he steps outside, he expects to find it covered with a layer of
sparkling frost. Not tonight . . . it's gone.*

Wednesday, 1 January 2003   4 Corners Bar

Time stands still for a couple of seconds and then that sickening
feeling wells up in the pit of my stomach. I stand motionless in disbelief. It's happened . . . it has finally happened. I walk around the
building just in case someone has moved it, but I know, I just know,
it's gone. I push out my search radius to include the wood line and
ditches now on the fringe of the light radiating from the bar. It really
has gone. I feel a sickness that slowly turns to anger. I swallow deeply
and take a couple of deep breaths before re-entering the festive
atmosphere of the bar.

I check my cellphone . . . no signal, but I knew that anyway as I'd
tried it when I first got here. I go and sit back at the bar. The jukebox
spits out good old country music very loudly as I order a glass of
wine. A local throws his arms around me, his breath a mixture of
beer and chewing tobacco. The barmaid brings me my drink: 'On the
house,' she says, still unaware of my predicament. I ask her for a
phone.

I don't know the police-post number so just ring 911 then explain
it's not an emergency but I need an officer to stop by as I've had a lot
of equipment stolen. I'm hit with 101 questions but have no intention of trying to thrash this one out on the phone as I know how
confusing it will get. As I try to suppress the raging firestorm inside,
I just try calmly to tell the woman that I really do need to see an officer in order that I can explain in detail what it's all about.

I sit and wait. This is one of the darkest moments I can remember.
I close my eyes as the enormity of the loss sinks in. My photos from
way back in Chile . . . all gone. I had a collection of maps from the

day I began the expedition, with every place I had slept marked on them with the date, covering the past four years . . . all gone. And Beast II, an old friend all the way from León in Nicaragua. The more I think about it, the more I can recall just how much I've lost.

'What's the matter with ya, come on, Happy New Year,' says an oil worker. 'Have another one on me, walker.'

Christ, I don't even want to tell them. How long will it take the police to arrive? The locals are shocked. Here! Now! In our community . . . they can't believe what has just happened under their noses. The festive mood turns to disbelief, anger and then to a succession of apologies. These people are genuinely outraged and ashamed. They insist that they don't lock their cars or homes, as this sort of thing never happens in these parts. This is why it probably happened to me, as I had never felt safer. This is the last place I can imagine this happening . . . you drop your guard just the once. Now what? Where do I go from here?

A thin layer of snow has fallen in the latter half of the evening and yet there are no tracks that may indicate where Beast II has gone. Christ Almighty! It started snowing around 20:00 so it could have been missing for hours. The party is somewhat subdued now. Well, aren't I the party-pooper.

Some time later the police arrive and take statements.

'So let me get this right. You left all your kit sitting outside the bar all night?' says an officer, almost incredulously.

I almost expect them to start sniggering. What can I say but 'Yes'. The cops look at each other. I know immediately that this is going nowhere.

'So what now?' I ask, as if I need to ask.

'Well, we'll have a look around, but it will probably turn up for sure,' one says.

'Turn up?' I feel my stomach tighten.

There then follows a rather confused conversation as I try to describe Beast II.

'A what? . . . a trailer . . . a what?'

They decide to have a drive out to the nearest settlements. I look down the pitch-black road now covered in a thick fog. You can't see Jack . . . I sigh to myself. I'm told I can sleep on the police station floor when I ask if I can go back with them. Locals offer to put me up, but I don't need to be stuck out here now, I need to be back in Shelby. If I am still at the 4 Corners when the officers get back they agree to take me.

I sit at the bar for what feels like an eternity. Others arrive having heard the news. There's a group that were here earlier. One is the girl who works behind the motel desk in Shelby and she suggests slipping to Kevin, which is just up the road, to see if anyone knows anything. It's nice of her – it also beats just sitting here like a sad puppy.

It's not a good road out to Kevin and the visibility is appalling in the fog. She swerves a little.

'You all right?' I ask.

'Yeah, just a bit pissed,' she says.

'How pissed?' I wonder.

'Ahhh . . . a bit.'

'Well just keep it slow,' I advise.

We finally arrive at a small bar, which is just closing, it now being about 03:00. Inside, another player from the 4 Corners Bar has got here before us, despite being extremely drunk. There's no further information to be had and so we head back. Not far from the bar my driver decides to pull into a house to speak to a youngster known to be a local tearaway. Following us back is the extremely drunken guy that beat us out to Kevin. As the girl slows to turn, the inevitable happens. There comes a crunching impact from behind throwing our car into a spin and we end up off the road, smashed car-parts spewing across the road. Bollocks! I jump out and check on the other guy . . . he's fine, but both cars are a mess. The night just can't get any worse than this . . . or can it? Well it does.

Who should show up at that very moment but the two cops. For fuck's sake! I'm all right, but these two people, who had set out tonight with only good intentions, are now in deep shit. It just goes from bad to worse. The police know these two very well, of course, as you can imagine in this small community, but they still go through the official accident procedure.

The driver of the rear car is so drunk he wobbles as he stands up, but they still ask him to perform some on the spot tasks, which, of course, he fails miserably, and both he and my driver are duly breathalysed. I stand shivering on the side of the road in only my thin T-shirt and jacket, neck rapidly stiffening up from the whiplash.

Christ, it's cold. Needless to say, on top of everything else I am feeling more than a little responsible for this mess. A policeman informs both drivers that they are over the limit, however, he will cut them some slack. The girl gets reported for no insurance and the guy for reckless driving. They could have both been in the slammer. The police then drive them both home while I sit in one of the wrecked cars until their return whereupon I'm given a ride to Shelby police station.

They give me a cup, a toothbrush and two little tubes of toothpaste, a bar of soap and two blankets. I then find myself a space on the floor. Losing everything is still taking its time to sink in. Ironically, for the first time ever I was truly happy with every bit of equipment I had. I'd been living more comfortably than ever before. I had the best waterproof Gore-Tex jacket and the best sleeping system, oh, and my radio as well. Arrgghhh, for Christ's sake! Well, I suppose I've still got my laptop so it's not all that bad. Actually, it is.

Karl speaks to the local TV news but neither the police nor the public have any word on Beast II. Locals call to commiserate and even put up a $500 reward for its recovery but to no avail. Fortunately, someone offers him the annexe in Tracy, a small community south east of Great Falls so at least he has a temporary base. Wasting no time, he then finds an engineering workshop in Helena that will build Beast III and he moves there.

Beast III is finished but he is unimpressed with the strength of the frame although it has a far superior box. Then just as he pays the bill – $400 – the police in Shelby call to say they've found the old one. What remains is just the frame; it's bent here and there, and there are some cracks in the welds but he decides that it is still sturdier than its replacement. Putting the new box on the old frame, he leaves the new frame with friends as a spare.

Thursday, 13 February 2003   The Canadian Border

Total distance to date: 12,014 miles (19,346 km)
Once again, I'm off with just nineteen miles to push to the Canadian border. It's good to be moving again. A bit on the cold side, at least

it isn't raining, which is good thing because my plastic waterproofs are crap.

The day goes well and ends with a climb over some small hills before dropping down into Sweetgrass and the crossing point. On the US side they know who I am and what has happened, so I don't get any grief over leaving without a visa. [*Stolen along with his passport in BII. The British Embassy had sent a new passport, but this did not have a visa stamp*]. Similarly, I've no problems on the Canadian side, and having asked if I can have an extended visa, I'm given one year.

Karl scours a Salvation Army store and a number of second-hand shops to reclothe and re-equip himself as cheaply as possible pending a re-supply of some decent gear from The North Face.

Chapter Nine

CANADA AND ALASKA

Friday, 14 February 2003   **Beyond the Border**

This morning a thick layer of snow lay on the ground and it is definitely still in the air. A lot colder than yesterday, I'm forced to don my new plastic waterproofs so I end up soaked in sweat. It's driving sleet and snow for a good number of hours. I find this area windy and just so bloody bleak. The flat landscape is depressing in some way. Out in this open world I find it a real problem even trying to have a pee in private, there's just nowhere to hide away from the traffic, there's no dead ground.

By the end of play I cross a river then find a culvert where I can hide under the road. I scoop up some clean snow to melt for water. Happily I don't have to use the tent, which isn't up to this climate at all. It won't free-stand and needs to be pegged down half the time. Unfortunately, the ground is so frozen at present I can't get the pegs in and they just fold in half.

In the darkness I listen to the coyotes howling close by. I have a mouse running around my kit, a noisy little bastard. I click on my torch to find it sitting right by my head, but the bright light right on top of him does not seem to worry him at all. He sits and nibbles on an empty food wrapper that he's stolen from my food bag. He's at it all night.

Thursday, 20 February 2003   **Towards Suffield**

Bleakness and so cold. There's a bitter wind that burns my face and leaves ice around my nose and mouth as my breath freezes instantly. Luckily, I have a spare woollen hat in which I cut holes for my eyes and

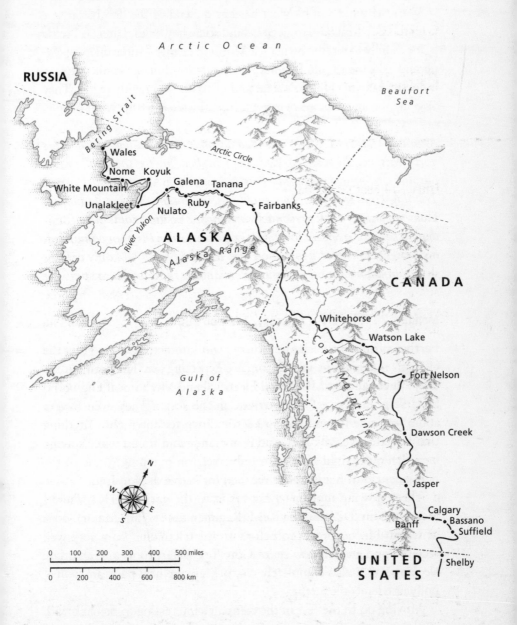

mouth in an attempt to limit the amount of exposed skin. The wind chill factor is below –40 °C today – winter has arrived in these parts.

With the wind still blowing hard at the end of the day I stop at a farm to ask permission to sleep behind some hay bales. Later, as I settle in for a chilly night, the owner – a Mormon farmer – turns up in a pick-up and asks me to join him and his family for dinner. Needless to say it doesn't take me long to accept and I end up sleeping there too. They also slip me an envelope before I turn in. Inside is $100. What people.

Although Calgary is Karl's intended destination north-west, he detours north-east, via the town of Medicine Hat, heading for the small prairie outpost of Suffield, Alberta. This is home to BATUS (British Army Training Unit Suffield). This small base maintains a large number of tanks and armoured personnel carriers for visiting units when they deploy here for overseas live-firing exercises. Given his poor equipment, his father thinks that it is a good idea to call in here. Not only will the troops boost his morale, they may have some superior kit to spare.

Monday, 24 February – Saturday, 1 March 2003   Suffield

I arrive, blistered to hell after thirty-eight kilometres, to find that the civilians manning the guardroom are expecting me. They call out the duty officer and REME (Royal Electrical and Mechanical Engineers) Staff Sergeant Steve Porett arrives on the scene. They even have a room set aside for me and so I settle down for the night. Anything that I need Steve will 'sort' and is my guide and friend while staying here. It's quiet right now with only skeleton manning, some of the permanent staff having been recalled for active duty in Iraq.

The following morning I am taken to the garrison HQ where I meet Captain 'DZ' and the RSM (Regimental Sergeant Major), both of whom I have spoken to before on the telephone. I am very well received and given a new set of Gore-Tex waterproofs and an arctic sleeping bag. I also completely re-stock my medical pack and some-body else lends me a tent.

Moving on to the rest of the camp, it's interesting to be back with the boys again. Theirs is a unique culture that few outsiders would understand and even I admit that, despite my twelve years' service, I could never quite click 100 per cent with the mentality of junior ranks. That said, I am enjoying seeing it in action again.

The first thing I realise, or rather I'm reminded of, is how mercilessly soldiers take the piss out of everything. No one or no thing is sacred. I am enveloped in the feeling that I'd never really left this environment, that perhaps I was just having a short break. Everything is so familiar, the cookhouse routine, the uniforms ... somehow I am just happy to be back. For a moment, I'm in a world that I know, recognise and feel safe in. It is somewhere that I understand.

Before I head off, I also get chance to chat to Catty over the Net, which after such a long time is a real boost. It seems it's not over yet. In a final effort she has sent her papers off to the Canadian embassy requesting a visitor's visa and is now waiting to hear. So I've now got something else to worry about. I find it is emotionally draining, all this building up my hopes and then being let down repeatedly.

Karl's father has decided that he and his son Ben – Karl's twelve-year-old step brother – are coming out on a short trip to Canada, between 6–13 March. They will be bringing a complete re-supply of equipment and will be staying with Bill Anderson in Calgary while they're here. Bill is another who has simply picked up on the expedition on the Web and offered to help. The plan is to meet them on 7 March at a truck stop near the small settlement of Bassano, not quite halfway towards Calgary.

Saturday, 1 March 2003   Leaving Suffield

It's about 116 kilometres to Bassano so I should be there well in time. I'm walking down the hard shoulder of Route 1, the Trans-Canadian Highway. Cutting across the open plains, the broad highway has a grassy central reservation and good hard shoulders, allowing me to keep away from the traffic lanes. This is just as well because in places the road is as straight as an arrow for miles and allows the massive trucks and trailers to set their 'cruise-control', so they don't expect to see the likes of me.

But having said that, at present I am enduring very high winds and snow storms, to the extent that sometimes it's a complete white-out, and needless to say very dodgy on this road. Luckily, and I say that reservedly, this snow is not the same type of snow that you see in

Britain. Because of the intense cold the snow almost seems to be dry, like a powder. If you get covered in it you can simply brush it off, with the clothes remaining dry, unlike at home where it soaks in. Given that it doesn't cling or pack down easily, the stuff blows about in swirling drifts across the road. Large trucks, travelling at speed, will have a maelstrom of spiralling snow clouds in their wake so the highway is kept clear of snow by both the wind and the vehicles.

I am glad of my new set of waterproofs as they deflect a lot of the bitter wind. One of the lads also gave me a neoprene face mask, but unfortunately I don't have any goggles, only a set of sunglasses, so I pick up some mild frostbite on the upper part of my cheeks. I'm well looked after by farmers. I spend most nights indoors as the people I meet are very reluctant to let me stay outside during this cold period. It's just as well really, because the tent I had borrowed, although better than the one I bought, would still have been blown apart in these winds.

Friday, 7 March 2003   Back to Calgary

The sky is a light grey, which then seems to merge with snow on the ground only a few hundred metres away so that the whole world is white. Now and then there is a flurry of snow. There's a stiff breeze blowing and with the wind chill factor it's below −30 °C when Bill Anderson's pick-up appears.

It's been four and a half years since I last saw my father, and yet within a couple of seconds it's as if it was only last week. Ben, of course, has shot up. It's even longer since I've seen him and that really does emphasise just how long I've been away. Not wanting to spend too long outside as it's absolutely freezing, we make for the shelter of the café. There's a chat and a couple of coffees, then we load BII into the back of Bill's pick-up and head off for Calgary.

Bill has a workshop at the rear of the house, and although it remains cold for the next couple of days there's bags of room (and a heater) in here so I can get comfortable. Dad and Ben are sleeping in Bill's study and we're all made extremely welcome by Bill's family.

Father has brought my re-supply from The North Face UK, which has replaced everything that was nicked in Montana. There's a tent, sleeping bag, waterproofs, fleeces, gloves, balaclava and much more spread all across Bill's living room carpet. I'm back in the major league again.

Sunday, 9 March 2003   Bassano

Dad hires a pick-up and we head off back to the truck stop where I'd met them. Apart from getting me back on to the road, the intention today is to use the opportunity to do some filming with the digital camcorder that Dad has brought with him for me. For a couple of hours or more I walk up and down the highway, waiting for the next big truck to pass so that I can mysteriously appear out of the swirling snowdrift.

Every ten to fifteen minutes, I have to defrost my un-acclimatised 'camera crew' in the café because there is a wind chill factor of −47 °C today. In these extreme temperatures, the batteries soon drain and once inside the humid atmosphere of the café, a layer of ice instantly forms on the frozen camera.

Monday, 10 March 2003   Beyond Bassano

Last night, Father and Ben went back to Calgary and I spent the night in a lone motel on the roadside.

I set off at around 10:00. This is maybe a good opportunity to try out my new camcorder for the first time on my own and I fumble awkwardly with cold hands, and then gloves, catching some footage on videotape.

The wind persists all afternoon, but starts to die down slightly at around 15:30, when I come across a few farmhouses clumped together in the middle of nowhere. I decide that this is fate. Not fancying erecting my tent in these chilly winds, I will ask if I can pitch it behind the barn, or somewhere that will give me a windbreak. I pull off the road on to what I think is stable ground, but unfortunately Beast II crashes through a snowdrift into a ditch, tipping sideways, taking me down with it into the snow. After a few minutes' rolling and thrashing about I manage to extricate it from the ditch and back on to two wheels.

Not wishing to push my luck I leave it there and walk the short distance to the nearest farmhouse. A kind, elderly lady answers the door and after my request, insists that I sleep in one of the barns tonight. Not long after I've set myself up in the barn, the wind drops off, but no matter, as I'm far better off in the barn than outside in a tent.

Tuesday, 11 March 2003   Gleichen

This morning my father and Ben are driving out from Calgary to join me on the road. It's cold again and although the sun is out at full strength, with just the odd little cloud, it is still quite nippy. After about an hour I begin to warm up and find that I can remove some items of clothing, including my gloves. However, around mid-morning the weather changes and a wind blows that causes the temperature to plummet. I'm forced to mask my face as the biting wind is very painful. Plumes of spindrift and white tornadoes swirl across the tarmac. It's by no means as bad as it was last week, but it's still making me work hard.

Father and Ben turn up in a jeep that they've hired to take a trip up into the Rockies. We sit in the warm cab for a while over a hot drink and talk about the preceding days' visit to the mountains. We attempt some more filming and then it's time for me to head off to a small gas station and café on top of the hill some six kilometres away. Ben decides that he will walk with me and also has a turn pulling Beast II. Dad drives ahead to meet us at the café. Back inside again, we have a coffee and get a chance to talk things over for a while. But all too soon it's time to push on and I say my final good-byes as they are flying home tomorrow.

In the late afternoon, another English person stops me when I arrive in the small hamlet of Gleichen. She has noticed the Union Jacks on Beast II and is naturally curious. She's Janet, a teacher, and she invites me to spend the night at her place with her and her hus-band, Keith. I accept the kind invitation and as soon as I've finished eating, pack up and move around to the address a block or two away. I'm in good company.

Wednesday, 12 March 2003   Gleichen

When packing up to leave, Catty calls me on my cellphone. She's in Bogotá and is preparing for her interview – her chance for a Canadian visa. She's going to call me as soon as she comes out of the interview.

Janet and Keith can see that I'm somewhat anxious and urge me to wait here for the call. It comes at 14:00 and I feel the pit of my stomach twist. My fears are confirmed when I hear her sad voice. Sure enough, the Canadians have turned her down yet again. The poor girl had been dragged back to Bogotá only to be refused once more.

I'm angry for her. I think that there is only one chance remaining. As she has already been granted a visa by the British embassy to visit the UK, perhaps she will have better prospects if she attends an interview with the Canadians in London having a British visa already in her passport. I email her this evening and ask her to pack her bags and fly to England as soon she can. I message my father asking him to look after her and to take her to the interview. If he can sit in on the interview and explain about the expedition, perhaps this will swing it.

When Karl arrives at the outskirts of Calgary on 14 March, rain is turning to heavy snow. He is met by Bill Anderson, who lets him stay in the workshop at his home again. Although not particularly luxurious it's quite snug and Bill gives him an old gas heater that keeps the place warm.

Catty, meanwhile, has flown to the UK. Staying at his father's house in Hereford, they go to the Canadian embassy in London on 31 March but, again, she is denied a visa outright.

An immigration consultancy company, Van Reekum Veress, takes up the case. Peter Veress, the firm's senior partner, is optimistic and, because he has already heard of the expedition, is prepared to do this work for free. He asks for papers, letters and documents, which his firm will need to prepare a crack presentation to the immigration service. This takes a month so, by now, Karl has been in Calgary almost four months. This concerns him and his back-up team at home. But Karl knows that once beyond Calgary there is little chance of Catty ever getting a visa.

Catty returns to Colombia and Peter arranges to accompany her to the Canadian embassy in Bogotá. It costs $1,000 to fly him down and, after some misgivings from Karl's father, the expedition pays. But despite these efforts, the final answer is still 'no'. In Canada, over 6000 Colombians were claiming refugee status and 3000 of them had come in on visitors' visas, each of which cost the government $40,000 to process.

As Karl starts to pack up again, he decides he must see his girl-friend, perhaps for the last time. Although he can ill afford it, he has reached the point where the money does not matter to him anymore. For the sake of his sanity he has to see her so he heads for Colombia, where they spend a very happy month together in Medellin.

Thursday, 24 July 2003   Back in Calgary

Total distance to date: **12,328 miles (19,852 km)**
After half a day of buggering about trying to finish off what I could not get done last night I'm finally set to go. Instantly, I find that Beast II is very heavy. This is a cause for concern as I'm heading again into the Rockies. It's a warm day, with just enough cloud to keep the sun from doing its thing. It's just right for walking but I know that I'm in for a kicking, having been static for so long. The roads into Calgary from the south had been mainly flat but as I leave town this quickly changes. It's not so much that they are 'big', it's just that they are 'rolling'. And God does it hurt.

I aim to crash at a gas station about thirty kilometres out of town, but as the day drags on it appears to have fallen off the edge of the world. Just as I'm about to quit for the day, it makes its appearance.

Saturday, 26 July 2003   Canmore

I am now in the Rocky Mountains, or at least just on my way in. In the distance there are huge plumes of smoke billowing into the sky, but luckily these are from controlled burning, unlike the forest fires that have been raging in other National Parks in BC (British Columbia) and up near Jasper. Today I feel better, I think I'm find-ing my road legs again. A car full of young guys passes and then turns around to come back. They had been reading *Hooked*, an outdoor magazine, and an article about the expedition only moments before they had come across me on the road. I'm asked to sign each copy.

I reach the town of Canmore. The afternoon is spent raiding the local fast-food joints before moving to the outskirts of the town to camp up. Canmore reminds me of a counterfeit Swiss village. Very picturesque, with its pleasant mountain views. However, it doesn't take more than a quick glance to spot that it's a tourist trap in the waiting, just so damn expensive.

Sunday, 27 July 2003   Banff

After breakfast I set off for Banff. It's very warm today as it has been for a few days, but I have the beautiful scenery of this part of the world to take my mind off it. Once in Banff, I am to meet an independent journalist, Kisha Ferguson, who has been commissioned by the Canadian Broadcasting Corporation (CBC), to put together an item for one of their radio programmes.

Kisha's plan is to walk with me until we reach Jasper, a good distance of about 300 kilometres. She had been an editor with a Canadian magazine called *Outpost*, which ran an article on me not so long ago. We sit, eat and talk until late. I'm very relieved to find that Kisha is easy to get on with, as I held some trepidation about walking a long distance with someone else. I am now going to be walking with a woman . . . but not the woman I had planned to or dreamed it might be. Somehow I feel as though life is mocking me.

Tuesday, 29 July 2003   Beyond Banff

All around the area of Banff the scenery is breathtaking. At the first chance we come off the highway and take a back road that parallels it. With a bit of luck we'll now leave the heavy trucks and traffic behind. It's a little tough on Kisha to start with, but she copes well. Hopefully this road will lead us to a series of campsites where we can pitch tent at the end of the day as it's illegal to just camp anywhere in the national parks. In dire need I suppose we can sneak off into the woods but it pays to be careful around here. The campsites themselves are small areas set aside in pine forests and cost about $17 per night. It has to be said they are well-kept, smell of pine and are surrounded by huge mountains. The place is infested with squirrels, not that they're a problem, however we are now well into bear country so at night all your food has to be kept well away from the tent and hung in a tree in a bear bag . . . just in case a hungry monster comes lurking.

Sunday, 3 August 2003 {Bow Pass}

Sunday, 3 August 2003   **Bow Pass**

Today we walk through some of the most amazing scenery. Clear blue lakes, smooth as table tops, stretch from the roadside to the base of the snow-capped mountains and glaciers.

We stop for lunch at an extremely posh lodge cum rich man's hotel on the edge of the lake. The Num-Ti-Ja lodge is a tourist hot spot from where people hike up on to the glacier. The manager has read about the expedition and so Kisha and I pick up a free meal in exchange for a photo op outside the main entrance.

From here we climb very steadily up on to the Bow Pass, at 2068 metres the highest point on this road. We have been climbing very slowly for many days now, since leaving Banff in fact. It's then down, down and down until we crash into the forest to camp.

Tuesday, 5 August 2003   **Saskatchewan River Crossing**

We now push on to Saskatchewan River Crossing. While walking along I spot what appears to be a large mass of black hair in the bush at the side of the road, and not far to our front . . . and it's moving!

'Kish, stop!' We pause.

A black bear's head pops into view, seemingly taken by surprise.

'Get the camera,' I whisper.

Unfortunately the camera is in BII and as she moves the bear makes a run for it, back into the forest. So, this is our first encounter with a bear.

Thursday, 7 August 2003   **Towards Jasper**

The ground is very rough and as we leave this morning I find it easier to push BII rather than pull it. It starts me thinking about these other people walking around the world and how much easier it is for them pushing their pram-like set-ups. What if, at the end of the day, they feel so much better than me because as well as pulling I'm also carrying a good deal of weight, not just in my rucksack but the weight of the Beast pulling down on my shoulders. By the time we get to the road it occurs to me just how much easier it has been to get down here, how about seeing how it copes with the road. I've never even thought about turning BII around and just pushing, it doesn't look as if it could be suited to such a thing.

However, over the next few hundred metres I'm absolutely amazed at just how easy it is. In fact the more I push and think about it, the easier it gets. Well, I'll be damned! I'm almost in shock. Kisha finds this puzzling.

'You mean you've never tried this before?'

'No, not at all!'

Despite being built with pulling in mind it moves very easily when pushed, all the weight being on the wheels. All I have to do is lift the two shafts and tip the box forward until the centre of gravity shifts to directly over the wheels. It then moves effortlessly and balances so well that I can almost hold it in place with just one finger while I walk. More importantly, I can place my rucksack across the two shafts and BII can now carry this added weight with seemingly no extra effort from me. And downhill, it's almost pulling me along. Oh my God, I feel sick. It means that after four and a half years I have at last realised just how much easier the thousands of miles might have been. Four and a half shagging years, it's hard to get my head around it. Possibly BI, with its different configuration, may not have worked like this, but on the other hand it might well have. I continue to push BII for the rest of the day.

Wednesday, 13 August 2003   **Jasper**

Jasper is vastly expensive and there just isn't anywhere to stay for under $100. Kisha immediately gets on to her contacts and very quickly has a place sorted out for us, and free of charge. They have got us another hostel, Hostelling International-Jasper. The only problem is that it's seven kilometres back down the road and I could do without that part. BII ends up staying at the workshop and we catch a shuttle bus to the hostel.

I have greatly enjoyed Kisha's company, she was definitely one of the guys, very smart and fun to talk with. After she leaves I move out of the hostel into a wood behind and, although sleeping in my tent at night, I'm allowed to use the hostel's facilities. I make some good friends within the staff and in reality I could have stayed in the hostel if I'd really wished, but I do not want to impose myself. I find it an interesting place to be stuck. I've not had a lot of experience in hostels and the last one I was in, before the Banff area, was in Quito, Ecuador. Unlike that one, here they have a very fast turnover with no one hanging around long at all, one or two days max. These places are just too expensive to hang out in and folk on vacation have limited time. They will rush in and dash about, before shooting off on a bike ride, a walk or rafting, etc., cramming in as much as they can in the time they have. With each turnover of occupants this place takes on a different feel. Some nights it's a continual party with everyone really chatty, then other nights it's dead. Full of people, but dead, with everyone just sat around reading.

At night I wander off back into the wood. This becomes a little creepy. There are elk and deer out here, as well as bears of course. The trick is knowing what it is that's crashing through the bush around your tent at 04:00. If you make a noise, things like deer and sometimes elk will run, but it's worrying when whatever it is does not, but continues to lumber heavily around. Now nearing the end of my stay I will go out on a combat elk patrol. Charge around the bush thrashing, yelling and throwing stones to move the group out of the area so that I can sleep. Unfortunately, they are now starting to breed and will occasionally emit a high-pitched scream. Not what you want when you're half asleep at 04:00. I chase the herd up on to the road and then along it. I am at one with nature, or at least have an understanding with nature . . . This is my wood, piss off out.

However, a bull elk in the rutting season is not likely to be intimidated by the likes of me. One night coming back to the tent, approaching the wood line where it's hidden, I stop dead in my tracks, sure that there's something in front of me . . . but I'm not sure as to whether it's a tree or simply shapes in the grass. Whatever, it's not moving. The night is pitch black and all I have for light is my small close-quarters torch, with no real beam at all. I walk on for a few more steps, then stop again, something is not right. A car passes on a nearby road and as it turns its headlights sweep across the area to my front. To my horror I'm right on top of a full-blown bull elk. Towering above me, with a full rack of antlers, the monster seems sure that it's going to stand its ground. Luckily the car comes to a halt nearby and as all the doors open and close, this beast of the forest decides to move on. Only slowly mind you, and as I stand there rock-like, a group of females, again initially unseen, moves past on my left.

Karl spends three weeks in Jasper waiting for various bits of electrical equipment to arrive, including a solar panel which he will use for recharging purposes.

Friday, 26 September 2003   Grand Cashe

It's been nine days since I left Jasper, nine days since I heard that my last attempt to keep Catty had failed before it even got sent! So now I've switched my hopes to Britain again, this time trying to fool myself into believing that my own country will find sufficient interest and incentive to pull some strings for me. Should I put everyone through this again? But then, after what I've been through over the last nine days it would appear that I have little choice other than to live by following that dim and distant star of hope. The alternative is to go back out there into a night of complete darkness. There are certainly no lights at the end of my tunnel. In fact it's so fucking dark in here right now I think I'm losing my way.

There is absolutely nothing to look forward to at all . . . nothing. Possibly the next city? To be stuck with people I don't know, to sit and smile, to tell the whole shagging story again and again like some form of a desk-bound, trained receptionist. To listen to them telling me how glorious this all is. 'What an amazing life you lead, how free you are!' I'm a prisoner of the white lines on the freeway.

The room I'm staying in becomes a happy retreat, and the rum and Coke I'm drinking is doing all I asked of it by numbing my senses a little and letting me fall into a timely sleep. Waking late, I then sit stewing over my twentieth coffee in a motel diner. My main problem is summoning up enough enthusiasm to begin thinking my way out of this. I need a plan, 'Plan X' will do, and this plan will kick-start my bloodstream. It doesn't have to be sensible or even possible, just as long as I can focus on something. What have we got then? I trawl back through the files on 'Forgotten Schemes'. Plan X is not to be a new idea but a resurrected one. It is to be direct action applied to my little problem and for that reason is a most appealing option. As with all cracking plans, it's really simple. Go and get Catty then bring her back with me! The only obstacles are:

1. Eight international borders we would have to navigate illegally.
2. The time it would take.
3. The money it would cost.
4. How everyone behind the expedition would view such a move.

The logical answers to the above are in order, impossible, for ever, there is none for this and they will freak. So . . . it's a go then! But it feels like the only hope for life. I'm not sure everyone else will see it that way, though, nor do I expect them to really understand how I feel, living like I do. To some this may appear very irresponsible behaviour for someone with a passing crush on a Latin girl. Actually, I fear losing her more than I will ever fear the ice of the Arctic Ocean or Siberia.

From Catalina's perspective this must seem like madness . . . frightening and overwhelming. Once I stood there, too. It's a little like that balloon cage on basic parachute training. All you have to do is . . . jump.

Friday, 3 October 2003   Beyond Grand Cashe

There's lots of wildlife out here. Beavers playing about and loping down trees, and early in the morning I had some wolves quite near by.

At night I throw a line up into the trees and haul up my food bag to keep it out of the way of the bears. Now you have to be pretty nimble (as well as keeping your eye on it) to get out of the way of a fourteen-kilogram food bag when the thin pine branch snaps and it whistles earthwards. Today I'm not! I'm nearly pile-driven into the ground. Bears 0 . . . Anti-bear measures 1.

Karl heads on via Grand Prairie, reaching the start of the Alaskan Highway on 22 October. He reaches Fort St John on 2 November and continues north-west via Pink Mountain.

**Thursday, 13 November – Sunday, 16 November 2003   Towards
                                                          Fort Nelson**

It's been a few days now of steadily dropping and climbing. I've stopped making fires of an evening because it's getting too cold. Let me explain. To combat the night chill I'm forced to get closer to the fire. As I do, small embers are spat from the fire and start to burn holes in my clothing. I suppose I could spend some time building a reflector behind the fire to send more heat in my direction, but to be honest it's just not worth the effort. Mostly, I just want to get into some warm dry clothing, have something to eat and then sleep. The routine now becomes tent up, get in, gas stove on! The tent then rapidly warms up to about 30 °C, which is heaven after a day of –10 °C to –20 °C.

Today it's Prophet River and again there's very little here other than a camp for the oil-rig workers (capable of accommodating a couple of hundred men), a gas station and café. After a quick chat I get to sleep in one of the mobile cabins.

Near by is a small Indian reservation that clearly has a few problems. On my way into the settlement I come across a group of young First Nation people staggering along the road, smashed out of their skulls . . . and it's only the early afternoon. I soon realise that just about everyone I see from the reservation seems to be blitzed or struggling to recover. The café and gas station was sold to the reservation to help with employment, however they cannot find any local folk capable of keeping the job so now it's run by white folk from Fort Nelson. It's just not good.

**Monday, 17 November – Wednesday, 19 November 2003   Towards
                                                            Fort Nelson**

Three more days now and I'm rapidly approaching Fort Nelson. The temperature during the day averages out at about –20 °C and I'm coated in a thin layer of ice from body moisture. I find that just wearing a base layer and fleece jacket allows the moisture to escape and freeze on the outside, rather than the inside, making my day far more comfortable. As long as I maintain a reasonable pace I can keep my body core warmish.

I sit pondering at the end of 19 November in a café/truck stop on an outskirts industrial area. My thoughts lie with Plan X . . . that overwhelmingly ridiculous task. I have given myself three months from the point where I will meet Catty in Panama to both of us arriving in Canada, crossing seven borders on foot and evading capture! I'm reasonably confident we can manage Central America, although I don't know how Catty will cope with the strain. In Mexico, we can piggyback on trains to stay off the roads and then there is an elaborate plan to sneak across the desert into the US and finally around the border into Canada. Once in Canada, then what? I think we'll just need to play that one by ear. However, for now, my immediate objective is Fort Nelson.

In December, having rested up in Fort Nelson, Karl decides it is time to pause the expedition and put Plan X into action. Getting a lift back to Fort St John, he catches a flight, first to Calgary and then on to meet Catty in Panama City. But the plan is to prove short-lived: Karl and Catty only get as far as Costa Rica before chancing upon a television documentary about the appalling treatment of illegal 'aliens' in Mexico. They decide it is too big a risk and give up, Catty returning to Colombia and Karl back to the frozen wilderness of Canada.

Thursday, 1 January 2004   Fort Nelson

Leaving Fort Nelson was not meant to be like this. It was intended to be a far happier day and going back on to the road alone brought all my fears and disappointments home to roost. However, I leave at about midday and I'm kept occupied and my mind busy by the fact that the air temperature is −40 °C, or even lower. I eventually come across a house that has a large space at the rear, so I approach the owner and ask if I can camp there. The day ends with them letting me use their camper van to sleep in, which is a real stroke of luck as it's bitter outside, in fact, evil would be a better word.

Friday, 2 January 2004   Beyond Fort Nelson

An absolutely horrendous day. Plastic items like buckles and clips on the Beast and my equipment freeze into an almost glass-like state and begin to break. I just can't wait to get off the road, into my tent and fire up the stove. Once inside my sleeping bag I'm happier, but my God, everything is covered in ice, and I mean everything. I have my sleeping bag pulled tightly around my face, except for a small hole that I can breathe through. Lumps of ice rapidly form around this small gap as my breath freezes.

However, while I'm warm enough in my sleeping bag, how I hate the mornings. I normally wake when it's light and then go through the routine of melting snow, cooking and then cleaning everything up. In these conditions it takes far longer than it ever used to. Actually getting started up is the real pain. It's so damn cold the inside of my tent is shimmering with ice, like a Hollywood set. Sticking one arm gingerly out of the sleeping bag I reach for my cooker then turn it on. It takes far too long to melt all the snow I need to cook, drink and then fill my flasks for the day ahead . . . and too much fuel as well. Within a couple of days I've blown half my fuel supplies, so I need to spend less time with the cooker on. The problem is, I will not be able to dry the clothes I have been wearing during the day and these will be covered in ice when I come to put them on. Admin, survival's all about personal admin.

Tuesday, 13 January 2004   Toad River

Now at Toad River on the Alaska Highway, population: seventy-five. My mileage has picked up since my last diary entry as I've refined my routine and got into the swing of things. Plus the temperature has crept upwards slightly to level off at between –20 °C and –30 °C during the day. In fact today has been a warm day at only –5 °C.

Karl walks on to Hot Springs Lodge, where he again breaks and heads to Colombia to see Catty. By the time he returns in late February, the bitter cold of earlier has gone . . .

Wednesday, 25 February 2004   Hot Springs Lodge

I'm pleased to find that there's been a serious change in the weather. The day I left it had been –38 °C, however today it is +1 °C, a world apart. Even so, how I hate being here again, just hate it. I get caught up for a few days, sorting out the next leg of my journey from Laird Hot Springs to Whitehorse. It's a long haul with very little in between – about 600 kilometres and very few places open to find food or fuel. So I start to assemble re-supply bundles that can be dropped off ahead for me to pick up.

I eventually arrive back at Hot Springs Lodge, where I am treated to one of the best displays of the Northern Lights I've seen since I was in northern Norway many years ago with the army. A full-blown display with all the colours and just so much movement. Awed by such a spectacle all I can think of is how much I wish Catty could be here.

Sunday, 29 February 2004   Towards Watson Lake

I set off for Watson Lake in relatively decent weather with the temperature at about –8 °C. It should be an eight-day trip, carrying all the food and fuel that I will need. I'm back on the treadmill. It doesn't matter where I stop on this road and look around, the scenery is just the same. It's as though I haven't moved at all.

Over the next few days the temperature drops down to –20 °C before rising back above freezing again. I get one night's sleep at a road maintenance camp where the folks have a spare heated cabin that I can sleep in. The days grow harder as hills come thick and fast, but as I say, at least it's getting warmer.

Sunday, 7 March 2004   Towards Watson Lake

A warm wind blows today and begins to melt the snow and ice from the roads. Along this stretch I meet up with the North American Bison for the first time. A herd of them is right beside the road. Trundling past at walking pace is pretty nerve-racking as these mighty beasts are fully wild, however it's not as if they've never seen people before. They are the star attractions around these parts, and as they live by the roadside they get plenty of attention from passers by. But today it's just me and I'm so close I can smell them. They just stare intently. It's impossible to deduce what they're thinking, but it's probably not too complimentary.

Sunday, 14 March 2004   **Towards Swift River**

After making a good distance yesterday and a couple of days of very pleasant weather, today is a lot colder and very blustery. The hills keep coming with monotonous regularity now and I'm having to work hard. Having said that, I'm still making better time than I expected. I have been planning distances with midwinter days in mind and now I find I'm moving much faster. Unfortunately, so is the traffic.

Today I should find my first fuel drop-off according to my map, but can't locate it. I can only think that someone else must have found it and waltzed off with it. It should be here according to the map, but myself I'm not so sure. Tonight, I'm sleeping on the road. I mean literally touching the tarmac. I ran out of time and then couldn't get off the road because I was snowed in. I now have twenty-four-wheelers zipping past my left ear. I'm as far over as I can get and very well marked, but not particularly happy. This is very unpleasant and a little nerve-racking.

Wednesday, 31 March 2004   **Whitehorse**

I am seized by the push for Whitehorse now. I move well and by 1st April I'm close to the town. I get stopped by an enthusiastic lady who knows who I am and invites me to stay with her and her boyfriend, both keen bikers and travellers. She had read about me in the *Outpost* magazine apparently.

I'm now only twenty kilometres from town, but end up staying over at their house through the next day in order that we can have a bit of a get-together with their friends the following evening. Stef and Brad look after me very well and it's good to be with a couple of my own age. They have travelled extensively and are interesting to talk to. Unfortunately I find that some of the folk up here do little travelling and consequently have a very limited view of the world.

Sunday, 11 April 2004   **Beyond Whitehorse**

An area of high pressure hangs over the Canadian/Alaskan border and so the weather continues to be cloudless and sunny. I'm in no hurry to wake as I've now all the time in the day to spare, plenty of light hours. My routine within the tent has changed accordingly and I'm on the road for 11:00. I remember my routine down in South America would include an hour-long break at about midday, something unheard of for so long now, but I decide to re-institute it. It's a chance to sit by the side of the road, among the sand and stone and do nothing. Now that the snow has receded I'm surprised to see just how much sand there is. At times this place looks, or could be, somewhere down in southern Utah. In fact, as I sit here I'm transported back to a place in northern Mexico and it feels magical. I can almost smell it and this triggers a memory of warm deserts, to the extent that there's a reluctance to come back to the real world.

I had promised Catty so much. And she had given up her job, twice, spent all of her money and worst of all believed in me. All these dreams have now been taken away from her.

Tuesday, 13 April – Wednesday, 14 April 2004   **Towards Haines Junction**

I awake to find the world covered in snow again, a good few centimetres at that. It continues to snow for the rest of the morning, with a brief break at about midday. To cheer me up slightly I bump into a guy who hands me a bunch of doughnuts. For the rest of the day it just rains and rains, remaining cold and very miserable. This is real Brit winter weather, and it sucks. Just hope it clears up tomorrow.

Tonight, at about 22:00 and just as it is getting dark, I am standing outside my tent. I'm surprised to find moose tracks that come right up to my tent which had not been there earlier. It's now so still and quiet, almost creepy. In the desert it was one thing, but out here, with all this forest and the huge mountains, it appears strange for it to be so quiet, unnatural. As I walk up the track from my tent towards the road, I come face to face with two large female moose. We all stand there, absolutely still, while staring at each other for a good ten seconds or so, before they turn slowly and slip into the vast forest. This is the time you'll find them out along the road, either early morning or last light. You rarely see them during the day.

Tuesday, 20 April 2004   **Sheep Mountain**

A good day's push finds me in an interesting place. Interesting because of its difference. Striking scenery that is some of the best I've ever seen. The road takes me right up to the very base of the snow-covered mountains. Again this wonderful scenery brings on an uncomfortable feeling. I'm tired of seeing it alone. Catty should be here, she should be here to see this and I get brassed off with it all. This is an extremely frequent experience now, be it the Northern Lights or impressive mountain ranges, I always immediately think of Catty and lose the magic.

The road takes me down on to Kluane Lake and I end the day at a tourist centre at the foot of Sheep Mountain. This early in the year the centre's closed of course, but it provides me with a clear area on which to pitch my tent. In fact, I pitch the tent on a wooden veranda, with an incredible view. There's a wide marsh area at the mouth of a river as it enters the lake. Its source is a huge glacier not far upriver and into the mountains. To the west the mountain range holds the largest icefields outside the Arctic Circle, with glaciers up to 700 metres deep that stretch from here to the ocean. On the aptly named Sheep Mountain itself, I can see Dall sheep grazing on the southern flank where the snow has melted.

Saturday, 1 May 2004   **Alaskan Border**

I leave for the border, only one day from here. I pass through Canadian immigration just outside Beaver Creek and continue pushing hard. The mountains are behind me now; I left them a few days ago. I'm now down into the low-lying hills, though still within the same old ocean of forest, which stretches for as far as your imagination will allow it to.

There is a certain buzz about the day. And this is not your normal day, but the day that I cross the line into 'Stage Five' of the expedition: Alaska and back into the USA. Almost symbolically just as the US immigration post appears to my front the Canadian Rocky Mountains disappear behind a hill and are gone like the chapter of a book.

I pant my way up to the border crossing to find two large, heavily set border guards. Before I even manage to remove my passport from its pocket the questions come thick and fast. Why? How? When? What for? And who? I explain my reason for being here as succinctly as I can, but this is a complete failure and only goes to create more confusion. We take it a little slower . . . And my intentions in Alaska? I lay it all out. I'm met with strange stares that proclaim I'm a nutter, and then an abrupt:

'No! You cannot stay longer than three months, so you can't go on, can you?'

I explain that I had a visa. Surely there must be some record of it being issued on their system? Someone checks:

'No . . . What's your job?'

'Well, I walk I guess . . .'

By the end of the day I've done thirty-four kilometres and reached 'Border City'. Not quite what I was expecting having seen a photo. That showed a bit more than this I'm sure and my hopes of a motel, truck stop and mini Vegas turn out to be a rather modest lodge and a rather crappy gas station. Wishful thinking seems to have got the better of me.

Monday, 3 May 2004   **Border City**

I am now back in the hills again and in fact this turns out to be a lot more work than the mountains. What I find among the mountains is that the road tends to follow the valley-bottoms, only climbing from one valley over into the next, but generally speaking the valley roads are pretty flat. Once out of the mountains you end up running at right angles to many water courses and it's a constant roller-coaster with no valleys running in my direction.

Friday, 7 May 2004   **Tok**

I arrive in Tok. On the way in I get stopped by an old man and his family in an RV. His name is Til and he stops to chat. An old traveller with adventures of his own and a special forces background, he's very pleased to hear what I'm doing. So much so that he drives off into Tok before I arrive and sets up a meal for me at 'Fast Eddie's' restaurant. He then drives back out to give me my meal ticket. Next I can see a young native lad running my way as I close on the town. He's wearing a US combat jacket, grey nylon trousers and dirty trainers. He carries two staffs decorated with sets of eagle feathers. As he closes on me then passes, he whoops loudly and screams, 'All the way to Panama, Whoooooooooo' . . . as he carries on running down the road. I stop and just watch with a smile, he made my day.

Wednesday, 12 May 2004   Beyond Tok

The weather has improved, however I've developed a stinking head cold. The road itself runs quite flat now and I'm feeling a lot happier after talking to Catty in Tok, a damn sight happier.

Come the evening, though, life begins to suck. My head cold enables me to go through a whole toilet roll worth of tissues to try and keep up with my running nose. My eyes are driving me nuts, burning like hell and itching. I feel like crap and get very little sleep.

Thursday, 13 May 2004   Dot Lake

I make it a half-day today and reach Dot Lake within ten miles. I sit in the café here looking like a mustard gas victim. My eyes, swollen and red, are still driving me crazy. My nose continues to stream. I give in to drugs and ask if they have anything that might help. I'm given something called Nite Time and this works a treat. It's then that someone mentions the trees are pollinating. Suddenly the penny drops. It's not a cold at all, it's a reaction. 1 thought it a little strange as colds don't usually affect my eyes to this extent. This is a new phenomenon to me as I don't have hayfever. Having said that, I can now think back to Canada where I had a reaction which must have been caused by tree pollen, though it was a lot milder than this. Anyway the medicine works as it contains, among other things, antihistamines. An hour later I'm as high as a kite and have never been happier.

Friday, 14 May 2004   Dot Lake

A very bad night. The drugs wore off far too quickly for my liking and although I've taken some more they don't seem to be working now. I swear to god it's like living in a gas chamber at the moment and this condition sucks big time. I feel as though I haven't slept for days.

A straight twenty miles (thirty-two kilometres) today and it's very warm at present, not a day to have such a heavy head. But when I do leave Dot Lake I set off at a rare old pace and somehow manage to maintain it. Ten miles just fly by, I mean gone before I know what is happening. I'm sure I must be high again! Ten miles in two hours, and the next ten in only half an hour slower. This is the fastest I can remember . . . four and a half hours for twenty miles . . . Whoooo. Not only that but I felt good. Even when I take a short break I'm pacing back and forth feeling as though I'm on speed or something. Very strange.

Sunday, 16 May 2004   **Delta Junction**

It's a twenty-three-mile (thirty-seven-kilometre) push to Delta Junction. I spend a number of days here, in a real state. Sleep is elusive and I lock myself away in a motel room. I've had bags of rest but then comes the day for me to get back out on to the road. For the first time I can remember, I simply refuse to get out of bed. Fuck it, fuck the whole world if it thinks I'm going out there again. Not until the following day do I muster the enthusiasm to move back out on to that shagging road; after all I know what's coming.

Finally I push on. It's strange to think that this is the last stretch of road I'll have the Beast with me. Maybe in the future there will be a BIII, probably will, but poor old BII's working life will end in Fairbanks.

I stop at a small place called North Pole and make contact with the local news and media groups in Fairbanks, now just a day or two up the road. A local newspaper sends a reporter out who interviews me at the local Pizza Hut but unfortunately I fail to get any response from TV stations. It rains during the night before I come into Fairbanks and the relief of clean air, as well as feeling just so damn good that this is truly the 'coming in day' of all 'coming in days'! Fairbanks is the end of this road. There will be more to come, but as far as the Americas go, no more highways. Wow.

In a run-down motel in Fairbanks, Karl plans his route across Alaska. Time is running out for a summer journey and the possible ways through large tracts of nondescript swamp interwoven with river systems look difficult. In contrast, a winter move looks far simpler on paper, with a definable route and a whole series of small villages that can be used as re-supply caches. Weighing up the odds, he settles for the chilly option.

Plans for his crossing of Alaska and then the Bering Strait are beginning to come together; ordering equipment from the UK, US and Norway, items begin arriving through the post, including two immersion suits and a sled from 'Bronco' Lane, the Army's Everest climber. Lane – who served with Karl's father in the Special Forces – has had a lot to do with running expeditions inside the Arctic Circle. The sled is 2.5 metres long and made of Kevlar, a bulletproof material, and was built in Gloucestershire by Roger Dayner of Snow Sled Limited. Karl will use it for the crossing of the Bering Strait. Quite coincidentally, the same company is also building him a less robust 2.3 metre fibreglass sled and harness, which he will use to cross Alaska.

With the arrival of the immersion suits, Karl is soon at the local swimming pool, practising swimming in them and handling the sled, which, happily, does float. Hooking up with the local fire department, he carries out further tests in the Chena River. Here, where there is some open water and ice, he practises getting in and out of the water, plus swimming for a decent distance. The suits perform well and don't leak.

A launch date of 1 December comes and goes. Equipment is still arriving by post, but the days vanish in a flash. New problems arise. It is taking longer than Karl had envisaged to pack and post all the food he will need to cache for the next four months (4000 calories per day) in villages along his route on the Yukon River. Timing is tight: in order to cross the Bering Strait, Karl needs to reach the coast by March, or the window of opportunity is gone for another year. On top of everything else, he falls while trying out his new ski-shoes, breaking his bridged four front teeth and losing them in the snow.

Thursday, 16 December 2004   **Beyond Fairbanks**

I take one last look at the distant, warm and ever so appealing lights of Fairbanks. I even take a photo. This is the first time I've had the chance to get a picture of a distant city's lights. Looking out towards the place with great expectancy, or like now looking back, remembering the people, places and times you've just had, it's always with that same feeling of sorrow, knowing that you will miss them. I've seen so many distant lights from so many places.

By 14:30 the sun has gone down but I push on until about 18:00, trying to get off the high ground. What fun it is in the dark, trying to get the sled (weighing nearly 100 kilograms) down these hills. It takes hours to find a technique that works. I spend most of the evening with the sled crashing into my legs from behind, knocking me off my feet time and time again.

In fact just letting the sled run in front and pull me down works best. It's a little hard to control . . . well, actually there isn't any control, but on a good straight run it's fun. The sled just does its thing and I'm pulled along behind as though I have my own dog team. I almost make it all the way down on to the flats before I quit for the night and, clearing a patch of snow, put up my tent.

Friday, 17 December 2004   Dunbar

I must find the point at which the trail I'm on meets the 'Dunbar Trail', as it is known. It runs north-south across my front, from a set of cabins called Dunbar and all the way north to Livengood, a small settlement on the Dalton Highway. Used by snow machines, tracing it is not a problem at first but it gets trickier when I come to a distinct fork in the trail. Both options have been used equally, making it hard to decide which is the main trail, so I stick with the one that continues in the general direction I have been moving.

A little later the snow-machine tracks end on a frozen river. I know that the river marks the bottom of these hills and the beginning of the flats, and had expected the trail to cross the river. It doesn't. Instead the tracks disperse up and down the river. I can tell from my map I have to head south but it still shows the trail clearly crossing the river. I push on. The wind picks up and is biting hard at my face. Wind-driven snow makes it harder to pull the sled. The river begins to wind left and right in a series of tight turns, and I grow concerned. I should have found something by now, but there is no sign of the trail leading west from the river. I push on for a few more hours, becoming increasingly pissed off.

A single, now very faint, snow-machine trail continues to run south on the river making me believe that if I push on for just that little bit further I will find the trail, but as time and distance go on I begin to lose faith. The going is hard, sometimes through deep snowdrifts, and I decide I have lost the trail and turn back. This really pisses me off as Dick, a friend from Fairbanks, is coming out to pay me a visit and the last thing I want is for him not to be able to find me because I've got lost . . . how embarrassing! Now three miles down the river I begin to march back, cursing to myself and trying to figure out where I've gone wrong. It must have been at that track junction, I think to myself. By now it is already starting to get dark.

An hour later snow machines come buzzing around a bend, it's Dick and his friends.

'You missed it,' they holler. 'It's about 500 metres back there.'

Dick has hot water, and foil-wrapped chicken and pork kept warm in the engine compartment while they travelled. After a short stop and a nibble at the food, the machines push on in front of me towards Dunbar. I have to keep moving – it's too cold to stand around once the sweat starts to freeze on me. As I push on, the group drive up to Dunbar, about twenty miles, breaking a good trail for me. They then drive back to find me. I stop, make a fire and pitch tent in a clearing in the woods at about 18:00. The evening is spent in good cheer, with friends and real food . . . steaks roasted on sticks, over the fire.

Saturday, 18 December 2004   Beyond Dunbar

The trail from Dunbar to Tolovana is hard to discern. A few days before setting off from Fairbanks, I met a chap called Simon, who had tried to reach the Tolovana hot springs on snow machines. His party had made it to within a few miles but had to give up on the Dunbar–Tolovana trail junction, unable to take the machines any further. They had marked their route with yellow tape. I find the junction and pitch tent about a mile beyond, where the trail ends at a frozen lake.

Sunday, 19 December 2004   Beyond Dunbar

The trail runs for nine miles, winding across these flats to the distant hills where I will find the hot springs. I get up in the morning, looking out across a frozen lake. The wind is blowing and there has been a snowfall so any tracks left by Simon are all but gone. I stick to the left of the lake, as that's where I think I'll find the trail. I inch out on to the ice and take a left but still cannot see any sign of a trail. The snow is deep. I have a real problem on my hands and often retrace my steps. I've only moved 400 metres.

Unhitching the sledge, I recce the treeline and ... wait, look ... there, through the grass. Is it my mind playing tricks or is that a faint hint of a track? Yes, a track, I'm sure.

I get the sled, dragging it back to the snaking, barely visible trace of a track and soon find more yellow tape and know for sure that I'm on the right route. I then find myself suddenly struggling like hell, hardly able to move at all in deep snow. I grow desperate.

This is mind-blowingly slow. I will lose the trail, then find it again every 100 metres or so, becoming obsessed with locating yellow tape, like some starving animal sniffing around every tree and bush, its nose in the air or down in the snow.

With gritted teeth and bent double, I use all my strength and weight but can hardly move the sled for more than a pace at a time. Have the snow conditions changed? Then I notice something is wrong. The rope brake is on! I can't help but laugh and laugh, out of sheer relief.

I come across a riverbank with a six-metre drop and climb on either side – a showstopper. I have to lower the sled down one bank with the ropes (or rather drop it down the bank as it pulls me face first into the snow), then empty the sled's contents and haul it up the bank piece by piece.

In three days Karl covers only about a mile. He regrets having chosen this more direct cross-country route between Fairbanks and Manley Hot Springs instead of taking the longer route by road along two sides of a triangle. He decides to ditch his sled and calls friends back in Fairbanks to ask if they will meet at the springs with a snow machine so they can retrieve the sled and have a rethink.

Thursday, 23 December 2004   Beyond Dunbar

It's –40 °C and bitching cold. I pull things from my sled that I might need. In these conditions I don't know how long it will take me to get to the hot springs on a compass bearing. There's no trail – I have to find three log cabins that are only five and a half miles away as the crow flies. I take my sleeping bag, a flask of hot chocolate, my sat-phone, a warm coat and my laptop (I'd rather die than leave this to the wolves). I also take two days' supply of food and a tank of gas to get a wood fire going if I need to, and throw everything into a large waterproof bag, which I attach to my harness like a rucksack.

After only 100 metres my breathing is pretty heavy as it's very hard going off the trail. These flats are criss-crossed with small ridges and rivers that have steep banks and once in these it's hard to get out. There is then an open area of fallen trees that is covered with snow. This part is definitely the worst. There might be only about twenty metres of fallen trees, but it's one helluva job getting across. I cross about thirty-five metres of forest to find another twenty metres of felled timber that is completely covered with deep snow. It is a minefield.

It's 19:30 and quite dark. I lose track of time, deep in my own thoughts or rather self-pity. At last I stumble across a firm piece of snow. I look up to find myself staring at a piece of tape . . . the track! About a mile from the hot springs I come across a track that leads all the way in to a cabin. The thermometer outside the door reads –45 °C. Heat . . . all I can think about is heat. There's a small wood stove, a pile of cut wood and some matches. Within the hour I'm sitting stripped to my wet but warm long johns, bathed in a bright orange glow and steaming nicely. My kit and clothing are drying above a roaring wood stove.

Karl's friends try to get to him but are driven back by strong winds and poor visibility. Karl has only two days' food supplies but his spirits rise when he finds two snow machines parked outside another nearby cabin. A man and a woman have made it through from another direction and when they depart, they leave him a stack of food.

After waiting for four days Karl decides to return to his sled and head north without it to Livengood. Using his GPS he locates it, hitches up and makes it to his campsite near where he had left the Dunbar Trail a week earlier.

Wednesday, 29 December 2004   Beyond Dunbar

Once out of my tent I find the Dunbar Trail is covered with deep snow as no one has used it for a number of days. This is not good news as even just a few inches of fresh snow like this mean slow, hard work and today I cover only five miles at best.

Saturday, 1 January 2005   Beyond Dunbar

A light appears up ahead . . . a shining beacon of hope . . . a snow machine!

The trapper is somewhat surprised to find me out here. Me, I'm overjoyed! The path created by his machine makes my life ten times easier, like Moses parting the Red Sea. I do not sink into the clear, compacted trail he has left and the sled seems to move as though it's hovering. I begin going at what feels like light speed and push as fast as possible, desperately trying to get in as many miles as I can in an attempt to make up for my disastrous performance over the last week. By the end of the day I've done well and am a happier man for sure.

A few miles further on, the Dunbar Trail intercepts the Alaskan oil pipeline, which runs from Prudhoe Bay in the north to Valdes in the south. Tracing the pipeline, which will take him to Livengood, he meets a security guard in a pick-up who urges him to stay in a camp nearby instead of going on to Livengood. The camp – an old construction site – is disused but has a solitary caretaker, Roy, who has lived here for thirty years. Karl elects to spend the weekend and is eventually resupplied when Ramey, a friend from Fairbanks, makes it here on Tuesday, 5 January, by road. He brings more food and fuel, plus his old tent and a $400 wood-burning tent stove, complete with chimney, which means that Karl is less dependent on white gas fuel as he pushes on along the road for Manley Hot Springs.

Wednesday, 5 January 2005   Towards Manley Hot Springs

I climb all day until about 14:30 when I find the junction that heads down towards Tolovana. Here I meet a large snowplough. At this point I'm about a mile from a looming summit. Beyond it is a ten-mile (sixteen-kilometre) stretch that runs across a plateau and is notorious for its high winds. The plough's crew say that it's been blowing a gale up there, with some real bad 'white-outs' above the treeline. Consequently I decide to cut the day short and camp here.

Tonight I can't light the stove, which is a real pain in the arse as it's been a big success. There's only green wood up here and not much of that. A few milder days have allowed the wood to get wet so it's a real smoky night, fighting with little more than a few pieces of smouldering twigs that won't burn.

Sunday, 9 January 2005   Manley Hot Springs

The moose I saw last night is close to my tent and still watching me. The temperature has now dropped again to –45 °C, making my start a bitter one. I make good progress and decide to keep pushing on into the darkness to get to Manley and not stop short and get cold. It's been a twenty-mile day and I finally arrive in Manley some time after 18:00. I'm coated in a thick layer of ice. This has frozen the layers of my clothing together and I have to force and rip them apart to get them off when I find the house of Art and Dee Mortvedt. Dee is a part-time teacher and her husband Art is an expedition logistics expert who generally works at the North or South Pole aiding scientific expeditions or the more crazy polar adventures.

His study is covered with certificates from thirty years of polar and non-polar expeditions thanking him for his assistance. Unfortunately he is away again at present, down in Punta Arenas of all places. I could have learned a lot.

Tuesday, 18 January 2005   Towards Tanana

At –45 °C, and with a wind chill on top of that, today is nasty and windblown snow forever covers the track in front of me. I push out all the way across Fish Lake, a wide, wind-scoured piece of frozen water covered with bars of hard snow that I need to negotiate and climb over. Somehow, when I crashed my way through the bush just prior to reaching the lake, I lost my snow shovel from the top of the sled and this really pisses me off. I used the shovel a lot and it was very useful out here right now.

Thursday, 20 January 2005   Tanana

The whole day is spent on frozen sloughs – small frozen rivers, as they are known in these parts – and there are some interesting ice states, most of them clear of snow. This is a little creepy at times as it's like walking on a glass table. The clear ice below me is very thick, looking as if it could be as much as a metre and a half, but through it I can see the river bottom.

I stick to the snow-machine trail and the track improves as I get closer to Tanana. I converge on the Yukon River. I then spend some time walking downriver before finally pulling out on to the opposite bank just a few miles short of the settlement. My contact is Ken Ostler, the Tanana police officer. He's not hard to locate. As I enter town I find him issuing a speeding ticket to a teenager on a snow machine.

On Sunday, 31 January, Karl overnights with an old Native American trapper, Roy Folger, who lives about twenty miles from Tanana. He has just bagged himself a wolf and its skinned body lies outside, as their pelts still fetch a good price.

It becomes clear to Karl how much he depends on snow-machine trails to make any sort of real distance at all. Over the next few days the weather is clear but still as cold as –50 °C and, on good days, he is happy if he manages to cover eight to ten miles. Soon enough the weather worsens: tracks disappear, white-out conditions ensue and Karl can't see his hand in front of his face. Luckily, he is close to a trapper's cabin at the time, which is at the mouth of Sunset Creek ... if he can find Sunset Creek in these conditions. His progress slows to a stagger as he can see nothing but a blank wall of white until at last, he catches sight of something man-made in the treeline – a cabin buried in the snow. He digs out the doorway and cracks open the door, 'like some ancient tomb'. It was last visited a year before. Inside are the basics: a large wood stove with a pile of wood, a makeshift bed, a chair, pots and pans and other knick-knacks. He is halfway to Ruby.

The following day he takes a large bowsaw and cuts some wood. With enough food for four or five days, he does not have enough to get to Ruby so needs a re-supply. Then for five days it doesn't stop snowing; he realises that he won't make much progress to Ruby unless someone breaks a trail in a snow machine as this part of Alaska is experiencing the heaviest snowfalls in decades. In desperation, he calls friends in Ruby and offers $300 a machine for two to reopen the route but, given the conditions, no one is keen.

A week goes by and the weather clears. At the sound of a low-flying aircraft Karl bolts outside to check his large red and day-glow orange bags hanging in the tree line. A pilot, Jay, comes out of the west in a white Cub aircraft and puts down near the cabin and unloads Karl's supplies. More bad weather is forecast, but in about a week the 'Iron Dog' snow-machine race will be coming through here with up to sixty machines blazing a multi-lane highway up the Yukon. This is the best news.

Saturday, 12 February 2005   **Towards Ruby**

Impatience gets the better of me and I pack up and make a desperately ridiculous attempt at a breakout. It's about a mile before I quit. I am now back in my tent. I have stopped where I can access the treeline on the southern bank of the river, and aim to hunker down and wait for the 'Iron Dog' race to pass. The day of their proposed arrival comes and goes, and nothing the following day either. There were no machines appearing out of the west to save my frozen arse and part the ocean of white. On the third day my patience runs out. Using valuable phone time again – my batteries are getting low – I learn, to my horror, that conditions are so bad on the Yukon that the route has changed and I won't be seeing them.

Friday, 4 March 2005   **Approaching Galena**

The days are getting longer now. It is light from 10:00 until 18:00 so I push on as hard as I can along the river. It's just like walking on a highway – nothing changes from day to day and boredom is the real enemy.

I come across some rather large wolf tracks. In fact when I step next to them the animal has the same stride length as I do. Later, as I round a bend in the river, I find the remnants of a wolves' ambush site in a very narrow slough. It's where they have jumped a moose. Blood and hand-size lumps of moose hair and skin are mixed in with the mishmash of moose and wolf tracks in a frenzied pattern that covers the snow-machine tracks. I follow the battle down the track. There's more blood and fur, but no body! It would appear the moose has managed to escape, or at least did not die here. Talking to the hunters in Ruby, I was told that the wolves are slaughtering the moose this year because the snow is just too deep for them to get away.

Owing to the weather and conditions underfoot, Karl realises that he will not reach the coast this winter. As the days pass, he comes to admit that he has just been going through the motions, and plans to call a halt this winter in Unalakleet, which is a little over halfway to Cape Prince of Wales.

Saturday, 12 March 2005   Nulato

In Nulato I visit the local school. It is not looking too good for the students in this part of the world – the native culture is in its death-throes. This is Athabascan country, a native group that occupies the central region of Alaska. Their root problem is alcohol.

I see lots of individuals, both native and white, fighting to keep the cultures in place but it seems a losing battle to me, mainly because it would appear that that's the way it's supposed to be. The gap between the younger generations and their elders seems so wide. I've heard the kids tell their teachers that they don't want to learn the native language. There is confusion among the staff. Do they teach the kids to survive here in the village or out there in the rest of the world? Is there life here for the kids? Teachers do their best to keep the kids interested in their past but they say it's getting harder. Learning to fish and hunt does not help the kids get a higher score on Grand Theft Auto 2.

They brought a large bull moose-kill into the school gym the other day and the whole school set to work skinning, butchering and preparing the meat. I chuckled to myself, thinking how this would have gone down at home at my old comprehensive in Hull.

Tuesday, 22 March 2005   On the way to Unalakleet

When I locate my stop for the night, 'Old Woman Cabin', I find a native guy inside stripped to the waist, putting up shelves. He's odd but seems harmless enough. He's been here overnight and his old snow machine sits outside. He explains he's moving on today but offers me a meal – some moose steaks – before he goes. As he does, he tells me his life story, which is dead weird. He's been to jail for 'terrible things'. I take this in as he hacks his way through frozen moose meat with a large butcher's knife. Oh Christ! I sit quietly in the corner, judging the distance to the door.

A day later, Karl is still in the cabin when a Frenchman, Dimitri Keiffer (DK), pulls up outside with a small sled weighing just twenty-seven kilograms. He is one of ten that set off from Anchorage, some on bikes, some on foot, in an annual 1100-mile (1775-kilometre) race to Nome using the Iditarod route. They are travelling much faster than Karl does, often as much as sixty miles, nearly a hundred kilometres, a day, only sleeping for three hours per night and carrying very little, which at first makes Karl feel his fifteen to twenty miles a day is pathetic in comparison.

DK is an endurance race specialist and, to Karl's disbelief, is wearing a pair of Gore-Tex training shoes. But, as Karl begins to reflect, this man is in 'race mode' and not walking around the world, which makes him feel better. DK even talks about the Bering Strait and wonders if they might attempt the crossing together.

Thursday, 24 March 2005   Unalakleet

DK plans to reach Unalakleet in one thirty-six-mile (fifty-eight-kilometre) push, but watching him go I find I'm champing at the bit. I set off about one and a half hours after he does. Despite telling myself to let him go, I do feel like a greyhound watching the hare burst from the slips and by 14:00 I can see his gold jacket and sled up ahead. Subconsciously I have moved at a clip. I stop to have my midday snack of candy bar and hot chocolate to let him put some distance between us. But when I set off I find that he has also stopped and is right there in front of me again. I catch up once more and sit on his heels for two miles without him even knowing I'm here. With hood up, goggles on and headphones in place he can neither hear nor see me even if he looked sideways. I'm kept amused if nothing else.

He stops to adjust his clothing and ski poles, while I stand behind him. I slowly place my foot on his sled so that when he tries to move he will find me. He feels his sled give a little and turns, almost leaping out of his skin. Hell, I would have freaked too. You get used to being very alone out here, with no one for tens or hundreds of miles around, so to turn and find someone right behind you is a shock.

I've been feeling like a serious wuss since I'd met DK and I need to know that I can do at least one of his days so that I can sleep at all tonight. I decide to walk with him. I'm really happy to be moving with someone and thoroughly enjoying this leg.

By 17:00 – the time I normally stop and tent up – I feel my energy levels turn off as though on a timer. I'm feeling empty and shaky as I rummage through my rations for the rest of my candy bars. DK, in contrast, just downs some magic pills. [DK *gives Karl a couple of caffeine pills and he perks up within minutes.*]

I'm not finding this hard at all, in fact I'm loving every minute of it. It is the best day I can remember this year and this has nothing to do with the fact that it is the last leg. If anything that makes me feel uncomfortable. It's just that everything about today is different – walking with someone else makes the hours just fly by.

Night falls but on we go in headlamp mode. There are some steeper hills to cross as well, the steepest I've encountered this winter. They're covered in a strange mix of deep and wet snow or bare sand as the temperatures are rising the closer we get to the coast. When Unalakleet's lights suddenly appear we toast our success with some more power bars and water. Stumbling down the other side of the hills we enter the village at about 22:30.

It is late March – the end of my road this winter. In a sense, I'm ashamed by the meagre effort I've made and now, right at the end, I feel belittled by DK's superb efforts. Next morning I just stand looking northwards, like a sled dog taken from the team and left tied to a tree. I'm already missing the trail but it will still be there next winter, it's not going anywhere, and I will be back.

Karl needs to leave the US to renew his visa, and returns to Colombia, where he spends the next six months with Catty in her new apartment in Medellin. Straight away, a dentist begins work on four new implants – a procedure that takes four to five months – and DK calls to say he would like to throw in his lot with Karl and take on the Bering Strait crossing. This is excellent news, as having a companion on the ice will increase Karl's chances.

Karl returns to Anchorage to meet Troy Henkels, a Belgian, who lives here. In March, Henkels and companion Dixie Dansercoer made an attempt on the Bering Strait, leaving from the same point that Karl has chosen. But soon after setting off they were swept southwards by the moving ice out towards the Bering

Sea where, nine days later, they had to be airlifted to safety by helicopter.

Henkels is helpful. He and his partner used skis, as did the Russians who successfully crossed in 1996. Karl is as yet undecided. Henkels highlights various factors, not least the improbability of success and also that they must be prepared to move well into the night as the ice drifts continuously. Of course, they will need to sleep but then there is a chance of being jumped by bears in the dark.

Expedition shopping begins in earnest. The list includes radios, new skis and boots, new clothing and headgear, monocular NVGs (night-vision equipment) plus new dry suits. Troy recommends Kokatat Gore-Tex dry suits, which because they are breathable can be worn all the time, unlike the one Karl has been training with, which must be removed once out of the water. But given that nothing is made specifically with the Bering Strait in mind, adapting and experimenting with different outdoors equipment is the way forward.

Timely information on the sea conditions in the Bering Strait is scant and there is no set route across as the ice moves constantly. Although weather satellites update weather situations every six hours and ice reports every other day, the two men need real-time information. Karl has a eureka moment. He wants to use a helium balloon to lift a micro camera into a position from where it might be able to relay images of the condition of the ice, enabling them to decide on routes. But given the winds on the Strait, his balloon soon becomes a kite and another friend, Cliff, who has his own workshop, builds one and even provides a camera.

Should they succeed, Karl and Dimitri will need special permits, as the north-east corner of Russia – a military buffer zone during the Cold War – remains a sensitive place. And as applications can take from twelve to eighteen months to process, he leaves it to his father to make inroads on Russian bureaucracy.

The whole expedition becomes a giant jigsaw puzzle; while ideas change course in mid-flow, slowly but surely a picture is beginning to emerge. Time, however, slips away so quickly and Karl begins to experience the parachutist's 'ground rush' as his departure date races towards him.

Monday, 12 December 2005   **Fairbanks**

DK flies in from Costa Rica – he's been in a cycling race – and we test our equipment. The kite flies and performs valiantly, so I'm quite confident we can make the camera work on the Strait. It's not 100 per cent but any problems are just details that can be sorted out. Dimitri is here for four days, which clearly isn't long enough as we shop for yet more equipment and talk over repeatedly every aspect of the crossing.

We take the kit out into the river but find there are so many details that need attending to that it's quite late when we get there. We carry on into the darkness, rehearsing our drills individually and as a pair in the frozen water. On the first day we wear our throw ropes, knives, utility pouches and a radio on our harnesses, as these must be on hand in an instant. The radio is carried high on your chest and as we swim on our backs, it is well out of the water. That said, after a few hours the radios are trashed – we never can get them or the throat mikes working anyway – and getting repeatedly in and out of the water at –28 °C coats everything in a thickening layer of solid ice.

The idea is to use the sled harnesses to pull each other from the water should we need to. I have used the simplest metal buckles possible, but I'm ill-prepared for these conditions. Although the buckles on the harness just need to be bashed with an ice axe to free them, the webbing is freezing solid and the straps won't pull through.

After dark we successfully test the NVGs, and Ramey – who has also come to help – devises a way of mounting them on two cycling helmets. In contrast, we have a serious problem with the Gore-Tex 'booties' of our dry suits. After a second night in the river mine appear to leak – my feet get painfully cold as well as wet. I've yet to confirm these are leaks, but I'm 99 per cent sure these suits will not make it across the Strait. This is a major headache. We need new suits that are capable of dealing with salt water that is colder and rougher than calm freshwater rivers. Added to this, I puncture one of my special sealed diving gloves, but I plug it with Aqua Seal.

On an improvised shooting range, we manage a practice. I have a shotgun, which I acquired last winter, and a new .44 revolver. It's soon clear that more time needs to be devoted to firearms handling.

On Wednesday, 28 December, Karl flies via Nome to Unalakleet where he overnights on a restaurant floor. Next morning, he leaves before first light – around 08:00 – heading for Shaktoolik, which is a two-day journey. After a second day in the hills, the weather closes in around 16:00 just as he starts to lose height. Determined to reach his destination in one fourteen-mile (twenty-three-kilometre) push across the flats, it is soon snowing hard, the snow is drifting and his progress is slow. Removing his goggles, as he can't see through them after dark, Karl's face is covered with driven snow. He is very tired.

Friday, 30 December 2005   Towards Shaktoolik

I spot lights up ahead. Snow machines are coming my way. I've never been happier when, seeing my headlamp, they stop. It is a man and woman – they saw me earlier in the day and are now heading back to Shaktoolik. Stoically I assure them that I'm just fine but I feel like death warmed up. I'm close to breaking into tears and asking for my mother.

Following their tracks, I'm feeling pretty beaten up; hours pass faster than the miles and my flasks of hot drinks have long run out. I press on as best I can. I pop two caffeine pills yet feel dead on my feet. What's wrong with me – it's only a few miles from here to the village? I feel my eyes close and snap open again as I catch myself nodding off. I can see a dim glow in the distance through the haze of the blown ground snow, which should be Shaktoolik.

The next few hours take their toll. I doubt whether I can make it tonight. I'm so cold and just want to sleep. I will find the trail and then lose it, find it again only to lose it once more until I find a section that leads me up on to a bank right on the coastline, a natural sea wall. With no protection from the wind up here the blown snow has piled up in banks over two metres high and creates a real challenge for the sled and me as I struggle like a penguin on my skis.

In high winds I stumble like some delirious drunk, while the faint, distant light of Shaktoolik never seems to get any closer. Suddenly I'm yanked sideways on to my arse. Before I can save myself, I'm being dragged across the snow. Wide-eyed, I grasp for anything that will stop this slide but my hands flail wildly in space. I stop but my sled has gone over the sea wall in the darkness. The ropes go tight and I take the weight.

I begin pulling . . . nothing moves. I scramble to my feet, working my way down the rope and finally see my sled down below among the driftwood. At last I drag it up again. I'm exhausted and almost immediately begin to fall sleep. I snap out of it, I dare not stop moving.

This feels like a death march. The snow is deep and walls of the stuff cross my path until, finally, the orange glow that is the village begins to take shape. It's now 02:00. Beyond care I go over to the first house that has a light on and bang on the door. A shirtless, sleepy local looks at me from the warm place where I need to be with a surprised look.

'You all right?'

'Well . . . actually no, I'm feeling a little rough and was hoping you might be able to help. I just need to get out of the wind.'

He opens the door and beckons me inside, where I just sit on the floor, panting. A native woman appears, a baby in her arms. I feel such a dickhead getting these people up in the middle of the night. I apologise repeatedly. Before I summon up the gall to ask if I can crash here, they invite me to. In the seven years I have been walking I cannot think of one day that has been anything like this one. This night I have been pushed to my limit. I almost quit on more than one occasion, willing to just sit and fall asleep in the cold rather than move another foot.

On Sunday, 1 January 2006, Karl leaves the village of 200 inhabitants and skis north-east into a stiff wind. He reaches the coast at sundown. With the wind still howling and whipping up the ground snow, the trail peters out so he camps on the sea ice in a small inlet called Reindeer Cove.

Next day the wind eases. It's cloudy and dull and there are no signs of a trail across the bleak windswept Arctic tundra. With only three days' food and fuel, Karl attempts to break a trail to Koyuk, north across the ice covering Norton Bay. It is hard going as the snow is soft in one spot, hard in another, with frozen bars of spindrift creating an uneven surface. The milky sunlight casts no shadows so it's hard to see texture on the ground, making it easy to miss his step on a surface resembling a white sheet of paper.

Monday, 2 January 2006   Towards Koyuk

I'm flying. As the sun sinks the surface is turning to smooth ice. I see the lights of Koyuk some twenty or so miles north. I'm overjoyed, singing along to my MP3 tunes – a new acquisition – which I can just hear over the roaring winds. In the back of my mind, this feels too good to be true. The sky is clear and the new moon is reflected on the ice behind me but, in the light of my headlamp, I can only see a few feet in front.

I suddenly feel the ice flex beneath me. I step back, but it is already too late: I'm going through. I manage a half-turn to my left then crash through the ice, the water coming up to the top of my legs. I scramble back towards the sled but the ice gives way again and this time I'm in up to my chest. I don't know how I did it but, like a cat out of hot oil, I'm out of the hole. My right leg punches through the ice again and I feel cold water on my skin as it has taken just a few seconds to permeate the layers of clothing.

I crawl fifty metres and unpack the tent. My hands are painfully cold as the wind bites hard. I quickly get my stuff inside and struggle with the stove. As I pump it, fuel is jetting out of a broken seal and forming a pool on the bottom of my tent. I look at the low flame now, wide-eyed, expecting an all-consuming fireball. I extinguish it before it comes. Shaking, I mop up the spilt fuel and, fumbling in the cold, switch over the bottles. At last, a flame roars as the stove comes alive. I whip off my wet clothing, dry off, change and get into my doss bag.

Should I call someone? Christ knows how but I don't have an emergency phone number on me. I call Ramey on the satphone – he's engaged so I get Catty (at 03:00 Colombian time), who eventually locates him and he gives me some numbers. I relax and try to sleep. How thin is the ice I'm sleeping on? If my tent goes through it, I've had it. I sleep little, sitting bolt upright whenever I hear or feel the ice move. It's like sitting on a waterbed.

Tuesday, 3 January 2006   Towards Koyuk

At first light I open up the tent and look around . . . Jesus . . . my tent is now only three metres from open water! I climb out and tiptoe around like you would on glass. I've been sleeping on thin, recently formed ice. Sea ice is different from its freshwater counterpart in that it's very flexible and spongy. It initially forms in small platelets that freeze together then form large plates and then pans. This ice is very new. In some places I can see the sea below me. This is really freaky. I pack up and, very slowly, try to retreat south, back the way I've come.

I hardly dare breathe. The route I took on to the ice last night is now open water and there's water to my rear and left. To my right is the open sea . . . just how the fuck did I manage to get out here?

In disbelief, two sea lions pop their heads out and stare. This is just too much. The pan that I'm on seems to be connected to the main pack ice in three places but I find that none of these areas can take my weight and between them is open water. I carefully try to make my way off the pan using one of the 'bridges' but leap back when I feel the ice give. I'm marooned, at least for the time being.

Koyuk is still eighteen miles away across the bay, while the nearest patch of coastline is nine miles. If I make a mistake now I'm in big trouble. Having decided to travel light, I've no dry suit or other specialist equipment as I'd been expecting the ice to still be hard frozen at this time of year.

The wind continues to blow strong and cold. Although he is loath to admit it, Karl is in a tight spot so he alerts a state trooper via satellite phone. The emergency services concur and ask if he needs assistance. Reluctantly, he says, 'Yes'. A helicopter is tasked.

But an hour later, he notices that the south-eastern corner of the pan that he is marooned on is drifting and being forced into – and then under – the main ice pack to form a pressure ridge. This becomes his escape route. In fifteen minutes he zigzags his way on to safer ice and into a field of massive pressure ridges. He is safe and moves as quickly he can to the south and east towards the shoreline.

Too late to stand down his rescuers, Karl is soon met by locals on snow machines and a helicopter puts down on the ice beside them. Karl apologises but there are no recriminations – they realise that he had no choice but to call for help.

Following the trails left by the snow machines, Karl continues north-easterly, towards Koyuk and connects with the main trail, which runs north-south. Still on the ice, he makes camp and, from his GPS, discovers he is three miles north and one mile east from where he fell in twenty-four hours earlier. This time, he is on thicker, more stable ice.

He leaves for Koyuk in a white-out. For four hours he battles with deep snow before it is replaced by hard ice, and he speeds the last six miles towards the village to be met by a youngster named Alex, dressed only in a T-shirt. Karl spends two days here recuperating at the home of Elvina Narango, an Inuit and the local Frontier Flying Service representative.

Monday, 9 January 2006   Next stop Elim

Having followed a land route, I now pick up on a snow-machine trail that again takes me across more coastal ice, which is more direct. The wind has died down considerably but Elim itself – now just eleven miles away – is hidden behind a spit of land.

It's getting dark by the time I reach the spit. I find there's a good deal of thin ice and open water dotted about, making me extremely nervous. I stick to the snow-machine trail as it wanders in and around the pressure ridges. The thing is, fast-moving snow machines have a much-reduced ground pressure, lighter than me in fact, and can even ski across short distances of open water. In contrast, I have to make some nerve-racking hop, skips and jumps before I arrive without incident.

Dan, the head teacher at the local school, offers me a room as my re-supply hasn't arrived and doesn't until Wednesday, 11 January.

On Thursday, 12 January, Karl sets off for Golovin and then White Mountain, which is about a four-day walk. With strong winds blowing the ice away from the coast, he must trek overland instead trying to follow the well-defined trails between villages, although these are sometimes confused with the tracks left by trappers.

Karl reaches White Mountain, but with blizzards and temperatures of –30 °C is forced to sit tight. When he sets forth on 19 January, the wind chill is still horrendous along this coastline. Gales have removed the snow, forcing him further inland and then back to the coast again as he searches for a white-covered trail. He makes it to Port Safety, and, next day, a fifteen-mile push sees him in Nome. Here he meets Dimitri – who, to enable him to acclimatise, will walk with Karl to Cape Wales – and a few hectic days are spent sorting equipment.

Tuesday, 31 January 2006   Leaving Nome

Breakfast at Fat Eddie's then we head off. It's cold – around –30 °C –
but a well-compacted snow trail leads west along the coast. The sun
is out and the sky a clear blue, but damn, it's bloody freezing. The
wind cuts to the bone at these temperatures.

We move well all day, carrying on into the night and making
about twenty miles. We've been making for a group of cabins but
can't find them – they would be preferable to the tent, as we could
get out of these winds. After years alone, I find it difficult to share a
tent, especially out here. We're also using a new three-man – not my
usual North Face – and I'm not particularly fond of it.

Thursday, 2 February 2006   Cape Woolley

We don't hear our wristwatch alarms and sleep in. It's easily done, as
it doesn't get light until 10:00. By midday, we're moving. Dimitri is
struggling to find his arctic legs – and he has ended up with frostbit-
ten fingers – but we are making better time. We need to – we have
five days' food and fuel to get us to Teller but at least the trails,
which are now taking us over hard sea ice, are in our favour. I'm
praying it doesn't snow – it would stuff us.

With temperatures as low as –42 °C, the wind-chill factor takes
this down to –68 °C. This really sucks and so does some of our kit.
I try to balance my temperature by not wearing too much clothing
when I'm moving – which means I don't sweat – but my windproof
isn't up to the job. I'm freezing to death because it's too short. My
midriff is exposed and the hood will not stay up.

Getting our facemasks just right is also a real balancing act and
already Dimitri has snow burn appearing under his eyes and around
the top of his nose. Even covered up, the air takes the skin off around
the nostrils as ice forms under your mask.

A mask completely covering your face and mouth is nice to start
with, as you can keep warm air in it, circulating as you breathe through
a vent. Unfortunately your goggles mist up. If you open up to clear
them, the warm air inside meets the cold and the whole mask freezes
and is useless. I've modified mine by cutting a hole to breathe through
in place of the vent. This allows most of the moist air to escape without

misting the goggles, although my lips and nose get burnt. That's the price you pay for being able to see where you're going.

Eventually, we make it to Cape Woolley. Five miles, less than ten kilometres, across the bay, we can see cabins on the shoreline and this motivates us to up the pace and beat the setting sun, as sleeping indoors appeals. That said, I'm feeling cautious – a set of polar bear tracks are heading straight for the same cabins.

Next day, Dimitri's fingers are looking nasty. Barely making ten miles, they reach Cape Douglas and decide to pitch tent on ice on the southern side of the landfall, where they are sheltered from the northerly wind. Only a few metres from the cliffs, Karl convinces himself that they are likely camping above sand rather than water so it seems safe enough. Besides, he is more worried about the risk of losing the too-flimsy tent to the wind.

They wake next morning at 9 a.m. It is blowing hard so they decide to 'sit this one out' and remain in their sleeping bags until it abates. Other than peanuts, they don't eat much and pee in bottles. This is a common enough practice in tent life, yet Karl still manages to spill his bottle in his sleeping bag.

Sunday, 5 February 2006   Ice camp

Peeping through a tent vent, I don't recognise the scenery.

'Dimitri, could you have a better look . . . can you see the coast?' I ask him to look as he is out of his bag.

'Yep, it's just a little ways off,' he confirms.

'That's a relief. Somehow, I thought we'd moved,' I reply, reassured.

After breakfast, we pack up and scramble outside. I'm certainly not prepared for what I see: distant mountains on the far horizon. Checking my GPS, I find we're twenty-eight miles, forty-five kilometres, out to sea. All through the storm, we've been drifting south-east. The implications hit home; we're surrounded by ice – not particularly good ice – and between us and the mountains are patches of open water.

We're in trouble. If we're drifting, it is in the wrong direction. We are low on food so we're looking screwed. I can't imagine there is a route left across the ice to the coast. What to do? I consider drowning myself. I don't. Instead I make an inevitable emergency call and, in less than an hour, our friends from Evergreen Helicopters put down – again – and pluck us off the ice.

Dimitri flies with them to Nome to get his fingers sorted out but I get dropped two miles from Cape Douglas. It is a different world; no sea ice at all, just clear open water for as far as the eye can see. Retracing our steps, I spot where we'd fucked up twenty-four hours ago. Had our tent been a few metres along the cliffs, literally metres, we could have saved ourselves all the drama because we pitched just where the ice divided in the darkness.

I continue. Before I know it, I'm in another white-out. There's neither depth nor detail, simply nothing. I repeatedly fall and stumble on the uneven ground that is criss-crossed with invisible piles of wind-driven snow. I think I only manage a few miles before I quit.

It's a fight to get the tent up and takes an hour to pin it down in the howling gale. Inside I groan, thinking of the expense of air rescue. The expedition must cough up and it won't be cheap. Then there's the local press. They must love me by now. I can almost see the headlines and shudder: 'Brit's Gone and Done It Again!'

By Tuesday conditions are calmer. After drying his kit and excavating his tent and sledge, Karl continues up the coast, which is somewhat flatter now, with visibility improving all the time. Switching to skis, he makes good progress and reaches Teller at 20:00, wrecked, blistered and exhausted, and checks into the school.

Dimitri arrives from hospital in Nome: two of his fingers have level-two frostbite and should recover quite quickly; the third has level-three for the length of its nail and is described as 'touch and go'. The final leg of the journey is held up as they wait for a plane large enough to fly in Dimitri's sled. This eventually arrives on Friday, 17 February, and the short but treacherous walk to Cape Prince of Wales can begin.

Saturday, 18 February 2006   Beyond Teller

The snow is deeper today and the coastline getting ever trickier. I'm very nervous in this blowing snow and bad visibility, remembering the white-outs I had around Cape Douglas and the falls and those small hidden crevices. We run out of shore, then find ourselves wedged up against high cliffs that drop straight into the sea. And as for the sea itself . . . try and picture this: take one seemingly endless car park and fill with wrecked white vehicles, six deep, then garnish with refrigerators. Half-fill your car park with semi-frozen water and cover with a thick blanket of snow. Leave to set overnight. My blood runs cold just looking at it.

With no other option we venture out on to the mass of pressure ridges and soon establish that this is going to be unworkable. It's like a minefield. With our ski poles we probe at every step the snow and ice, for often beneath it is open water or a crevice between slabs of ice. It's hard to find a place just to put your feet, let alone pull these damn sleds. At one point, Dimitri is leading when he finds himself in a dead end, hemmed in by thin ice. As he turns to withdraw, the ice gives way and in he goes. By the time I have scrambled from my harness he has managed to pull himself out, gasping and cursing in French. He shrugs it off and says as long as he keeps moving he'll be all right. We push on, but not long after that Dimitri goes in again. He is lucky that this is the warmest day we've had in a while, just above freezing. A short time ago it could have killed him pretty quickly.

Before it grows too dark we find a patch of ice that looks as though it can take our tent. Neither of us is thrilled by the idea of sleeping on the sea ice again, even under the best of conditions, so we keep a watchful eye on our surroundings.

After another fruitless attempt along the coast, Karl and Dimitri decide to cut back inland for the York Mountains. The climbing is hard, but as the weather clears, they are finally making good progress. By Tuesday, Wales is in sight.

Tuesday, 21 February 2006   **Cape Prince of Wales**

There is no wind at all, not a whisper, but it's cold, −17 °C. We are moving swiftly now and have Wales in our nostrils.

Images of my first day's walk spring to mind, looking back at Punta Arenas as it disappeared, when I was green as grass and full of beans. The journey so far has been everything it was supposed to be, and much, much more. But for all that this 'coming in day' is supposed to mean to me, ultimately it's just another leg and not the end. In fact not by a long shot.

Wales, population approximately 130, finally comes into view. I stand for a while waiting for Dimitri to catch up and eye this village at the end of a world. There is just a fleeting moment's contemplation: a feeling of pride? Achievement? Then the crunching of skis and ski poles from behind snaps me back to the real world. I try getting footage of this great day, my hands cold, these damn ski boots crippling my feet and my frozen nose running. The video camera fails within moments, to be followed swiftly by the stills camera. Bugger it! We push on. There's going to be no dropping to one knee in the arctic water or weeping tears of joy before planting a Union Jack.

So here it is, crunch time. Now we have to prepare, watch, wait and pick our moment to cross the Bering Strait. Our aim is to move forward aggressively, cutting down rest to a minimum. Being stationary on the Strait means being carried away from the objective by the tides. We know the odds are stacked against us. No one here believes we can make it. They've seen it all before. One guy even told Dimitri he would bet $10,000 against it. That's right people, you keep it coming. You can only fuel the fire. Victory is having the means plus the will to fight, and at this point it bleeds from our skin. If there's any luck going spare we'll be there to pick that up, too. Like our forefathers before us, when the whistle blows we go over the top, bayonets fixed.

Do what thy manhood bids thee do, from none but self
expect applause
He noblest lives and noblest dies who makes and keeps his
self-made laws

Sir Richard Francis Burton

property of
L.E. SHORE
MEMORIAL LIBRARY
THORNBURY, ONTARIO, N0H 2P0